AF595861
TG977
ANZ-979
ARB
4X4 ACCESSORIES

First published 2013

Updated 2022

Published and distributed by
AFN Fishing & Outdoors
PO Box 544 Croydon, Victoria 3136
Telephone: (03) 9729 8788
Email: sales@afn.com.au
Website: www.afn.com.au

ISBN: 9781 8651 3341 6

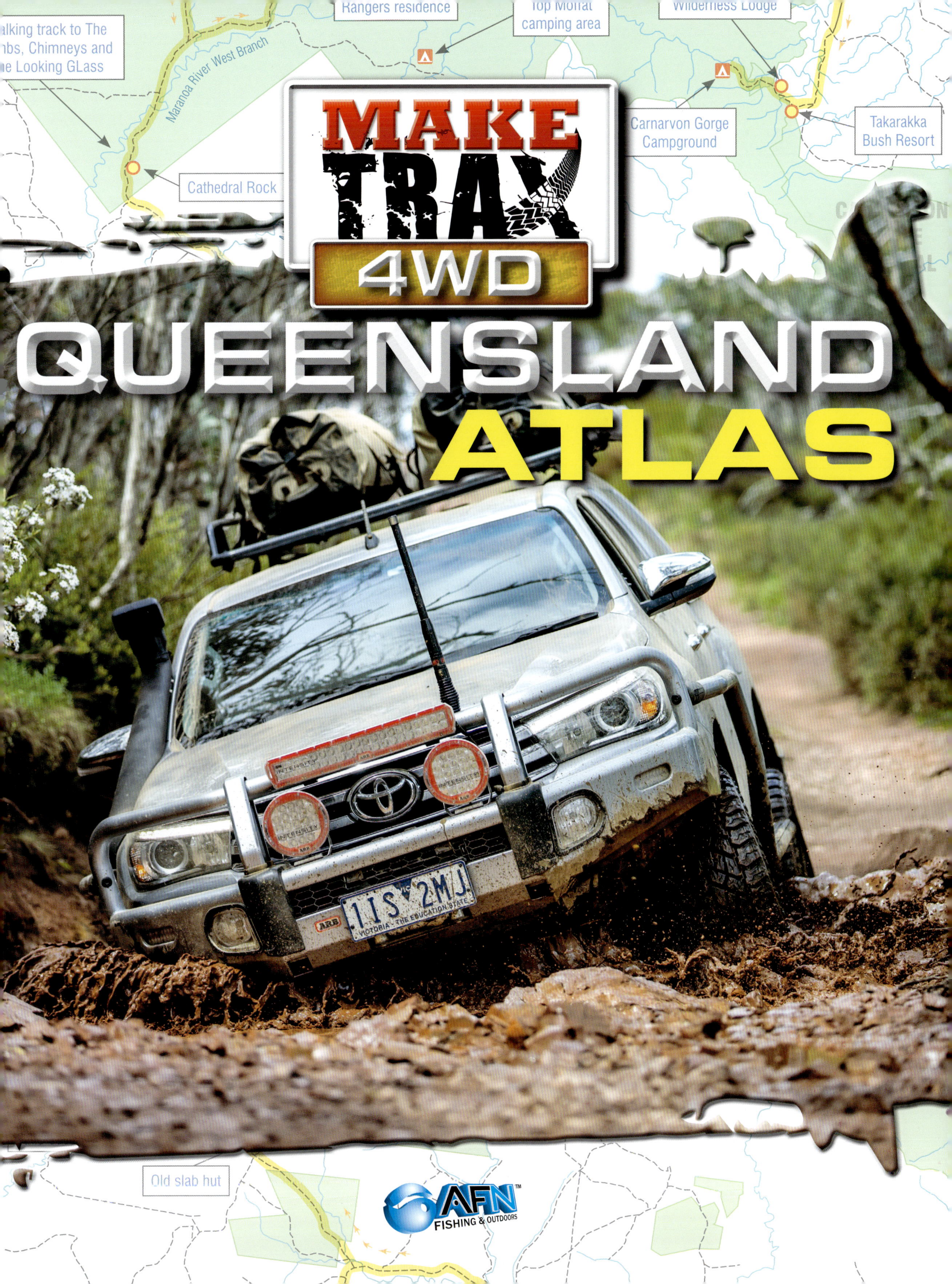

MAKE
TRAX
4WD
QUEENSLAND
ATLAS
Rangers residence
Top Moffat camping area
Wilderness Lodge
Walking track to The
Chimneys and
Looking GLass
Maranoa River West Branch
Carnarvon Gorge Campground
Takarakka Bush Resort
Cathedral Rock
Old slab hut
AFN
FISHING & OUTDOORS

LAND ROVER
XFB·655
LAND ROVER
XKE·409

CONTENTS

ABOUT THE CONSULTANTS

John and Anne Morton, have been four-wheel driving for over 30 years clocking up nearly 700,000 kilometres around Australia.

John is a qualified mechanic while Anne is an editor and writer. Their knowledge of four-wheel driving tracks around Australia is comprehensive and in their home state of Victoria, they have pretty well covered every track and 4WD adventure.

In 1995 they started Lifestyle Video Productions, and produced their first video documenting their month-long adventure on the Canning Stock Route. Their videos now document the four-wheel driving, the route and track conditions, mud maps of daily travel, as well as the sights, history, landscapes, scenery and the camaraderie of travelling with others.

Over the years Lifestyle Video Productions has grown into an award-winning business. Together John and Anne have completed a multitude of 4WD adventures – they have travelled Cape York 4 times, Canning Stock Route 3 times, Simpson Desert 7 times, plus dozens of trips on tracks all over Australia and more recently trips in New Zealand and Africa.

They are currently planning further explorations in NSW and Queensland.

Travel Videos of Australia

Explore Discover and Experience using these videos as your guide

travelvideosofaustralia.com

Fraser Island and the Sunshine Coast | **Long Road to the Alice - Port Augusta to Alice Springs** | **Namibia Experience - African Adventure** | **Vistas to Valleys - High Country Adventures** | **Wild Southern Land - New Zealand's South Island**

The Old Ghan Heritage Trail | **Simpson Desert - 50 years on** | **Canning - Stock Route Adventures** | **Savannah Way - Across the top** | **High Country - The Victorian Alps** | **The Madigan Line - Crossing the Northern Simpson** | **Colours of The Kimberley**

The Binns Track - Savannah to Simpson | **Desert Highways - The Roads of Len Beadell** | **New Zealand - Down South** | **On the Track of Burke and Wills** | **Tasmania - The Devil's Playground** | **The Magic of the Flinders Ranges** | **Cape York - Still the Great Adventure**

HOW TO USE THIS BOOK

MAKE TRAX QUEENSLAND presents all of the information that you will need to undertake a safe and enjoyable 4WD trip into the back blocks of this State.

Our TRACK SNAPSHOT identifies the vital requirements for each trek, listing them in a boxed format.

The detailed maps are all oriented with north to the page top, and an integral distance bar to give a sense of scale. Towns, together with the road and track network linking them are clearly displayed, with broken lines indicating unsealed surfaces. For the sake of clarity we have omitted contour lines, but have included waterways and State / National Park boundaries. Camping areas, lookouts and other points of interest are indicated by boxed captions, and the tour route and direction are highlighted in yellow with orange arrows.

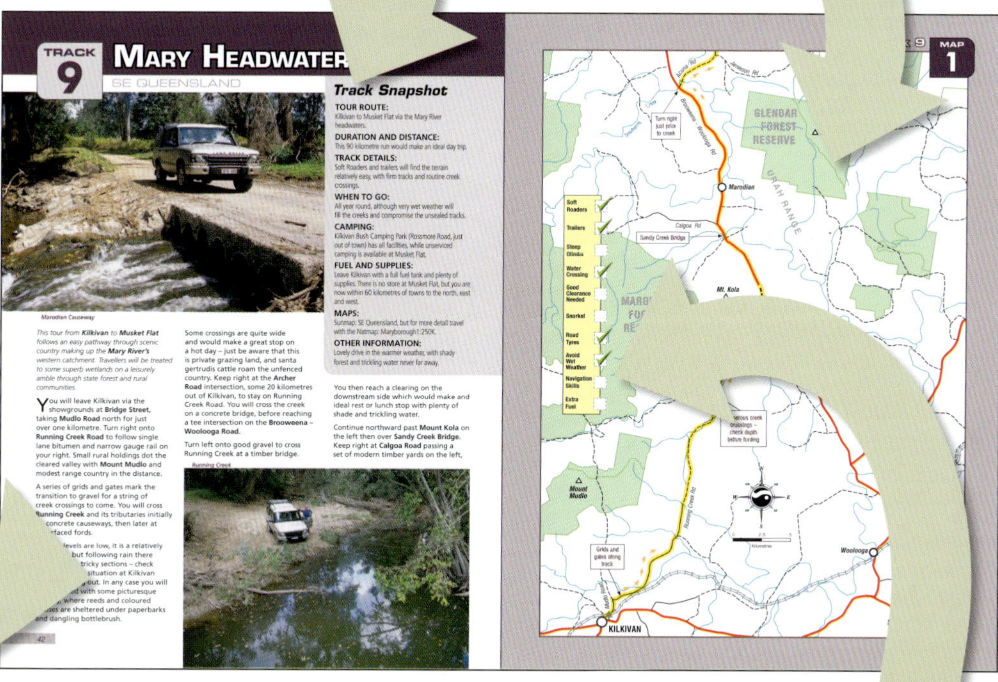

The text follows the vehicle journey using landmarks and intersections as stepping stones through the trek. The intermediate distances mentioned can be compared with your own progress, but it will be necessary to read ahead through the text to identify the next "stepping stone". Those running a GPS unit within the vehicle will have an advantage here, as they can easily compare their position in relation to the maps provided. (A GPS is recommended on any tours where the "Navigation Skills" box has been ticked). In any case, try to keep a record of your odometer readings as you reach the various landmarks described in the text.

A "tick the box" list of tour hazards and basic requirements is included with Map 1 of each trek. This list cannot account for every combination of driver, vehicle and weather combination, but rather attempts to provide a guide for what is likely on the tour. For example a tick in the "Steep Climbs" box cannot indicate how steep the climbs are, but if there is a tick in the "Soft Roaders" box as well, then they are likely to be climbs that will not require low range.

Similarly, a tick in the "Water Crossings" box, but without one in the "Snorkel" box would indicate relatively shallow crossings (although it is customary for travellers to check out an unknown water crossing on foot before plunging in – with the exception of waterways that may be the habitat of salt water crocodiles).

Introduction

MAKE TRAX QUEENSLAND describes 29 of the best 4WD destinations and tours from across the state. From the tropical expeditions of Cape York and the Gulf Country to shorter treks just out of Brisbane, there is no time frame that cannot be satisfied. We will travel station country tracks to the channel country rivers, and return to the coastal islands for some relaxation.

Each trek is graded, allowing travellers to choose a suitable tour matching their experience and vehicle's capability. Camping details, together with practical notes, encourage you to plan your own itinerary, with one eye on the information presented here, and another on making the trek a personal adventure.

These tours visit many of Queensland's well known destinations, but broaden that appeal with some forays into the lesser travelled regions. Whether you are a local looking for something different, or an interstate visitor searching for new and exciting destinations, we know that you will find Queensland to be much more than just the Sunshine State.

THE PRACTICALITIES:
This book has been produced as a guide book and does not attempt to cover the technique of 4WDing in any detail. Some of the treks described require a little more knowledge than that to drive a conventional car, but others will require a much greater level of skill. It is important to understand that a novice is unlikely to drive their new 4WD up a rocky climb with any more "natural ability" than somebody reversing a trailer for the first time.

An experienced instructor can dramatically flatten the learning curve. Travel with such a person in the early days – or better still join a 4WD Club or undertake a commercial training course. It is an unfortunate irony that most newcomers underestimate what their vehicle is capable of, but overestimate their ability to reach that limit.

VEHICLE CHOICE:
These tours have been field checked in full sized conventional 4WDs, occasionally towing a trailer or boat, and regularly with a utility based camper outfit. I have also travelled to many of these destinations in soft roaders with reasonable success.

Ground clearance, rather than gearing would be the limiting factor for 4WDs on most of these tours, so tactical driving can compensate for some dimensional restrictions. Choosing a suitable line over rough sections will elevate the underbody of any vehicle, while robust tyres and traction control assist in the grip department.

Each of these tours indicate whether a full size 4WD (with low range gearing) is necessary, or whether a soft roader could undertake the journey. In some cases a well driven AWD will complete the tour routinely, but recent rain for example can scour troublesome ruts into what may have been an easy track.

Equally, full size 4WDs are not automatically guaranteed easy travel. Driving experience and track conditions are variable, so always drive within you and your vehicle's ability and turn back (or exit via an easier track) if the conditions demand.

NAVIGATION:
These trek notes and associated maps should be used in conjunction with a compass and preferably a vehicle mounted GPS. Our maps provide the essential information, but can be supplemented with the relevant 1:50K or 1:25K topographic maps if you need contour lines or more detail. A GPS is also invaluable for locating your position quickly and allowing it to be plotted on a paper map.

It should be noted that the accompanying maps indicate more tracks than may be accessible to the travelling public. Follow the described route for each tour and only use other tracks if they are known to be for general use, perhaps seeking local knowledge or permission.

The trek notes utilise fixed locations such as rivers, T-intersections, items of interest etc as the reference points for distances throughout the tour. By working with intermediate distances, rather than a cumulative distance from the trip start, a number of inaccuracies are reduced. Variables such as odometer changes due to worn or non-standard tyre sizes, or loose surface slippage can be significant, so follow the kilometre readings with a degree of caution and lookout for other defining features as described in the notes.

TRACK ACCESS:
Most of these tours follow public roads through national parks, state forests, and station country. In some cases (national parks, and especially in state forests) a permit to traverse is required. Elsewhere access is generally both free and unrestricted – providing you stay on the designated tracks, and not venture onto management vehicle only tracks, which are usually locked or clearly signposted.

Access into Aboriginal Land will require permission (and sometimes a fee) while station country tracks linking multiple homesteads are generally open to the public, providing that you stay within the roadside reserve.

In all cases it is essential to behave in a respectful manner. Do not drive on closed or rain affected tracks, obey all road signs, leave gates as found, and do not drive "off road" especially over vegetated sand dunes.

CAMPING:
Bush camping sites have been detailed in most of the treks and may be private or national park based. The former have all of the usual facilities, while the latter vary from just a plot of dirt, to formal campgrounds with all facilities.

Camping in national park or state forest (if permitted) normally attracts a fee of $6.85 per person per night (no charge for children under five), with family rates available. Bookings are usually made online www.parks.des.qld.gov.au/camping or by phone on 13 7468, although cash payments may still occur at a few national park registration boards.

You may not camp on station property without permission, however informal camping occasionally occurs within the roadside reserve at some river crossings for example. Seek permission if an overnight stop is necessary (try using the station channel on your UHF) and respect any restrictions mentioned. No shooting is a universal rule, and fishing / campfires may not be welcome. Always select a site well away from stock watering points, and leave no trace on departure.

TRAILERS:
Trailers can be successfully towed along many of the tours presented (check our TRACK SNAPSHOT for an overview), but will limit your progress in tight country (sharp creek crossings, overgrown tracks and obstacle bypasses etc) and are a particular burden on soft sand or muddy sections – while slippery descents and failed climbs can be disastrous.

If a trailer is considered essential, gain some experience on the easier treks, before undertaking a more difficult tour. Travel in company if possible, as vehicle recovery can be tedious when travelling solo and substantially more difficult with a trailer in tow. However it is sometimes possible to unhitch a bogged trailer / vehicle combination and continue to drive out without the additional weight hampering progress – it is a good idea to fit a skid plate underneath the trailer's leading "A" frame structural member to facilitate the subsequent trailer recovery.

It is very desirable to select a robust trailer with a similar track to the towing vehicle and preferably ride on the same wheel / tyre combination. An extended articulation coupling is essential and it is important to adjust the trailer tyre pressures in proportion to those needed by the towing vehicle. In soft sand for example, a typical front and rear pressure may be 18psi and 22psi in the vehicle, but the trailer may only require 16psi for the weight it is carrying.

SAFETY:
Touring by 4WD is not without risk in itself, so travellers should minimise any hazards within their control. Always travel in a roadworthy vehicle, on good tyres and at a speed consistent with the terrain ahead. Full size 4WDs tend to be more top heavy and require longer braking distances than a conventional car (or soft roaders), so drive conservatively, particularly on side slopes and on wet bitumen.

Secure any load within the vehicle, preferably behind a cargo barrier, and use the roof rack for light weight items. Keep a fire extinguisher and first aid kit handy, together with a satphone or new generation EPIRB. A UHF radio is very desirable for convoy chatter, but can be a lifesaver in station country too. Regular outback travellers should consider fitting a HF radio for longer distance communications.

Recovery gear should always be carried, with shovel, axe and heavy duty jack being mandatory items. A snatch strap together with rated shackles and suitable anchor points (definitely NOT a tow ball or vehicle tie down point) may be useful when travelling in company. All items of recovery gear should only be used by experienced people, noting especially that snatch straps should not be joined together by any type of metal coupling.

Always carry adequate water, fuel and food on even the shortest of trips; a breakdown or accident can happen anywhere. On longer tours top up with water and fuel wherever possible, as track closures can mean lengthy detours, and rain can close tracks for days at a time.

ABBREVIATIONS USED IN TEXT:

N.P. National Park
S.F. State Forest
H.S. Homestead
M.V.O. Management Vehicle Only

TOUR LISTINGS BY REGION:

BRISBANE AREA

D'Aguilar Range • Moreton Island • Kandanga • Conondale • The Condamine • Blackbutt

SOUTH EAST QUEENSLAND

Sundown • Brisbane River • Mary Headwaters • Wongi • Burrum Coast • Cooloola • Fraser Island

CENTRAL QUEENSLAND

Salvator Rosa • Mitchell to Culgoa • Carnarvon Gorge • Expedition Range

CHANNEL COUNTRY

The Diamantina • Haddon Corner • The Georgina • Min Min Way • Dowling Track • The Paroo • The Thomson • The Barcoo

NORTH QUEENSLAND

Lolworth Creek • Lawn Hill • Lakefield • Telegraph Track

CHANGING CONDITIONS:

Please be aware that track conditions, campsites, locations and many other aspects of access can change. It is the responsibility of individuals to ensure and enquire about the current status of these possible changes prior to departure.

DISCLAIMER:

The publisher and consultants cannot accept responsibility for any errors or omissions in this guide as track conditions can change overtime. Every effort has been made to ensure the information in this book was accurate at the time of publication. The representation of roads and tracks on maps is not evidence of right of way. This publication is

Chapter 1
BRISBANE AREA

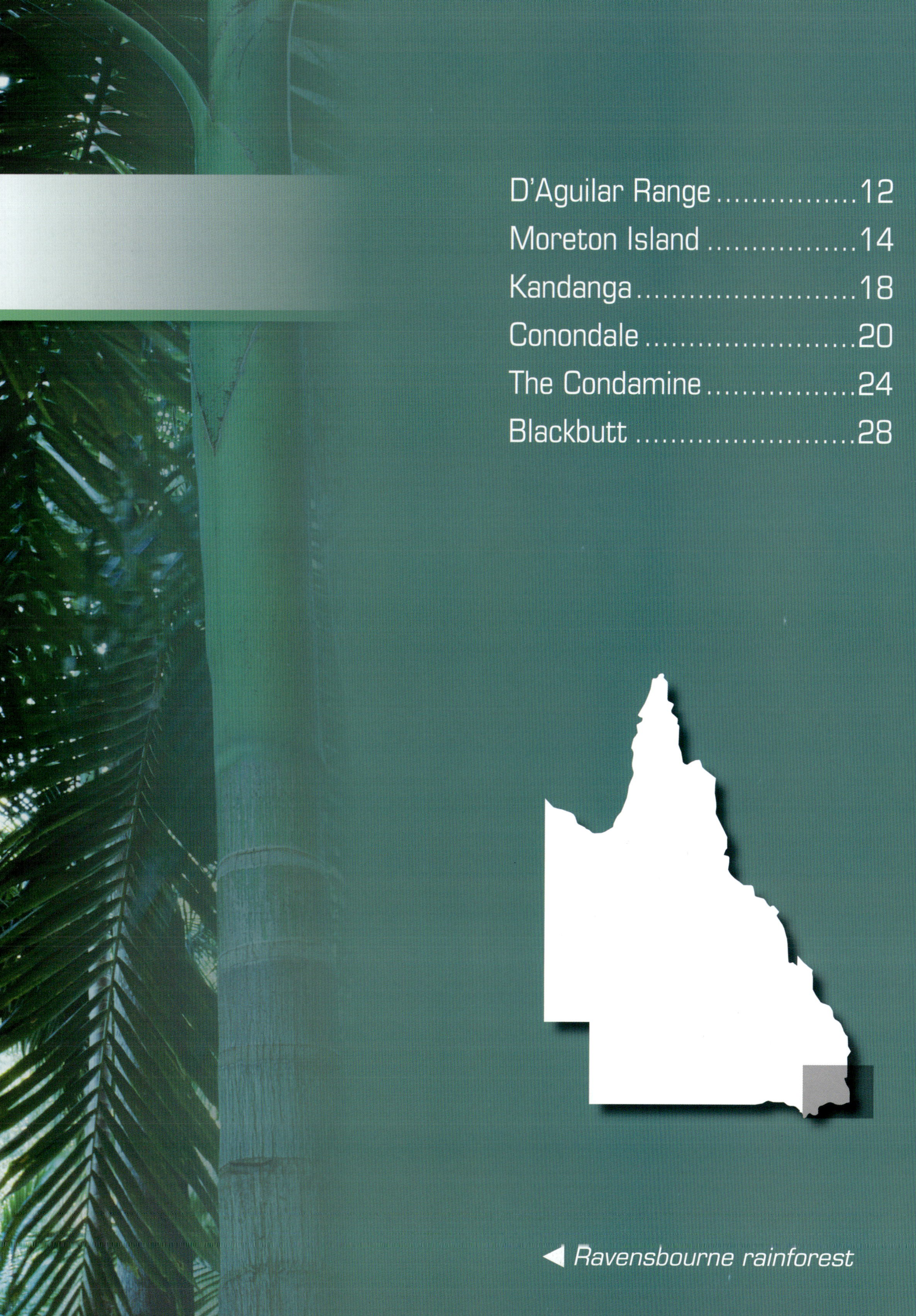

◀ *Ravensbourne rainforest*

TRACK 1 D'AGUILAR RANGE

BRISBANE AREA

__D'Aguilar NP__ is one of the closest destinations to __Brisbane__ where 4WDers can point their wheels onto dirt. This trek could be done as a day trip out of Brisbane, but an overnight camp would be even better – and there are plenty of opportunities for that.

Views from the __D'Aguilar Range__ extend over rural land to the __Glass House Mountains,__ while there are numerous walks throughout the forestry areas. A couple of swimming holes will prove popular over the summer months, with a waterfall and abandoned timber cutter's relics providing interest for the less energetic.

Our starting point is **Kilcoy** where you head east on the **D'Aguilar Highway,** turning right two kilometres later onto **Neurum Road**. A bridge spans **Sandy Creek,** before you reach the **Stanley Arm** of **Lake Somerset** and its much longer bridge.

The community of **Neurum** is spread out at the foot of **Mount Archer,** with horse paddocks and rural houses. The road deteriorates beyond Neurum Creek, and you will turn right onto **Stanton Road,** some 17 kilometres from Kilcoy.

Turn right again onto **Rasmussen Road,** signposted **"Neurum Creek Bush Retreat"**, to cross a grid and begin the unsealed run. You will head toward the heavily treed, but distinctive rocky crest of the D'Aguilar Range.

A concrete causeway over Neurum Creek flags a private bush retreat, with camping available on the waterway, or on grassy sites further away. You will continue for a couple of kilometres to the boundary of D'Aguilar NP, taking **Lovedays Road** to the **Archer Camping Area** on your right.

Basic facilities and grassed sites make this an ideal tent based camp for small groups, although vehicles cannot access the actual camping area. There is a day use area opposite the camp at Broadwater Picnic Area, again with toilets and fireplace. Follow a short walk from here through jungle vegetation to a swimming hole.

Beyond Broadwater, begin a sustained climb past a set of old yards and MVO tracks to either side. Veer left following the main road to an elevated look out some 4.8 kilometres from Broadwater, to enjoy views over the Glass House Mountains.

Keep right at the Neurum Creek turn off to enter state forest and pine plantation. (This area was harvested of red cedar, blackbutt and hoop pine, together with hardwood species from the higher slopes. Replanting has established the state forest reserves of today).

Continue past other MVO tracks to the **Western Escarpment Forest Drive,** and veer left here. You will reach a four way intersection 1.3 kilometres later, turning left onto **Neurum Creek Road.** A carpark and old log mill mark the junction, with excellent facilities available at **The Gantry** day use area. Walking tracks radiate to the south and west, while the sawmill offers an interesting peek into the area's history.

We will take Neurum Creek Road north from The Gantry on a one way return drive to **The Falls** and **Rocky Hole,** but will return here to continue the trek. If time permits head north with The Gantry on your right, to reach state forest 700 metres later.

The signposted **"Falls Lookout"** is found one kilometre from The Gantry, with a 200 metre drive and 500 metre walk bringing you to a viewing platform over **Bulls Falls**. There is unlikely to be much action unless recent rains have fallen, but there is scenic forest to appreciate on the hike.

Return to Neurum Creek Road passing the **Mill Rainforest Walk** on your right (a pretty creek walk of one kilometre, sheltered by remnant rainforest). Climb via a couple of switchbacks to another creek crossing, flagging D'Aguilar's second bush camping possibility (and a better choice for vehicle based camping).

Neurum Creek Camping Area is located just beyond the crossing, some six kilometres from The Gantry. Turn right into the camp to follow a loop drive past sheltered campsites and a trickling creek. The 750 metre **Lophostemon Walk** commences at the camp, and basic facilities are provided.

Track Snapshot

TOUR ROUTE:
Kilcoy to Dayboro via D'Aguilar NP.

DURATION AND DISTANCE:
This 80 km tour will take a day, or more if you choose to camp in or near the national park.

TRACK DETAILS:
Easy driving on dirt and gravel – suitable for all vehicles and trailers.

WHEN TO GO:
All year round; closed in wet weather.

CAMPING:
Private camping at Neurum Creek Bush Retreat and Neurum Creek Camp, Archer Camping Area within D'Aguilar NP. Organise camping permit online at www.qld.gov.au/camping.

FUEL AND SUPPLIES:
Kilcoy and Dayboro.

MAPS:
Natmap: 1:100 k Caboolture, Nambour.

OTHER INFORMATION:
D'Aguilar NP offers cool respite from the low land heat on hot days.

Back on the main road continue north for a couple of kilometres to Rocky Hole – a sizable swimming hole that is tempting in hot weather. We will retrace our steps from here to The Gantry, although Neurum Creek Road does continue through to Broadwater, completing a circuit drive through the park.

From The Gantry follow the **Dayboro sign,** veering right onto **Peggs Road,** one kilometre later. Continue through a potentially locked gate (in wet weather) to make a sustained winding descent to a creek crossing. You will climb out through subtropical forest to a junction 6.5 kilometres from The Gantry.

Turn left here at the signposted **"Dayboro via Mount Pleasant Road",** then turn right 500 metres later to cross a creek and leave national park. Serpentine bitumen paves the way down past small land holdings and valley views. Keep left onto Laceys Creek Road for the final run into the undulating town of Dayboro.

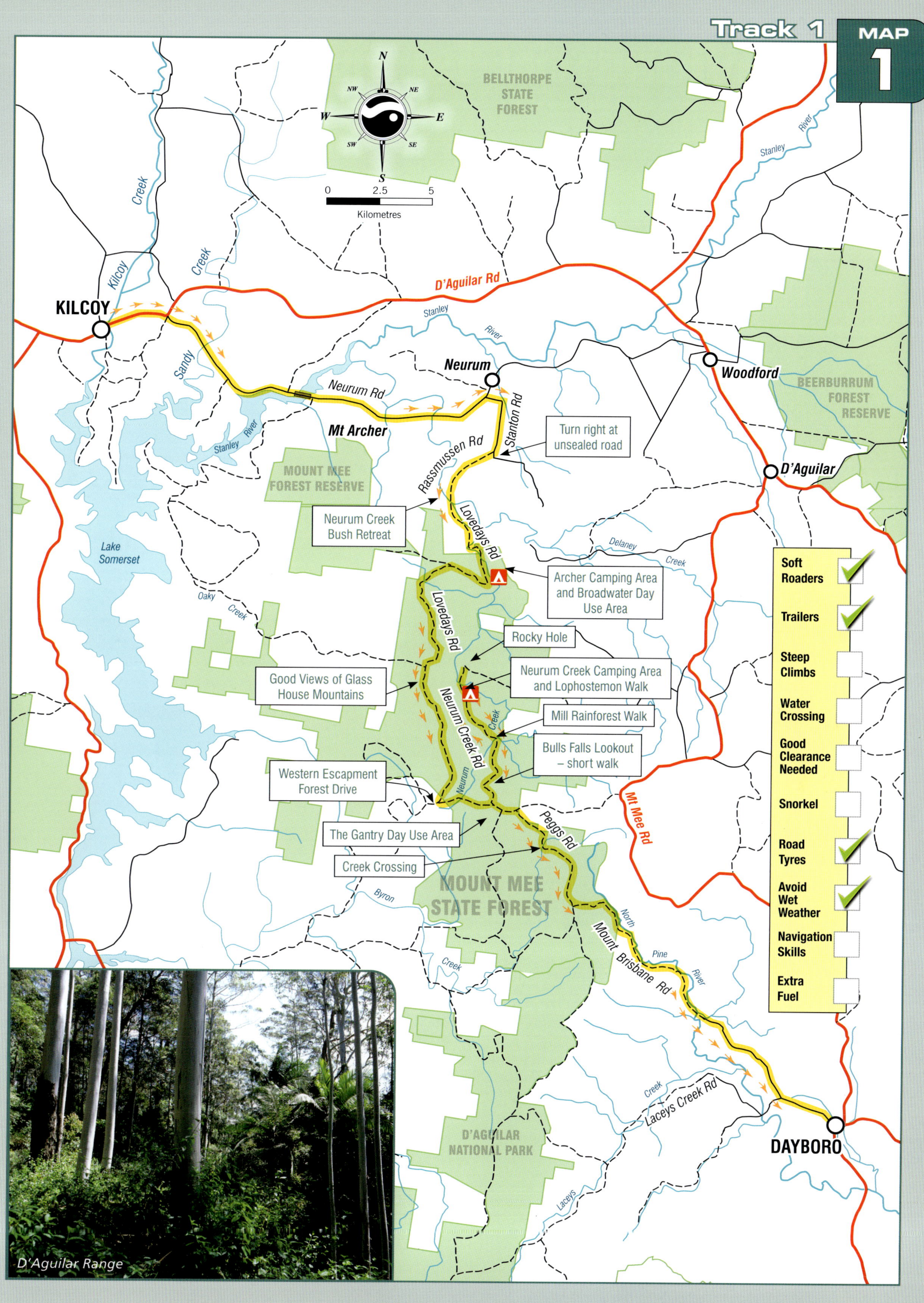

Track 1
MAP 1
N
NE
E
SE
S
SW
W
NW
0
2.5
5
Kilometres
BELLTHORPE STATE FOREST
KILCOY
Kilcoy
Creek
Creek
D'Aguilar Rd
Stanley
River
Stanley
River
Sandy
Neurum
Neurum Rd
Mt Archer
Stanley
River
Woodford
BEERBURRUM FOREST RESERVE
Stanton Rd
Turn right at unsealed road
Rassmussen Rd
D'Aguilar
MOUNT MEE FOREST RESERVE
Neurum Creek Bush Retreat
Lovedays Rd
Delaney
Creek
Lake Somerset
Archer Camping Area and Broadwater Day Use Area
Oaky
Creek
Lovedays Rd
Rocky Hole
Neurum Creek Camping Area and Lophostemon Walk
Good Views of Glass House Mountains
Neurum Creek Rd
Creek
Mill Rainforest Walk
Bulls Falls Lookout – short walk
Western Escapment Forest Drive
Neurum
Mt Mee Rd
The Gantry Day Use Area
Peggs Rd
Creek Crossing
MOUNT MEE STATE FOREST
Byron
North
Mount Brisbane Rd
Pine
River
Creek
Creek
Laceys Creek Rd
D'AGUILAR NATIONAL PARK
DAYBORO
Laceys
Soft Roaders
Trailers
Steep Climbs
Water Crossing
Good Clearance Needed
Snorkel
Road Tyres
Avoid Wet Weather
Navigation Skills
Extra Fuel
D'Aguilar Range

TRACK 2

Moreton Island

BRISBANE AREA

Courtesy of vehicular ferry access from the ***Port of Brisbane, Moreton Island*** *can be reached in under two hours. The transition from bitumen to sand driving is achieved without fuss, and interrupted only by the 75 minute cruise.*

Travellers will enjoy the mostly national park island (only 2% of the land mass is privately owned) and be treated to a range of activities including fishing, hiking, sand boarding and of course 4WDing. Many visitors come here to simply relax, and will find a quiet beach away from the bustling mainland.

This trek follows the shoreline of **Moreton** from the barge landing at **Tangalooma,** north to **Cape Moreton,** then south along the surf coast to **Kooringal**. There are only two major sand roads crossing the narrow wedge shaped island, and a number of village bypass roads, leaving the majority of travel as beach driving.

You will leave the Port of Brisbane by barge (having first arranged a vehicle permit and camping permit. Book online at www.mulgumpincamping.net.au. About an hour later, the old whaling station of Tangalooma comes into view as the ferry prepares to land.

You will exit the ferry onto soft sand (air down your tyres on the barge prior to landing) at a location known as **The Wrecks**. These are simply old rusting vessels (15 in total) that have been deliberately sunk, forming a break to shelter other craft from westerly winds.

Cape Moreton Lighthouse

Nearby Tangalooma is now a private resort only open to residents, so head north along the beach (there is no vehicular access on the beach in front of Tangalooma). There is also no vehicle based camping at The Wrecks, but there is at **Ben Ewa**, about 1.7 kilometres to the north.

Ben Ewa also marks **Middle Road** – two parallel one way tracks that cross the island to **Eagers Beach** on the east coast. There is a U turn area near the **Tangalooma Bypass** track that allows travellers to head south along **Moreton Bay,** or visit **The Desert** – a fenced off sand blow with walking access to a sand boarding area. This location also marks the end of the **Rous Battery Track**; a ten kilometre hike to the eastern beach of Moreton.

We will however continue north from Ben Ewa to pass **Cowan Point** (look out for dugongs), and reach the **Cowan Cowan Beach** bypass track, about 3.8 kilometres from The Wrecks. You must turn right here (no beach driving is permitted at the settlement of Cowan Cowan), then return to the beach a couple of kilometres later.

Several creek crossings punctuate the next kilometre (low tide access only – use bypass otherwise) as you weave around dead trees and driftwood. You will cross **Craven Creek** preferably near where it fans out to meet the ocean, rather than at the sharp step cut into the beach up higher. A beach camping area heralds the island's largest community of **Bulwer** in the north west corner.

A network of sandy residential streets criss cross the tree shaded town, which includes a store (good range of supplies) and barge access to the mainland on Tuesdays. Camping is available at nearby **Comboyuro Point** with good facilities, and a popular fishing and snorkelling area. There is no beach access for vehicles beyond the point.

You will leave Bulwer via the bypass track, taking the signposted option to **North Point.** Turn left toward **Tailor Bight** about three kilometres later to head on a lovely wetland drive through paperbarks and sedges. This area of Moreton is mostly swampland, and home to frogs and some of the 120 bird species that call this island home.

The track ends at a broad, rather windswept beach, with a long variable spit of sand stretching to **Heath Island.** Retrace your steps turning left at **North Point Road,** to reach the **Blue Lagoon** junction two kilometres later.

Turn left here (right option is an eight kilometre run to Blue Lagoon on the island's east), to follow a corrugated path to the signposted **"Five Hills Lookout"**. It is well worth the steep 200 metre climb here, to look out over the island's northern reaches, and as far as the **Glass House Mountains** on the mainland.

Track Snapshot

TOUR ROUTE:
Moreton Island; coastal run clockwise from Tangalooma Resort and return.

DURATION AND DISTANCE:
This trek requires about 100 kilometres of driving and would be best spread over three days – more if you are looking to kick back a little.

TRACK DETAILS:
Sand tracks only; these vary from loose dry powder to firm beaches at low tide. Soft Roaders can tackle this tour, but trailers are best left to experienced drivers at the wheel of a powerful vehicle.

WHEN TO GO:
All year round, but the school holidays are busy. The sand flies and mosquitoes are voracious over the humid summer period.

CAMPING:
Beach camping without facilities in the zones permitted, and at several defined camping areas with basic facilities.

FUEL AND SUPPLIES:
Bring all food & supplies from mainland – fuel top ups (in drums) and basic food stuffs available at Bulwer.

MAPS:
Sunmap: Moreton Island

OTHER INFORMATION:
Vehicle access and camping permits must be organised on the mainland. Firewood to be carried onto the island (no open fires at North Point), and rubbish to be taken off. Micat Ferry bookings ph: 07 3909 3333 or www.micat.com.au

North Point
Honeymoon Bay
North Point Camp Area
Cape Moreton
Lighthouse
Cape Cliff
Five Hills Lookout – steep walk but extensive views
Lots of wildlife in swampland
Yellow Patch
Nice camp but no open fires allowed
Tailor Bight
NO BEACH DRIVING BEYOND THIS POINT
Bulwer – North Point Rd
Lake Jabiru
Five Hills Lookout
Braydons Beach
Comboyura Point
Spitfire Creek
Bulwer
General Store and ferry access to mainland on Tuesdays
Blue Lagoon Camping Area – short walk to Blue Lagoon nice swimming location
Blue Lagoon
Bulwer Rd
Honeyeater Lake
Beach drive at low tide only
Soft Roaders
Trailers
Steep Climbs
Water Crossing
Good Clearance Needed
Snorkel
Road Tyres
Avoid Wet Weather
Navigation Skills
Extra Fuel
Cravens Creek
Through traffic must use beach bypass track
Cowan Cowan
Look out for Dugongs at Cowan Point
Telegraph Walking Track
Mt. Tempest
Ben Ewa Campground
Eagers Creek Camping Area – Beach Only
The Wrecks
ONE WAY TRAFFIC
Middle Road
ONE WAY TRAFFIC
Eagers Beach
Barge Landing Point
Tangalooma Bypass Track
TANGALOOMA RESORT
N
NW
NE
W
E
SW
SE
S
0
1
2
Kilometres
Sandboarding
The Desert
Soft sand

MORETON ISLAND

Above: *Eastern Beach*

Right: *Palms at Rous Battery*

Continue toward North Point to reach the beach at **Yellow Patch**. A prominent sand blow gives the area its name, but there is a lovely lagoon system with tannin stained waters and sheltered beach camp sites, although no facilities are provided and open fires are not permitted.

North Point Camp Area is nearby and marks the limit of vehicle access to the north. You can walk around the rocky outcrop at North Point (good fishing from the rocks, but dangerous conditions make it only suitable for experienced and well equipped anglers). A series of scenic coves mark the beaches of **Honeymoon Bay** to the east.

Continue the drive past North Point Camp to signposted "Cape Moreton" and its historic lighthouse on the island's hazardous north east tip. A carpark allows visitors to walk a short loop trail around the sandstone tower, built in 1857 and still operating today. A lofty viewpoint near the lighthouse offers expansive views of the eastern beaches, and a staffed information centre is housed in one of the keepers cottages.

Return from the carpark and turn left down a corduroy track to the beach at **Cape Cliff.** Turn right at the surf to follow a southerly run past **Braydons Beach** and over **Spitfire Creek**. You will reach **Blue Lagoon Campground** 2.7 kilometres later, at a signposted track heading into the foreshore dunes.

Blue Lagoon is accessible via a short heathland walking track inland from the camp. This large window lake has been formed by the water table penetrating an undulation in the coastal dune system. Annual rainfall of 1600 mm can lift the water table above sea level, making this location a lovely freshwater swimming spot.

Continue south from Blue Lagoon to the **Bulwer Road.** This road links Blue Lagoon to the island's western shore with a 13 kilometre winding forest drive through bloodwood and scribbly gum. **Honeyeater Lake** is passed on the journey, with its elevated timber look out surrounded by banksia and grass trees. Unlike Blue Lagoon, Honeyeater is a perched lake – formed by a layer of leaf litter lining a sand depression and filling with rain water.

You may wish to take a look at Honeyeater, then return to the eastern beach, to continue south to **Eagers Beach.** There is good camping amid the foreshore dunes here, but camping is not permitted at **Eagers Creek** at a culturally significant site. Indigenous people lived at Moreton for at least 2000 years, leaving shell middens and bone scatters at numerous locations across the island – please obey all instructions in relation to these sites.

Beyond Eagers you will reach the twin cross island tracks of Middle Road (northern most track is the one way track for west bound drivers heading to Ben Ewa), so continue south past **Jason Beach** and its camping possibilities. Human scribblings at the prominent feature of **White Rock** flag the concrete bunkers of **Rous Battery.**

Moreton Island was an important defense base during the world wars – especially WW2, when construction of the Rous site was undertaken. The concrete structures provide historic interest for travellers of today.

Follow the coast past the **Little Sandhills** for a winding run in and around dead trees. Try to time your progress around the larger obstacles with receding waters, rather than be swamped by an oncoming wave.

Some eight kilometres from Rous Battery, you will turn right onto a bypass track to avoid **Mirapool Lagoon.** Native pines and sheoaks frame the rather pleasant wetland and shoreline – home to many species of birds.

You will pass **Short Point** enroute to the village of Kooringal and this trek's conclusion. Mangroves and variable sands make the drive from Kooringal to Tangalooma an uncertain prospect. Progress can be impeded even at low tide, so it will be advisable to head back the way you have arrived.

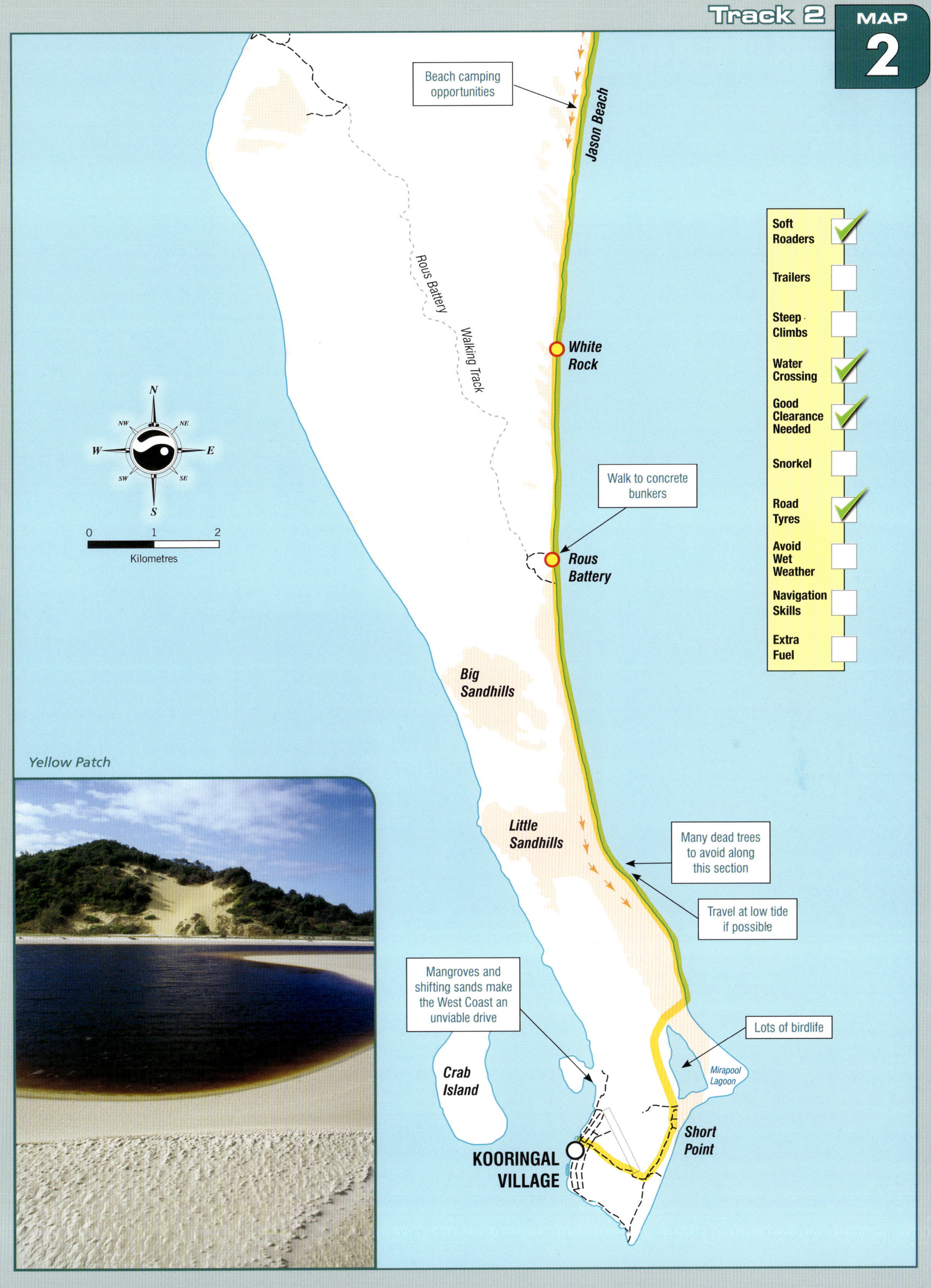

Yellow Patch

KANDANGA

Track Snapshot

TOUR ROUTE:
Kandanga to Imbil via the Kandanga Range

DURATION AND DISTANCE:
You can drive the 100 kilometre trek in a day.

TRACK DETAILS:
Routine 4WDing makes this trek suitable for competent Soft Roaders and trailers. You may need low range for one section, although an auto would be quite capable of a high range climb if pressed.

WHEN TO GO:
Anytime as long as it is dry.

CAMPING:
Good camping with facilities at Lake Borumba Dam or at Borumba Deer Park.

FUEL AND SUPPLIES:
Kandanga and Imbil.

MAPS:
Natmap: Gympie 1:250K is adequate, although a vehicle mounted GPS would be useful.

OTHER INFORMATION:
An excellent (long) day trip from the Sunshine Coast – but better as a weekend.

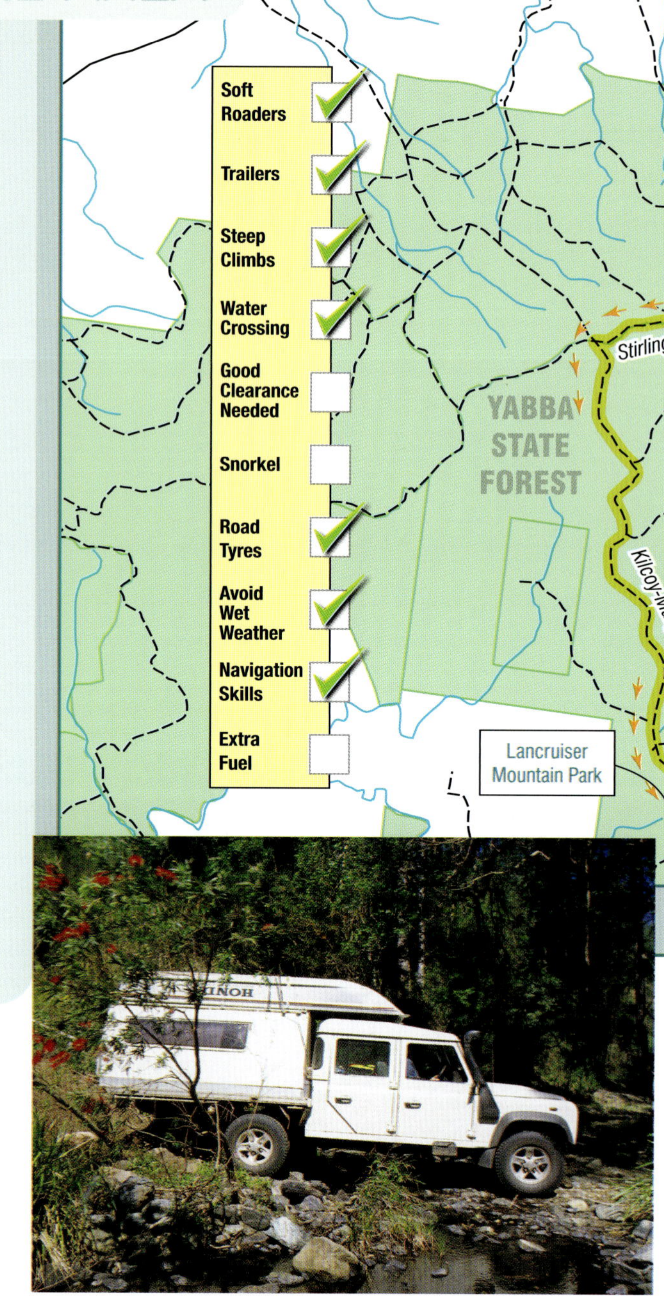

Crossing Kandanga Creek

This trek links the ***Sunshine Coast*** *hinterland hamlets of* ***Kandanga*** *and* ***Imbil,*** *not with the usual 10 kilometre bitumen run, but with a 100 kilometre journey through the ranges. The scenery is verdant and with a little bit of 4WDing thrown in to keep the driver alert, there is sure to be something for everyone.*

Kandanga is well know as a siding for the tourist steam train that puffs its way from ***Gympie*** *to Imbil – an historic route that owes its origins to timber harvesting and pioneering pastoralists. These days the small village boasts of shops, cafes and hotel, catering for an increasing tourism demand.*

Leave town via **Kandanga Creek Road,** passing under the rail trestle bridge, and following bitumen over feeder creeks in cattle grazing country. Dams and sheds dot the rural landscape, as you keep left at **Happy Valley Road.**

Doyles Bridge spans **Kandanga Creek,** some eight kilometres west of Kandanga, where winding road penetrates a broader part of the valley. Bellbirds are often heard through here as you pass **Kandanga HS** on **Faragon Creek.**

Gravel paves the way now so look out for logging trucks, and cattle roaming the unfenced country. You follow Kandanga Creek as it is funneled between the **Amamoor** and **Kandanga Ranges,** under the jungle-like vegetation colouring your arrival onto **Oakwood Station.**

A series of causeways flag an airstrip on the right, some 28 kilometres from Kandanga. You will need to veer left onto a lesser used track here, about 1.5 kilometres beyond the airstrip (public access is prohibited on the main road).

A gate heralds the boundary of **Wrattens NP** two kilometres later as you climb out of the creek with good views through boulders and jungle foliage (although unfortunately lantana is also growing well). Grass trees colour a steep winding pinch over a cattle grid to a marker **"AS 97".**

Turn right at the marker, keeping left at the next junction 1.8 kilometres away. Follow a descent on the main road past several tracks on either side (no access). Then trace the boundary of national park, keeping right away from a gate in state forest, some seven kilometres beyond the AS 97 marker.

Keep left through a gate 500 metres later, passing through three more gates in quick succession. The wet sclerophyll forest thickens now as more leaf litter

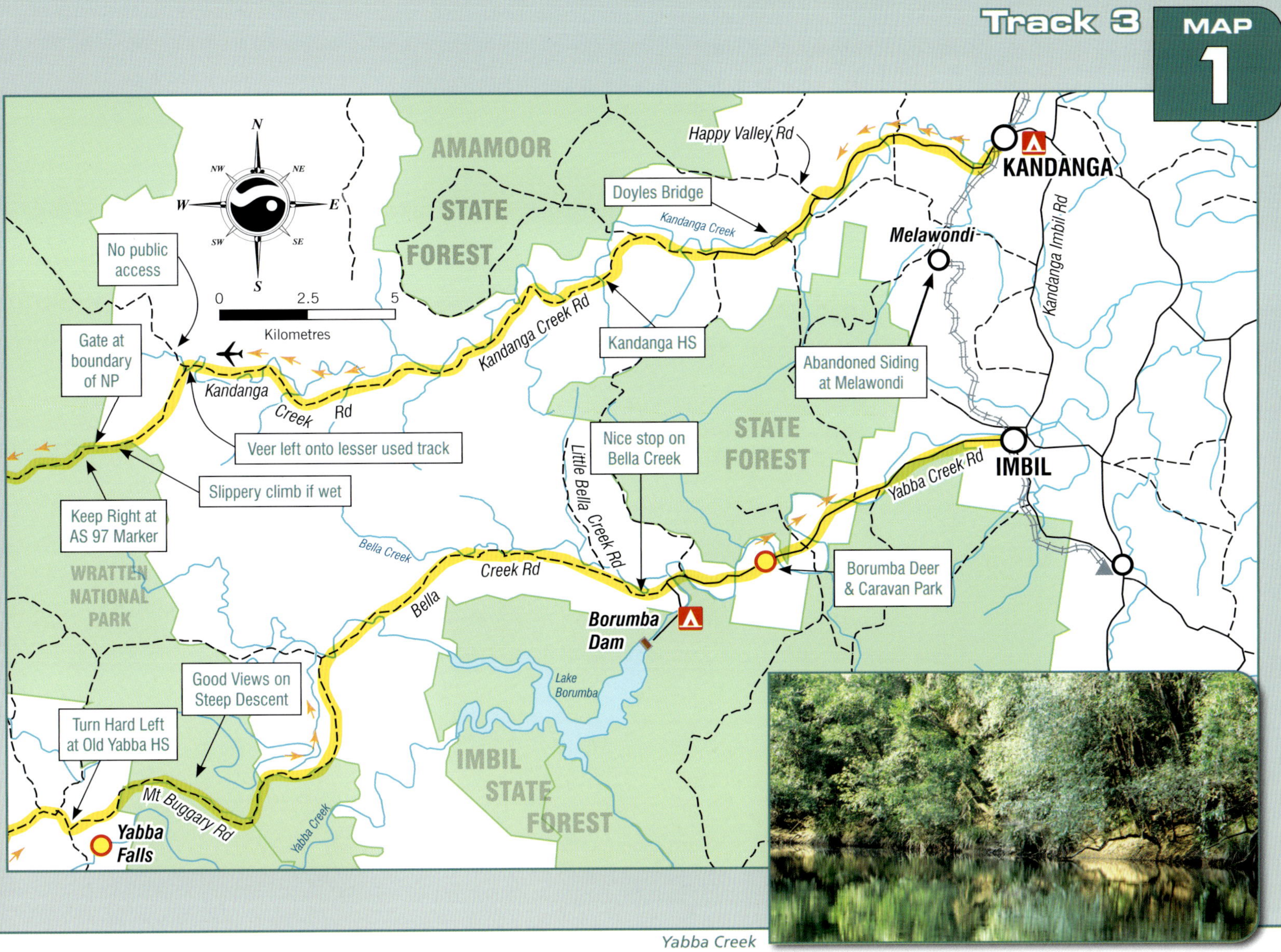

Yabba Creek

carpets the earthen track. This would be very slippery following rain, so time your trip accordingly. (Rain is plentiful around here at times – nearby **Yandina** saw nearly 4500 mm of rain in the big wet of 1892, with more than 2 metres drenching the district in February alone.)

You will reach a tee intersection on **Stirlings Road** just after the last gate, where you turn left to reach another tee, some 2.4 kilometres later. Turn left here onto the main **Murgon – Kilcoy Road,** following the winding gravel through **Yabba SF** to **an intersection,** about 13 kilometres further on.

Swing left onto Kingham Road (Landcruiser Mountain Park on right), to pass a dam on the right. A signpost at the turn indicates that the run over **Yabba Forest Reserve** is 4WD only – this would certainly be the case following rain, but the relatively steep descent and especially the climb are routine in the dry.

You will cross the headwaters of **Yabba Creek** and enter an open grazing area. Tall fencing surrounds the deer farm at **Kingham HS** with stockyards and dams framed by range country on both sides.

Swing hard left away from Old Yabba HS onto **Mount Buggery Road,** about 8.4 kilometres from the beginning of Diaper Road. You will follow a spur with broken views on either side, perhaps pulling back to low range for the steeper section of track.

The heavily treed valley has pockets of grass tree and reedy plants, as a couple of minor creek crossings precede the more significant **Bella Creek.** Houses together with old stockyards and a disused cattle dip herald a major road cutting (good views), where irrigated volcanic soils support ginger plantations and other cropping.

Keep right at **Little Bella Creek Road** to cross Bella Creek at a major causeway. A minor track follows the creek south to a large pool, which would make an ideal rest stop or swimming opportunity. A few hundred metres later, turn right at a tee to reach the spillway at **Lake Borumba Dam.**

Follow bitumen through hoop pine plantation to a grassed camping area with shaded sites and good facilities. Fees are payable for campers, but there is a boat ramp and scenic lookout over the dam spillway, together with colourful exotic trees and a day use area.

Return to the tee on Yabba Creek Road, swinging right for a number of bridge crossings on the final run into Imbil. Another camping possibility is located at **No. 6 Crossing bridge.** You can turn right into **Borumba Deer Park** to find a terraced private campground with absolute water frontage. Plenty of trees line the creek here, with a less formal layout than the Borumba Dam area.

Continue through grazing country over the single lane bridges and past a sawmill. The township of Imbil marks the conclusion of this tour with hotel, cafes and shops available. Imbil is also the beginning of our more demanding Conondale trek, so those looking for adventure may well read on...

TRACK 4

CONONDALE

BRISBANE AREA

Above: *Conondale access track*

Track Snapshot

TOUR ROUTE:
Imbil to Kilcoy via the Mary River and Conondale NP.

DURATION AND DISTANCE:
The 100 kilometre run can be done in a day.

TRACK DETAILS:
Routine driving apart from a short section climbing up onto the range that will demand low range and good clearance. A difficult section for trailers, and out of the question for Soft Roaders.

WHEN TO GO:
All year round but avoid wet weather.

CAMPING:
You can camp on the Mary River at Kenilworth, or choose from a range of options at Kilcoy.

FUEL AND SUPPLIES:
Kenilworth and Kilcoy.

MAPS:
Natmap: Gympie 1:250K provides most detail, but a vehicle mounted GPS and the Natmap: Nambour 1:100K would be very desirable.

OTHER INFORMATION:
Lovely sub-tropical rainforest is one of this tour's highlights. Bring a sense of adventure (and direction) as signage on this trek is poor.

*This tour on the **Sunshine Coast** hinterland follows a scenic path along the **Mary River** valley, before climbing up and over the **Conondale Range** to drop down into **Kilcoy.** There are dense tracts of jungle, open river and creek valleys, together with great camping opportunities. You will enjoy a relaxing amble over much of the journey, but revel in the demanding drive that penetrates the Conondale Range.*

The village of **Imbil** – some 37 kilometres south of **Gympie** – marks our starting point (and the final destination for the **Mary Valley Rattler**; a steam tourist train that runs out of Gympie). Head south from Imbil via **Diggings Road** to follow the rail line**,** crossing a creek and tracing the bitumen into **Imbil SF**. A rail trestle bridge precedes a car park on the right, from where bellbirds may be heard.

A rail siding indicates your arrival in the hamlet of **Brooloo**, where you turn left into **Parry Street**, then right on the main **Mary Valley Road**. Follow the **Kenilworth Road** south for 400 metres, before turning left onto **Moy Pocket Road.** Winding bitumen paves the way along the Mary Valley, with good views over the river on the left, and **Kenilworth Bluff** on your right.

Continue to a tee intersection on the **Eumundi – Kenilworth Road,** turning right at the locality of **Gheerulla.** You will pass state forest and a picnic spot on the left, as you cross **Gheerulla Creek** and its canopy of jungle.

A campground on the right marks the **Obi Obi Road** on your left (lovely scenic run into **Mapleton**). You will again cross the Mary River at a substantial bridge as you swing left into **Kenilworth** and its bottleneck main street.

A number of cafes and weekend tourists are now a feature of this former forestry town.

Follow the main road south past a tea house to **Sunday Creek Road** on the right (forest drive to **Jimna**). A carpark and picnic spot near the junction allows

Right: *Mary River*

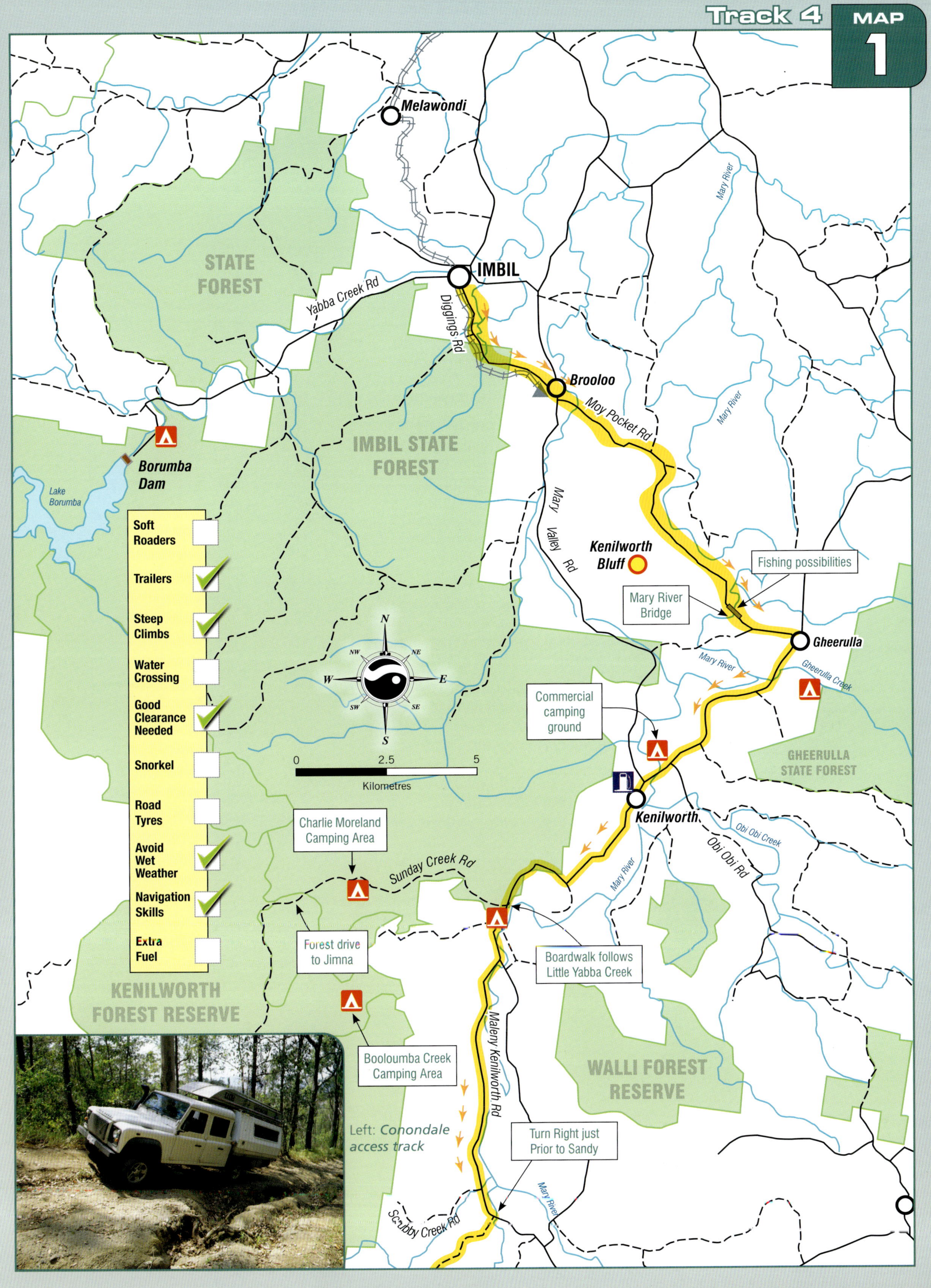

Left: *Conondale access track*

visitors to access a boardwalk following **Little Yabba Creek** under the shade of Moreton Bay fig trees. Beware of the infamous "stinging tree" on this stroll – its generous leaves are covered with barbs that can leave itchy welts on exposed skin.

Two kilometres further south you will pass the turn off to **Booloumba Creek** (camping area, swimming hole and walks). Continue south to pass the Mary River Bridge on your left and a winding valley run following the river (watch for motor cyclists who also like this section of road).

You will pass **Scrubby Creek Road** on the right, some 6.4 kilometres south of the Mary River Bridge, then reach another junction on the right 800 metres later. Turn right here, onto Grigors Road (may not be signposted) just prior to **Sandy Creek,** passing the Keith and Ivy Boon Memorial Park.

A cluster of cottages on the corner mark the transition to gravel and dairying country before the road narrows to track status, after approximately 3 kilometres. Bracken fringes the lesser used continuation which crosses Scrubby Creek some five kilometres from the bitumen.

A rather nasty eroded climb will pull you back to low first to pick a suitable line over the next kilometre. There are good views to be had from a series of switchbacks as you reach **Conondale NP** and its jungle vegetation. The most demanding part of this trek is now over, and you can probably select high range again.

You will reach a tee intersection 9.3 kilometres from the bitumen, where you turn left to descend through a magnificent forest of bluegum, stringybark and picabeen palms. Fig trees and vines run rampant in the tree tops, while an understorey of ferns shade the forest floor.

Turn left again one kilometre later onto the the dry weather only **Bellthorpe – Jimna Road,** to travel approximately 8 kilometres past a section of pines and across Sandy Creek (scenic stop), to reach a large triangulated intersection.

Turn right at the fork onto Bellthorpe Road. Keep straight past views on the left on a winding descent through palms and subtropical rainforest.

After approximately 10 kilometres, you will reach a concrete bridge **East Kilcoy Creek** (its origins lie just a few kilometres away at Mount Langley), where you will find a small park. Step out to enjoy this tranquil spot, where a jumble of trees have been washed into a rocky bend, and a nice pool has formed downstream from the bridge.

Conondale Rainforest

Kilcoy Creek

Approximately seven kilometres beyond the bridge you will reach another large triangulated intersection (the result of log trucks needing plenty of space to turn), where you swing left to begin a sustained descent along **Traves Road**. Follow the main track over some quite substantial erosion damage, with elevated views over the **Kilcoy Valley.**

You will exit national park onto better road with concrete causeways at the creek crossings. Sealed road is flanked by range views on either side as you reach the outskirts of Kilcoy. While this township was established in the 1890s, it originally grew from a 35 000 acre spread, selected 50 years prior.

Today smaller holdings and hobby farms dot the valley past **Mount Ann** as you turn right over Kilcoy Creek, then left

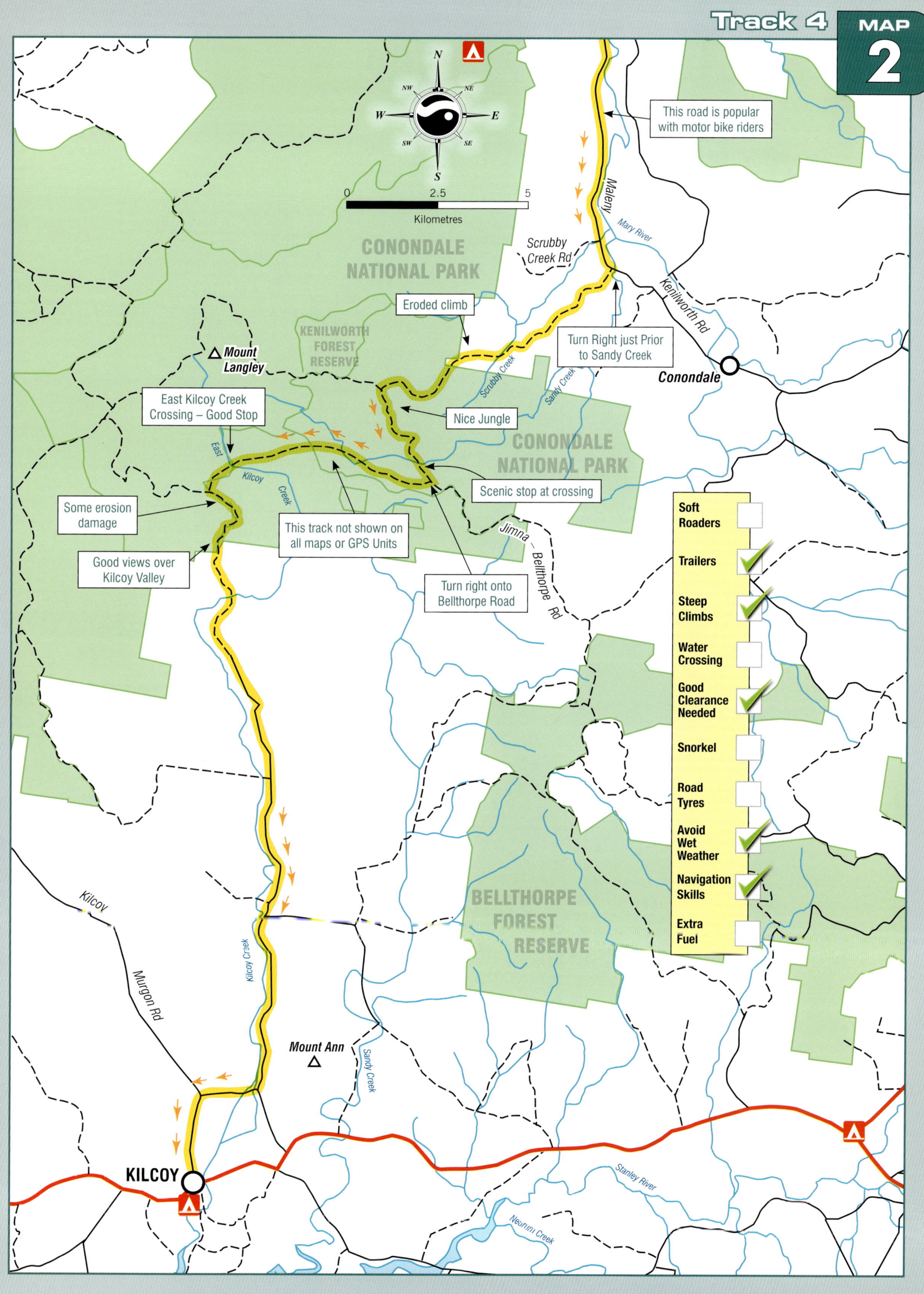
N
NW
NE
W
E
SW
SE
S
0
2.5
5
Kilometres
This road is popular with motor bike riders
Maleny
Mary River
Scrubby Creek Rd
Kenilworth Rd
CONONDALE NATIONAL PARK
KENILWORTH FOREST RESERVE
Eroded climb
Turn Right just Prior to Sandy Creek
Conondale
Mount Langley
Scrubby Creek
Sandy Creek
East Kilcoy Creek Crossing – Good Stop
Nice Jungle
CONONDALE NATIONAL PARK
Scenic stop at crossing
East Kilcoy Creek
Some erosion damage
This track not shown on all maps or GPS Units
Jimna – Bellthorpe Rd
Good views over Kilcoy Valley
Turn right onto Bellthorpe Road
Soft Roaders
Trailers
Steep Climbs
Water Crossing
Good Clearance Needed
Snorkel
Road Tyres
Avoid Wet Weather
Navigation Skills
Extra Fuel
Kilcoy
Murgon Rd
BELLTHORPE FOREST RESERVE
Kilcoy Creek
Mount Ann
Sandy Creek
KILCOY
Stanley River
Neurum Creek

TRACK 5

The Condamine

BRISBANE AREA

Track Snapshot

TOUR ROUTE:
Boonah to Killarney via the Condamine River

DURATION AND DISTANCE:
This 90 kilometre tour will take about a day.

TRACK DETAILS:
Routine driving for the most part, with a number of river crossings marking the Condamine Gorge. Trailers are not permitted and Soft Roaders will need good clearance for the rocky river crossings.

WHEN TO GO:
Anytime, but not following heavy rain as the river crossings may be high or flowing rapidly.

CAMPING:
Campgrounds at Boonah and Lake Moogerah enroute, with popular camping available at Queen Mary Falls Tourist Park, south east of Killarney.

FUEL AND SUPPLIES:
Boonah and Killarney

MAPS:
Natmap: Warwick 1:250K.

OTHER INFORMATION:
While the Condamine Gorge is scenic and offers attractive river crossings, it runs through private property and camping is not permitted.

Above: *Main Range National Park*

Right: *The Condamine*

Queensland's Scenic Rim** began life eons ago as an enormous volcanic extrusion. Erosion over the centuries has moulded the land mass into a string of ranges that intersect with the east coast's **Great Dividing Range.

*This dramatic country is shared across the NSW border, and attracts visitors with its lofty viewpoints and plunging streams. The steep terrain spawns the **Condamine River** – and with it the beginnings of Australia's longest river system, the **Murray-Darling.***

*Our tour will take you from Boonah in south east Queensland, through the Scenic Rim, and just touch the NSW border, to follow the Condamine River into **Killarney**.*

Leave Boonah on the **Rathdowney Road** to pass the **Dugandan Hotel,** and head in the direction of the signposted **"Maroon Dam"**. A Lutheran church marks the crossing of **Teviot Brook** as you pass vineyards, cropping and grazing country. The rich volcanic soils here support a variety of pastoral pursuits, with valuable water from Teviot Brook irrigating broad acres.

Turn right onto **Mount Alford Road** to cross a complex system of waterways at the **Frenchs Creek** confluence. Good range views extend in an arc from the distinctive **Moogerah Peaks** cluster (Mounts: French, Edwards, Greville and Moon) to the more distant peaks of Mount Barney in the south.

Turn right onto gravel at **Tunstall Road,** some 11 kilometres from Boonah, at the locality of **Mount Alford**. Follow the narrow road through scattered pine trees toward **Mount Edwards**. You will reach a tee intersection on bitumen seven kilometres later on the shoreline of **Lake Moogerah.**

Turn right here to follow the signs to a day use area on the lake. BBQs and toilets are located in the dam reserve, while access to the spillway picnic area offers a nice waterway, fringed with grassed areas and bottlebrush.

Return to the last junction and continue to follow the lake shoreline south past an outdoor education centre to **Muller Park Road.** The **Moogerah Caravan Park** is located on the lake here, but we continue for another 2.6 kilometres to turn right toward signposted **"Mount Edwards".**

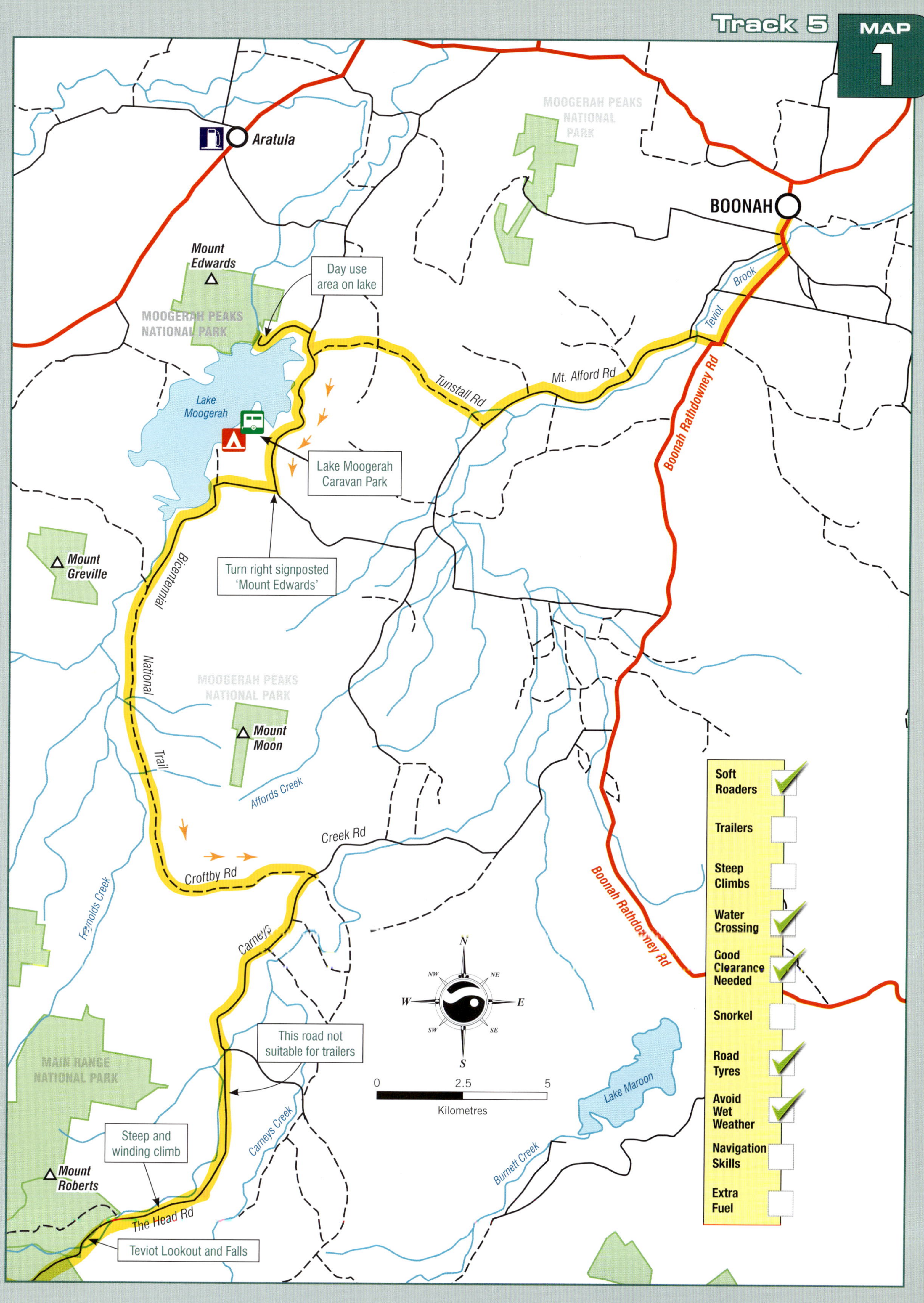

Aratula
BOONAH
MOOGERAH PEAKS NATIONAL PARK
Mount Edwards
Day use area on lake
MOOGERAH PEAKS NATIONAL PARK
Lake Moogerah
Lake Moogerah Caravan Park
Turn right signposted 'Mount Edwards'
Tunstall Rd
Mt. Alford Rd
Teviot Brook
Boonah Rathdowney Rd
Mount Greville
Bicentennial National Trail
MOOGERAH PEAKS NATIONAL PARK
Mount Moon
Affords Creek
Creek Rd
Croftby Rd
Reynolds Creek
Carneys
Boonah Rathdowney Rd
MAIN RANGE NATIONAL PARK
This road not suitable for trailers
Steep and winding climb
Mount Roberts
The Head Rd
Teviot Lookout and Falls
Carneys Creek
Burnett Creek
Lake Maroon
N
NE
E
SE
S
SW
W
NW
0
2.5
5
Kilometres
Soft Roaders
Trailers
Steep Climbs
Water Crossing
Good Clearance Needed
Snorkel
Road Tyres
Avoid Wet Weather
Navigation Skills
Extra Fuel

THE CONDAMINE

Follow the bitumen past the south arm of Lake Moogerah, veering left just prior to **Reynolds Creek** on **Croftby Road**. Gravel now paves the way along the **Bicentennial National Trail,** with **Mount Greville** dominating the skyline on your right, and smaller farms dotted along the valley.

You will climb past **Mount Moon** to a tee intersection at **Croftby.** Turn right onto **Carneys Creek Road** to reach **The Head Road** about five kilometres later. Turn right at this junction (left option follows a parallel path through **Main Range NP**), and pass a sign indicating "not suitable for trailers and caravans".

The pasture gives way to bush as you wind through substantial cuttings into **Teviot SF.** A causeway at **Goldys Corner** flags entry into Main Range NP and its tall eucalyptus forest. Bellbirds may be heard along the way, although the once plentiful cedar trees are few and far between on the ranges, with most falling to timber cutters of the 1900s.

The road narrows to a steep winding climb over the next few kilometres, as you reach **Teviot Lookout** on the right. You are now standing at the watershed of the **McPherson Range,** with the single drop of **Teviot Falls** plunging almost 100 vertical metres over the **Dividing Range** to begin its journey toward **Moreton Bay.**

Views to the north take in **Mount Roberts**, while **Mount Superbus** dominates the western skyline at an impressive 1381 metres. Continue beyond the lookout on a gradual descent past **Wilsons Peak** on the left, and the character buildings of **Bretts Crossing**.

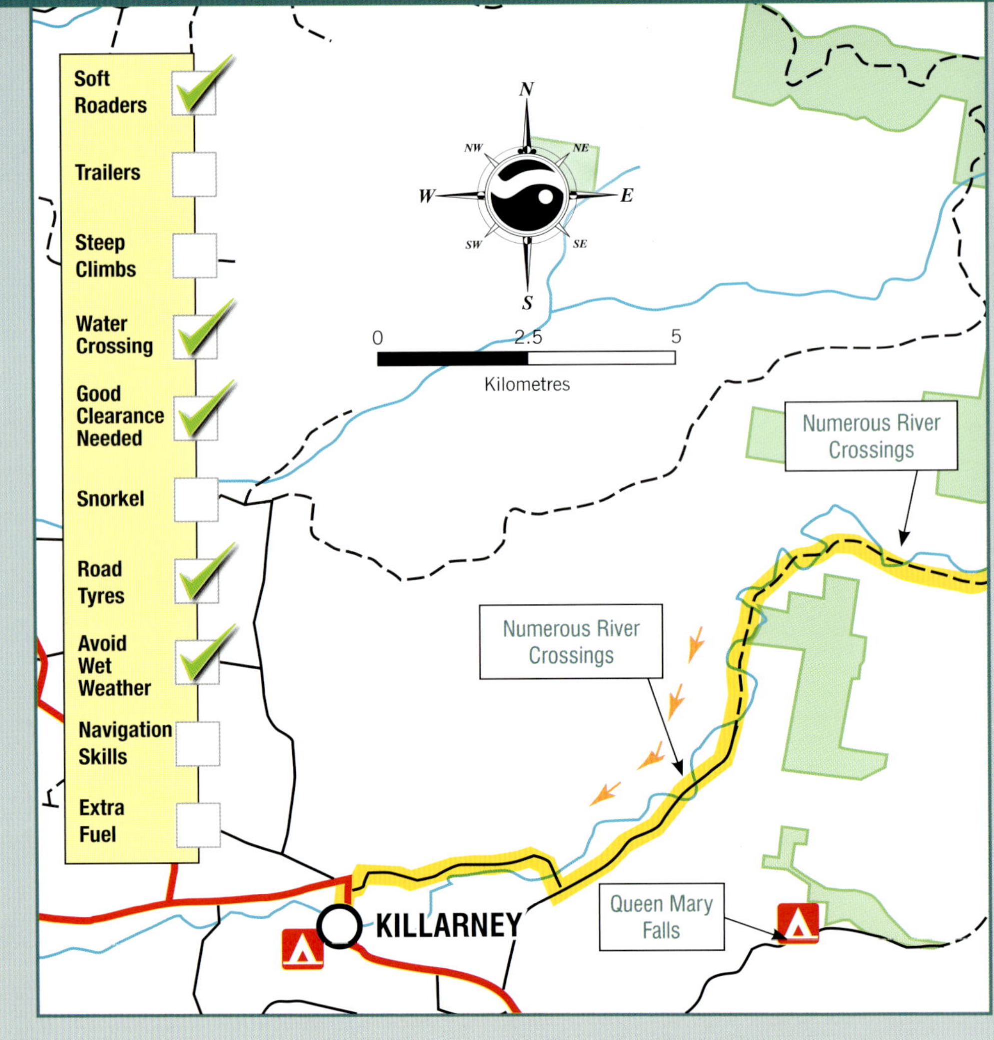

The infant Condamine River gathers pace here on its westward journey away from the ranges, and through pockets of remnant rainforest. You could throw a stone into NSW from here, as you reach a major junction 800 metres further on.

Veer right onto the **Condamine River Road** (left option leads to Main Range NP and **Queen Mary Falls**), and drop down past the telephone exchange. Gravel paves the way past a Bed and Breakfast at **Oaklea,** with the Condamine River on your right. Old stockyards precede a homestead at **The Head,** before you reach a sign warning of the 14 river crossings to come.

While the crossings are usually routine, it does not take much rain to funnel a sizeable quantity down the gorge – do not continue if water levels are high or fast flowing.

A network of waterways converge through clumpy grass and rocks as you descend from an elevated view, through some massive fence posts to a sheoak forest.

A couple of weekender cottages precede the first river crossing, with an almost vertical gorge of sheer rock looking down from perhaps 200 metres above. Subsequent water

Lake Moogerah Area

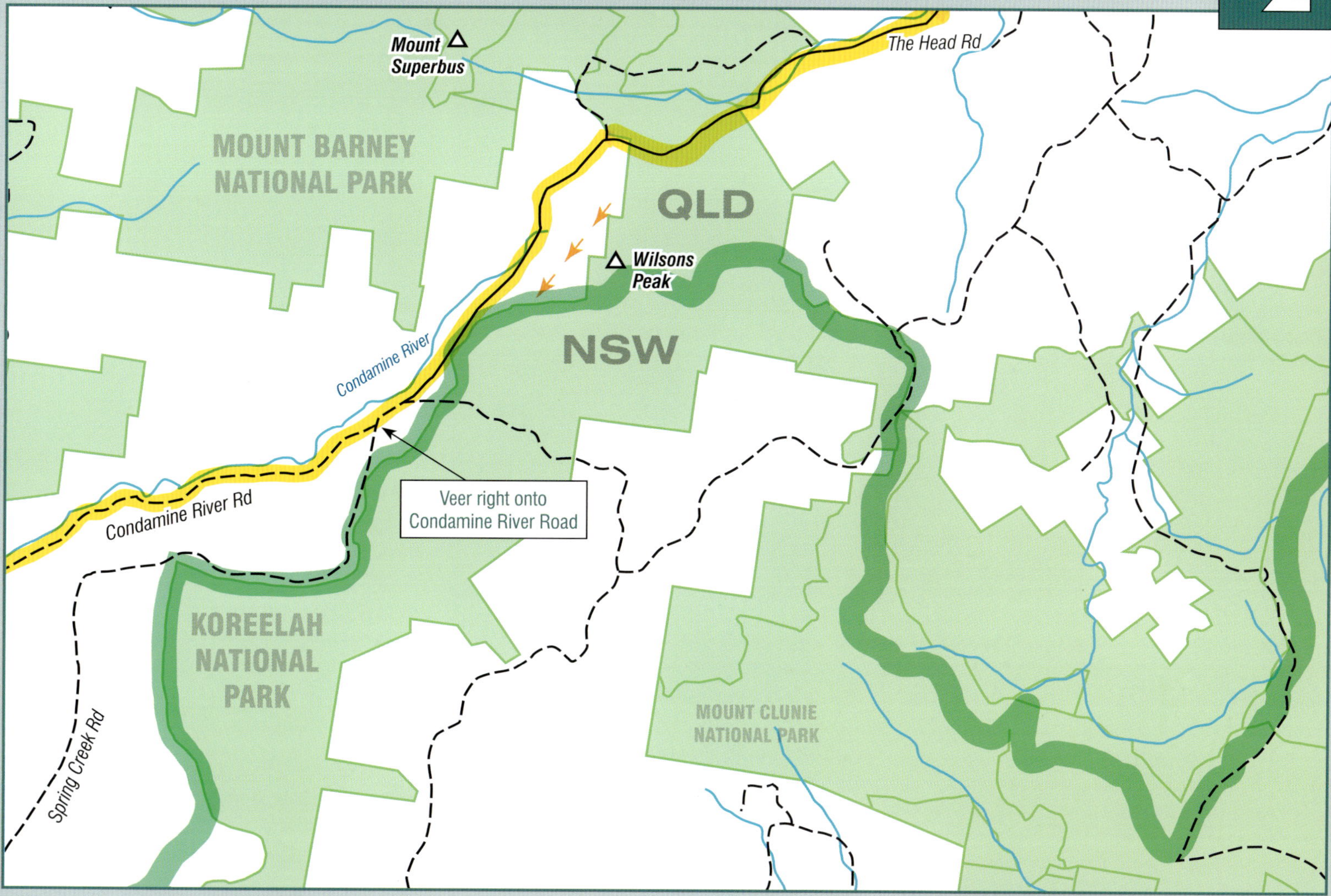
Mount Superbus
The Head Rd
MOUNT BARNEY NATIONAL PARK
QLD
Wilsons Peak
NSW
Condamine River
Veer right onto Condamine River Road
Condamine River Rd
KOREELAH NATIONAL PARK
Spring Creek Rd
MOUNT CLUNIE NATIONAL PARK

crossings are punctuated with signage (Double Crossing, Mawhirts Crossing etc.), and there are some uneven sections – watch for wheel placement and clearances in lower slung vehicles.

Keep straight at **Ajinbilly Road** (Rainforest Retreat Cabins) to pass a notable peak on your left just after **Bullocky Crossing**. The track improves beyond **Reis Crossing,** returning to bitumen about a kilometre later.

Keep right on the Condamine River Road at the signposted "Killarney" junction. Follow the river through potato growing country to the town of Killarney, separated into distinct north and south

Cambanoora Gorge
Condamine River
You are about to cross the Condamine River 14 times.
SUITABLE FOR HIGH CLEARANCE VEHICLES ONLY

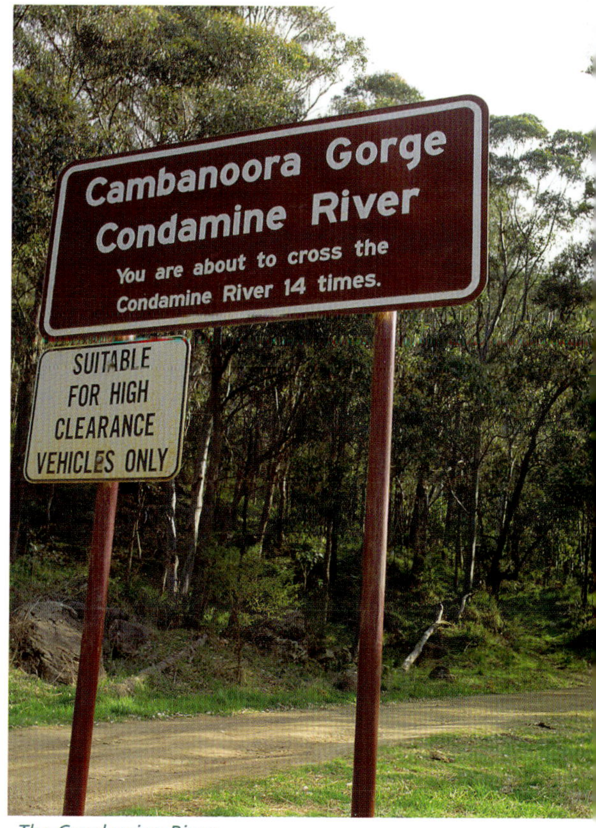

The Condamine River

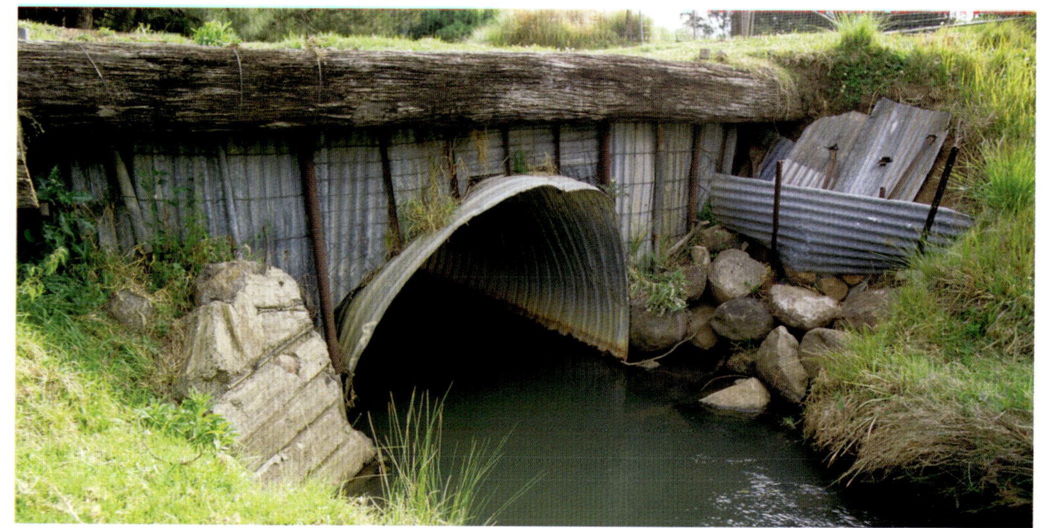

TRACK 6 BLACKBUTT

BRISBANE AREA

Track Snapshot

TOUR ROUTE:
Hampton to Blackbutt via Ravensbourne NP and Lake Cressbrook

DURATION AND DISTANCE:
You could drive the 110 kilometre run in a day trip or make it a two day tour with an overnight stop at Lake Cressbrook.

TRACK DETAILS:
Easy driving on a mix of forestry tracks and some bitumen. Suitable for all vehicles and trailers.

WHEN TO GO:
All year round unless heavy rain has filled the creeks.

CAMPING:
Excellent camping with good facilities at Lake Cressbrook. Other possibilities at Crows Nest and Blackbutt.

FUEL AND SUPPLIES:
Toowoomba, Crows Nest and Blackbutt.

MAPS:
Sunmap: SE Queensland, but better detail on Natmap 1:250K Ipswich and Gympie.

OTHER INFORMATION:
An easy drive packed with the right ingredients – forests, lakes, nice creek crossings and good bushwalking at Ravensbourne.

*The **Blackbutt Range** owes its development and track network to forestry operations over the past 150 years. Cedar and bunya pine harvesting proved viable enough to establish several towns, with timber plantations now sustaining the small communities. This trek follows in the path of those pioneering wood cutters, but takes in pockets of rainforest and a couple of man made lakes.*

You will begin the tour at **Hampton** – a quiet country town 32 kilometres north of **Toowoomba** on the **New England Highway**. Turn east on the **Esk Road** to follow a winding descent over **Perseverance Creek**. Turn right about six kilometres out of Hampton at sign posted **"Perseverance Falls"**, then veer right onto gravel 1.5 kilometres later.

Keep left at the tee (the right option leads to walks along Monroes Tramway) to follow **Palm Tree Road** past hobby farms and retreats. You will reach the locality of Palm Tree at the "School Road", where you will swing left on a descent to a culvert crossing of the creek, where 20 metre high Piccabeen Palms compete with adjoining eucalyptus species.

Lowland views continue to the **Esk – Hampton Road,** where you turn right back onto bitumen for a short run to the signposted **"Ravensbourne National Park"** on your right. It is a 1.5 kilometre drive to **Beutels Lookout,** where good views extend through cleared land toward **Lake Wivenhoe** (the local area was harvested of cedar trees in the 1900s).

Visitors with energy to spare can follow a network of foot tracks through remnant rainforest taking in a feel for this country prior to European settlement. The options vary from short to lengthy hikes on moderately steep terrain, but are well worth the effort.

Ravensbourne is a day use only area with toilets, tables and shelter shed.

Return to the Esk – Hampton Road, turning right back on the bitumen, then left a few kilometres later, at the signposted **"Perseverance Dam"**. Swing

Ravensbourne rainforest

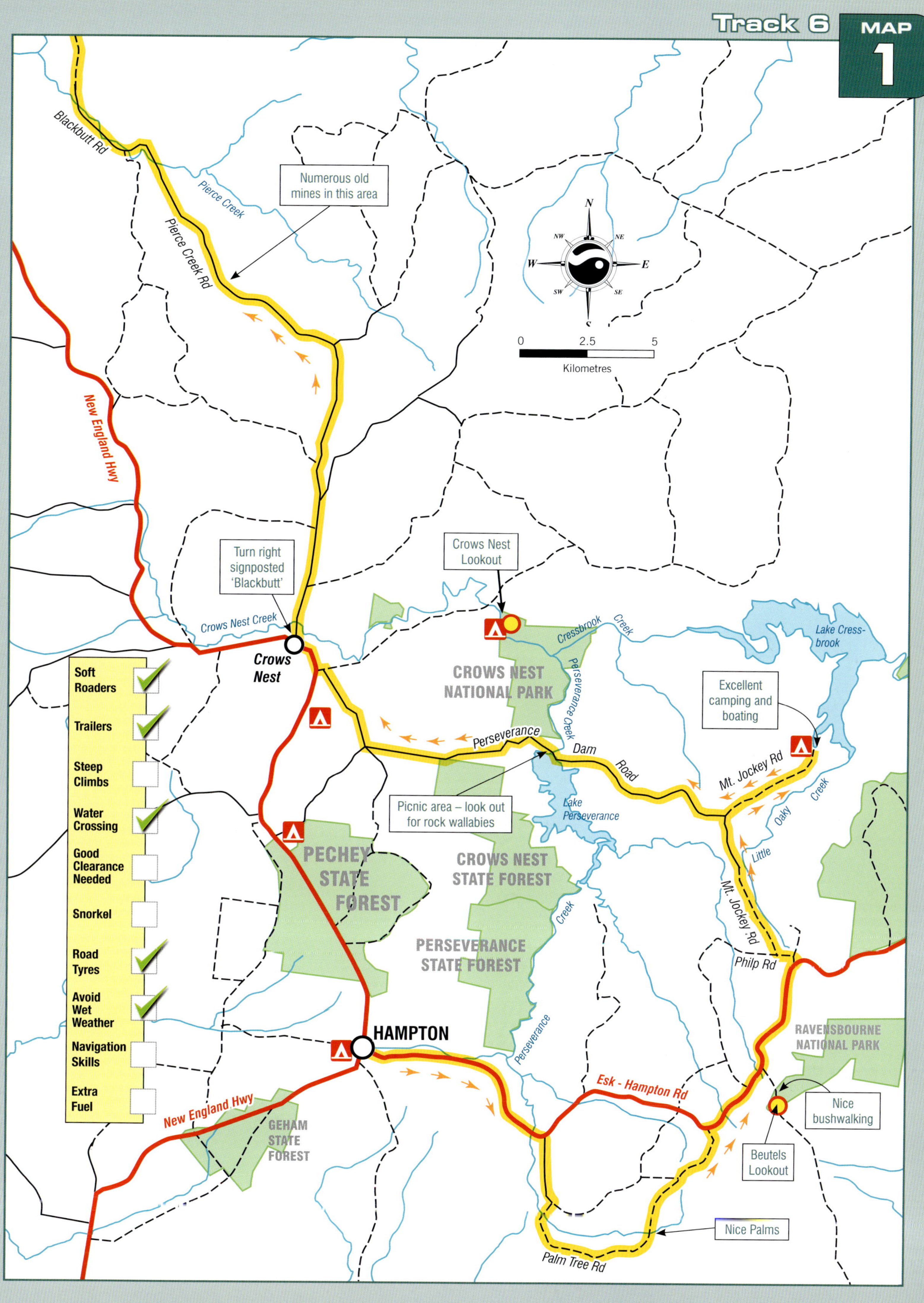

Blackbutt Rd
Pierce Creek
Pierce Creek Rd
Numerous old mines in this area
New England Hwy
N
NE
E
SE
S
SW
W
NW
0
2.5
5
Kilometres
Turn right signposted 'Blackbutt'
Crows Nest Lookout
Crows Nest Creek
Crows Nest
Cressbrook Creek
Lake Cress-brook
CROWS NEST NATIONAL PARK
Perseverance Creek
Excellent camping and boating
Perseverance
Dam
Road
Mt. Jockey Rd
Picnic area – look out for rock wallabies
Lake Perseverance
Oaky Creek
Little
PECHEY STATE FOREST
CROWS NEST STATE FOREST
Creek
Mt. Jockey Rd
PERSEVERANCE STATE FOREST
Philp Rd
Soft Roaders
Trailers
Steep Climbs
Water Crossing
Good Clearance Needed
Snorkel
Road Tyres
Avoid Wet Weather
Navigation Skills
Extra Fuel
HAMPTON
RAVENSBOURNE NATIONAL PARK
Perseverance
Esk - Hampton Rd
Nice bushwalking
New England Hwy
GEHAM STATE FOREST
Beutels Lookout
Nice Palms
Palm Tree Rd

Right: *Blackbutt pub*

Below: *Late afternoon on Lake Cressbrook*

left again almost immediately onto **Philp Road,** turning right at the **Mount Jockey Road** intersection for a winding descent toward **Lake Cressbrook.**

You will reach a toll gate after nine kilometres, where a small fee allows day access. Camping is permitted here with grassy terraced sites, shade and excellent facilities. An additional fee is required to camp, and although swimming is not permitted (algal blooms), fishing and boating are popular activities.

On leaving Lake Cressbrook, retrace your steps to Mount Jockey Road, continuing in a westerly direction past a picnic area and power station at Lake Perseverance. You may spot rock wallabies at this location, where the spillway drops away in spectacular fashion.

A winding climb through thick forest thins out into rolling hills closer to the township of **Crows Nest**. Turn right five kilometres beyond the spillway, following road signage back onto the New England Highway. Most services and supplies can be found at Crows Nest, with the nearby **Crows Nest Falls NP** perhaps enticing some travellers if there has been recent rains.

Continue the trek by veering right at the town centre onto **Pierce Creek Road** signposted **"Blackbutt",** keeping left at a fork some eight kilometres later. Old mines dot the bush on a winding run over floodways and creeks. Keep straight past Emu Creek, where stockyards and windmills are flanked by rocky outcrops. There is a small parking area at the Emu Creek causeway if you would like to stretch your legs.

Bitumen gives way to gravel beyond Emu Creek, as you skirt the eastern foothills of the Blackbutt Range. Keep right at the **Mount Binga** turn off, to reach **Googa State Forest** on the right. Rich volcanic soils now contrast with the earlier stony substrate, as hoop and plantation pines usher your journey into a sheltered network of forest trails.

Follow the main track, keeping left at **Googa Creek Road** for broken views at some elevated sections. Continue through the Googa locality and past **Nukku Road,** before veering right at the signposted "Blackbutt" turn off. Cropping and irrigated country with Queenslander style houses heralds your arrival into the township of Blackbutt.

Bigger than most people expect, **Blackbutt** now looks to tourism to supplement forestry income, and visitors will find most services in the town. From here, the popular **Bunya Mountains** lie to the west, while our **Upper Brisbane River** trek begins here.

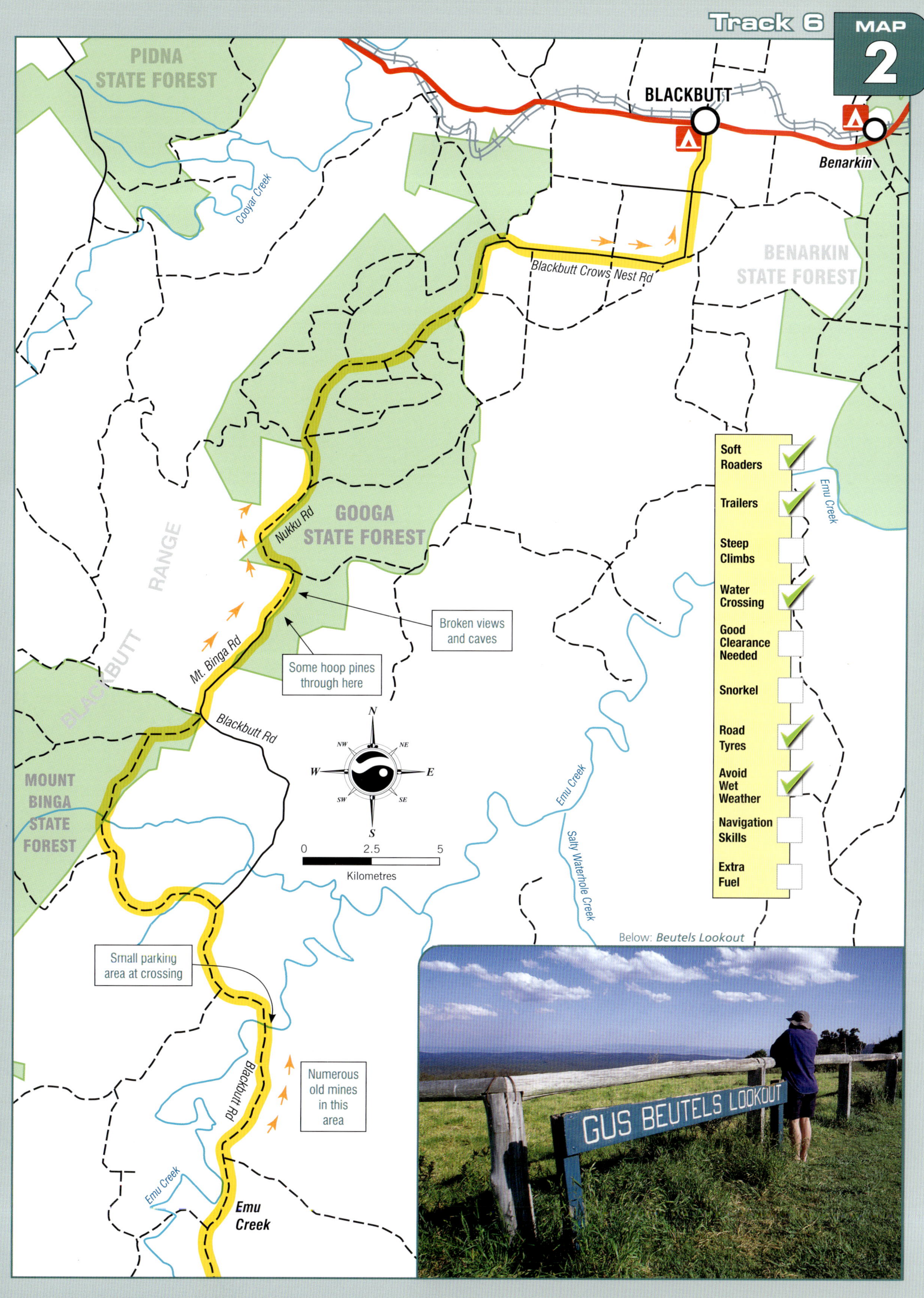

Below: *Beutels Lookout*

Chapter 2

SOUTH EAST QUEENSLAND

◀ *Coast Range view*

TRACK 7

Sundown

SE QUEENSLAND

Above: *Red Rock Gorge*

Track Snapshot

TOUR ROUTE:
Stanthorpe to Sundown NP via Girraween.

DURATION AND DISTANCE:
The 80 kilometres from Stanthorpe to Burrows Waterhole in Sundown will take at least two days to complete – three if you camp at both Girraween and Sundown.

TRACK DETAILS:
Easy driving through Girraween and to the boundary of Sundown NP, but rough and rock strewn beyond that. The steep hills demand low range, and rough sections will require good clearances. Trailers must be robust and towed by an experienced driver.

WHEN TO GO:
All year round, although winter nights will be cold. Avoid wet weather as the final descents to the Severn River are slippery. Wildflowers are at their best throughout Girraween over spring.

CAMPING:
There are opportunities with facilities at Girraween and Summerville. There is bush camping at Sundown (unserviced at Reedy Waterhole and basic facilities at Red Rock Gorge and Burrows Waterhole.

FUEL AND SUPPLIES:
Stanthorpe, Ballandean.

MAPS:
Hema: Girraween, Bald Rock and Sundown NP.

OTHER INFORMATION:
Travel in company with recovery gear into Sundown, as there are few visitors and some difficult terrain.

*The **Granite Belt** of Queensland runs across the border into NSW in spectacular style, with massive extrusions of weathered rock jutting up from the earth's crust. Nearby **Sundown NP** encompasses some additional granite features, but is mostly covered with traprock geology – sedimentary rocks crushed and cooked into a hard landscape cap.*

*This trek follows a rocky trail through the granite tors of **Girraween**, then descends to the **Severn River** at Sundown NP for an action packed 4WD adventure.*

We begin the trek at **Stanthorpe** (a stonefruit and winery region) on the **New England Highway**, taking **Sugarloaf Road** south east from the town at the signposted **"Eukey"** turn off. Keep straight past the **Summerville Caravan Park** and **Storm King Dam** (fishing, swimming, but camping prohibited).

Sundown access track

Turn left onto **Breens Road,** some 15 kilometres from Stanthorpe, just prior to **Eukey.** Follow this road to a tee intersection, turning right onto **Pyramids Road**. Cross a creek through grazing country, where giant granite eggs flag the approaching national park.

Follow the boundary of **Girraween NP** to a fork 2.5 kilometres later, keeping right at the signposted "Park Headquarters". You will reach **Dr. Roberts Waterhole** and **Underground Creek** walks 800 metres later (both fairly short walks), then follow a winding drive over the **Bill Gobel Bridge** with **Mount Norman** and **Castle Rock** visible on the right.

A ranger's station and adjoining camping areas allow visitors to

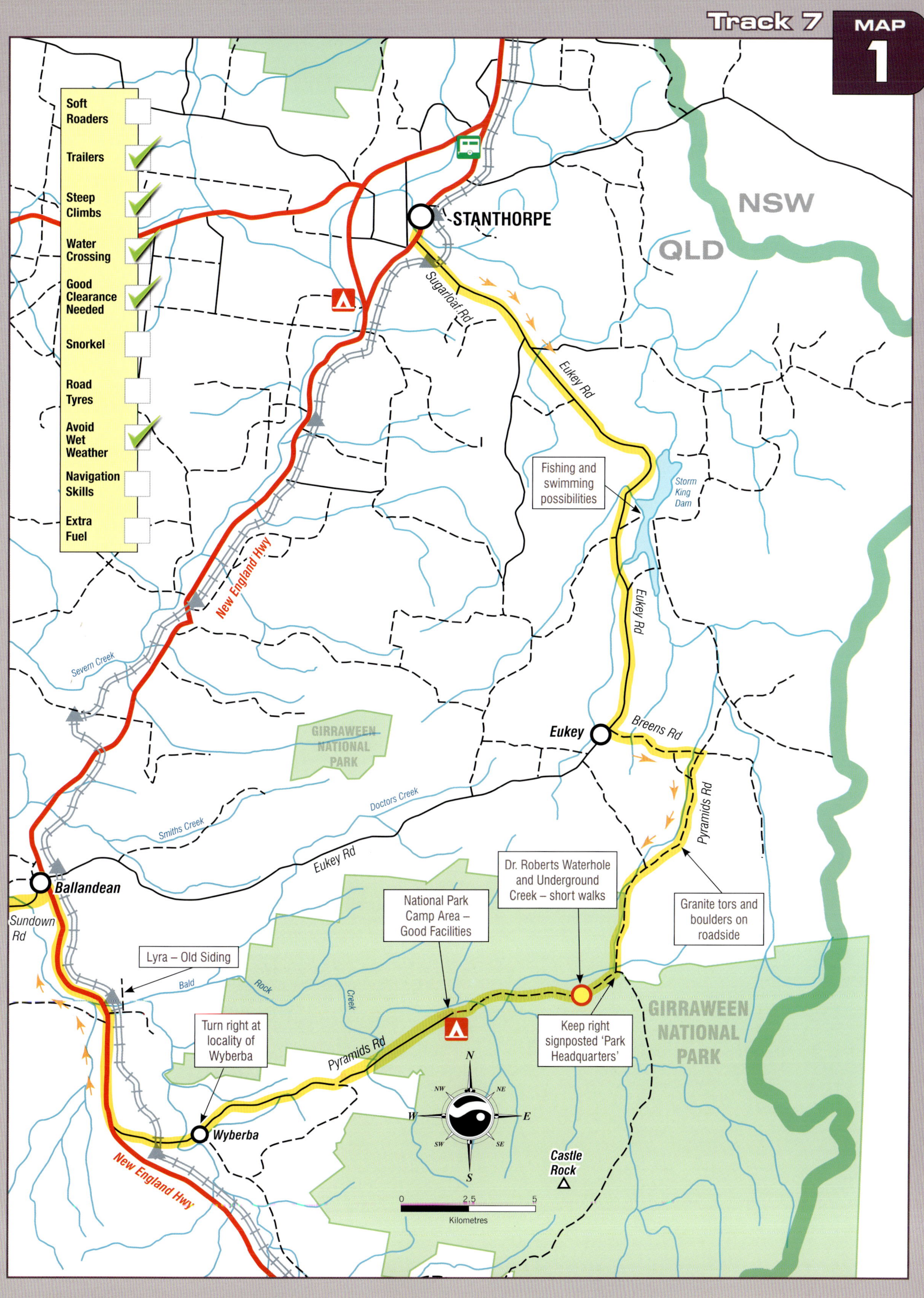

Soft Roaders
Trailers
Steep Climbs
Water Crossing
Good Clearance Needed
Snorkel
Road Tyres
Avoid Wet Weather
Navigation Skills
Extra Fuel
STANTHORPE
NSW
QLD
Sugarloaf Rd
Eukey Rd
Fishing and swimming possibilities
Storm King Dam
New England Hwy
Eukey Rd
Severn Creek
GIRRAWEEN NATIONAL PARK
Eukey
Breens Rd
Pyramids Rd
Doctors Creek
Smiths Creek
Eukey Rd
Ballandean
Sundown Rd
Dr. Roberts Waterhole and Underground Creek – short walks
National Park Camp Area – Good Facilities
Granite tors and boulders on roadside
Lyra – Old Siding
Bald Rock Creek
Keep right signposted 'Park Headquarters'
GIRRAWEEN NATIONAL PARK
Turn right at locality of Wyberba
Pyramids Rd
Wyberba
New England Hwy
Castle Rock
N
NW
NE
W
E
SW
SE
S
0
2.5
5
Kilometres

undertake walks to the weathered smooth dome like formations, coloured by abundant wildflowers in season. Good facilities, but no power, are a feature of Girraween, so campers can pull up for a day or two to further explore the area.

Further on from the ranger's station you will ease out of the granite country as the formations become smaller and sparser. Leave the national park and pass some holiday lodges on your way to a tee intersection at the locality of **Wyberba.** Turn right to reach another tee intersection two kilometres later on the busy **New England Highway,** where you carefully turn right again toward **Ballandean.**

Follow the rail northward past strawberry farms to the old siding of **Lyra.** The rural themes continue to Ballandean, where you turn left on **Curr Road.** This township features a tavern, shop and fuel outlet, with numerous vineyards in the district.

Follow **Sundown Road** on the town's west to cross **Accommodation Creek** with its permanent waterholes, two kilometres from town. You will travel through **Ballandean Station** (selected in 1840) to cross **Washpool Creek** just after a grid.

Turn left onto the gravel of **Sundown Road,** to reach national park boundary six kilometres later. Continue through a gate (keep closed) and fill out camping permits at the information board. It will take at least an hour to reach any of the camping areas, so make sure you decide whether you will be stopping in the park or not.

Continue into the park on a slow run to a tee intersection six kilometres later. Turn right to **Red Rock Gorge** – a dead end track that leads to a lookout and camping area about two kilometres away. The access track is boggy in places, but bypasses skirt the worst of it, and kangaroos and deer are commonly seen.

There is a 500 metre walk to the lookout over Red Rock Gorge, and whilst the falls may be dry, there is a spectacular view of the sliced granite wall, with native pines and tea tree colouring the foreground.

Camping is permitted here, but most people prefer the riverine options of **Reedy** or **Burrows Waterholes** further into the park.

Retrace your steps to the last intersection and turn right (west) through stringybark and box forest. Keep left some 2.2 kilometres later to reach a saddle and old yard on the left (Sundown was established as a national park in 1977 from surrendered sheep grazing properties, and now encompasses 16 000 hectares of remote range country).

Thick forest precedes a fenced off area where tin, copper and arsenic mining occurred from the 1870s. Extraction proved difficult and the mines were decommissioned leaving poisonous mining residues and collapsing shafts to be reclaimed by the bush. These areas are not open to the public.

Continue past the two main mining and treatment areas to a cleared view over pine cloaked valleys. You begin a steep rocky descent a couple of kilometres later, veering right away from a lesser used track to the left.

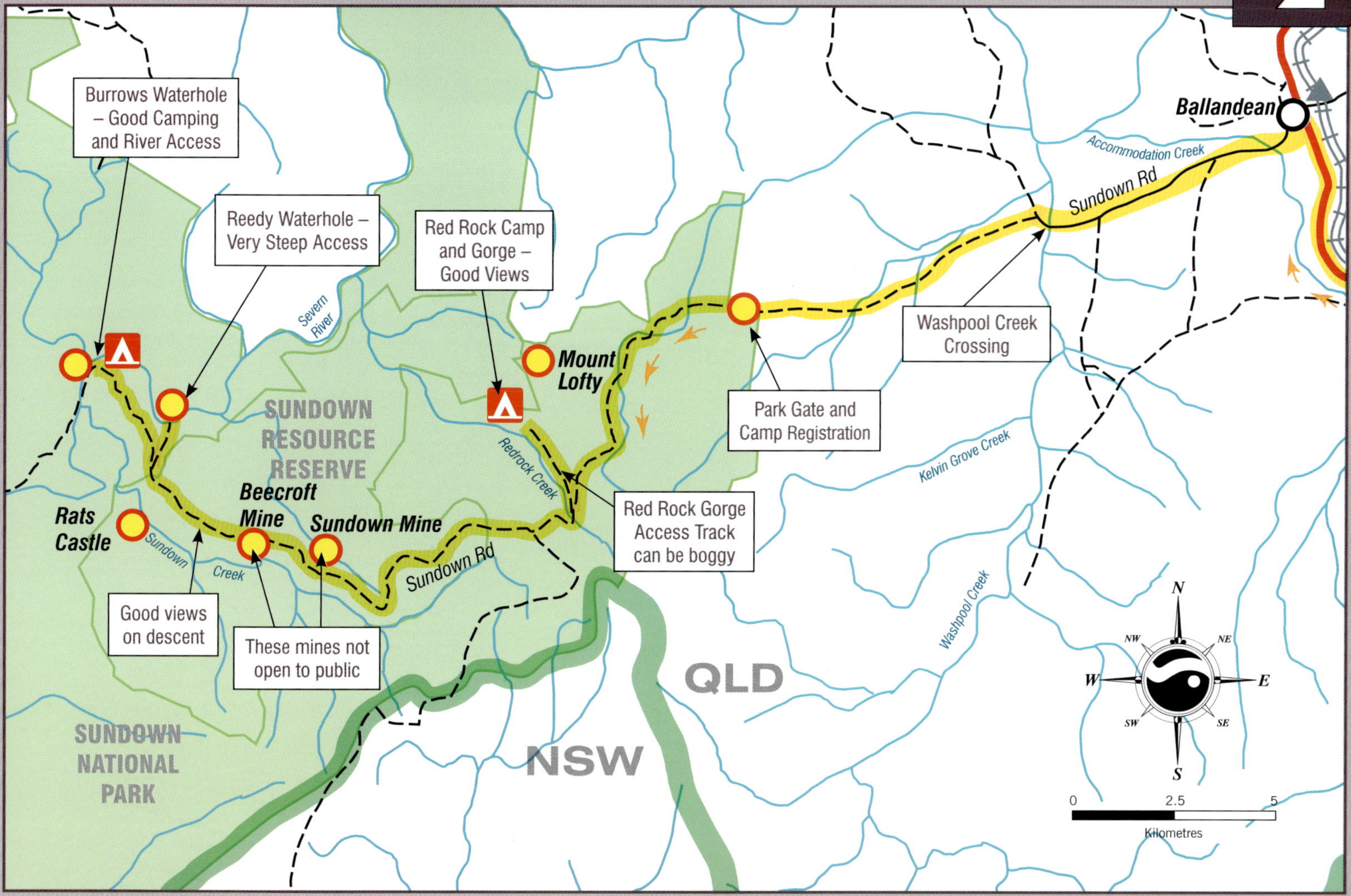

Burrows Waterhole – Good Camping and River Access

Reedy Waterhole – Very Steep Access

Red Rock Camp and Gorge – Good Views

Ballandean

Accommodation Creek

Sundown Rd

Washpool Creek Crossing

Park Gate and Camp Registration

Mount Lofty

Severn River

SUNDOWN RESOURCE RESERVE

Redrock Creek

Red Rock Gorge Access Track can be boggy

Kelvin Grove Creek

Rats Castle

Beecroft Mine

Sundown Mine

Sundown Creek

Sundown Rd

Good views on descent

These mines not open to public

Washpool Creek

QLD

NSW

SUNDOWN NATIONAL PARK

N NE E SE S SW W NW

0 2.5 5 Kilometres

A tee intersection is reached 600 metres later, where you can turn right to **Reedy Waterhole.** This intersection is located at a set of old yards, where hand woven wire is stretched across locally cut timber posts.

Reedy Waterhole is reached following a very steep low range access track, some 2.4 kilometres long. Its slippery surface is made even more treacherous following rain, so check out the descent on foot if necessary, as turning back would be difficult. You will descend to another set of yards with river access on the left, and a grassy camping area on the right.

Return to the sheepyard junction and continue north to **Burrows Waterhole,** along a similarly steep access track, which drops down two kilometres later to a nice stretch of the **Severn River,** complete with pit toilets and grassy sites. Shelter and shade complete the picture, while a swimming hole makes life pleasant over the warmer months.

Above: *The Severn River*

A walking track to **Rats Castle** allows energetic hikers to look over the **Severn River** from a red granite outlook. Rock wallabies may be seen in the area, while iron barks and native pine cloak the range.

Burrows Waterhole is as far as 4WDs can go within the northern part of Sundown, so you will need to retrace your steps on the way out. Visitors looking to explore the park further will find other opportunities at **The Broadwater;** a well appointed camp in the park's south, just off the **Texas – Tenterfield Road.**

TRACK 8 BRISBANE RIVER

SE QUEENSLAND

Track Snapshot

TOUR ROUTE:
Blackbutt to Kilkivan via the Brisbane River

DURATION AND DISTANCE:
A long day trip will cover the 200 kilometre tour

TRACK DETAILS:
The string of forestry roads and station tracks are well surfaced in the main with numerous river crossings to contend with. Soft Roaders and trailers can undertake the tour if water levels are low.

WHEN TO GO:
All year round, but avoid wet weather.

CAMPING:
Camping at Blackbutt and Kilkivan (Rossmore Road to the east of town). Bush camping can be arranged at Mount Stanley Station.

FUEL AND SUPPLIES:
Blackbutt, Moore and Kilkivan.

MAPS:
Sunmap: SE Queensland or Natmap: Gympie 1:250K for better detail.

OTHER INFORMATION:
The butcher at Kilkivan is well known for his delicious smoky bacon.

Left: *Linville Township*

*This trek from **Blackbutt** to **Kilkivan** ticks most boxes for an ideal day trip. Plenty of water crossings, a superb lookout, some history and a character pub thrown in. There is some impressive scenery across the route, and it is likely that you will have it all to yourself.*

Leave Blackbutt via the **D'Aguilar Highway** heading east toward Kilcoy. Narrow bitumen cuts a path between the **Blackbutt** and **Balfour Ranges**, while bunya and hoop pines share the stage with other plantation timbers. Old stone huts mark the crossing of **Wallaby Creek,** before you reach the township of **Moore,** some 22 kilometres from Blackbutt.

A couple of cafes are found in this small and tidy community, so perhaps make a stop here before beginning the haul northward. You will exit town via the **Linville Road,** following a disused timber rail, and the adolescent **Brisbane River.**

Six kilometres north of Moore you will reach **Linville,** and its two storey hill top pub. Memorabilia literally oozes from every pore of the old Cobb and Co stop, as indeed it does throughout the town. The abandoned rail siding is well worth a look, and with a general store, rotunda and toilet, this town is another good stop.

You will leave town via the **Mount Stanley Road,** crossing **Blackbutt** and **Sandy Creeks** on their timber bridges. Avocado farms and brahman cattle begin the rural themes along the **Brisbane Valley.** Veer left seven kilometres from Linville, remaining on the Mount Stanley Road, to pass old yards and green hilly country. Keep straight away from **Avoca Creek Road,** passing a character Queenslander HS with its meathouse and rusting tanks on the left.

You are now 12 kilometres north of Linville, and will cross the Brisbane River 10 times in the next 10 kilometres. If water levels are low it is an easy run as concrete causeways pave the river bed. If it is raining or the water is elevated, get local advice, as the tracks still to come will deteriorate quickly.

You will reach a fork in the road some 25 kilometres from Linville, as you enter **Mount Stanley Station.** This fork marks the confluence of the Brisbane River's **East** and **West Branches.**

(It is possible to turn right and follow the East Branch from here for about 17 kilometres past old timber cutter's camps to a MVO track in State Forest. This trail was opened up in the 1930s to extract hoop and bunya pines for plywood production – an endeavor that continued until the 1970s with the timber pulled to a sawmill and rail head at Linville. These days deer hunters use a few private huts and shelters across the property, while graziers run stock on the river flats.)

You will swing left at the junction to pass **Mount Stanley Hut** with the Brisbane River's West Branch just metres away. The track squeezes through a gap created between the **Mount Stanley Forest Reserve** and the Brisbane Ranges to your west.

Cottages and stockyards usher a picturesque run past **Venilla HS** and side tracks toward Mount Stanley. Keen eyed travellers may notice concrete footings and the odd telegraph post that remain from the early timber cutting days.

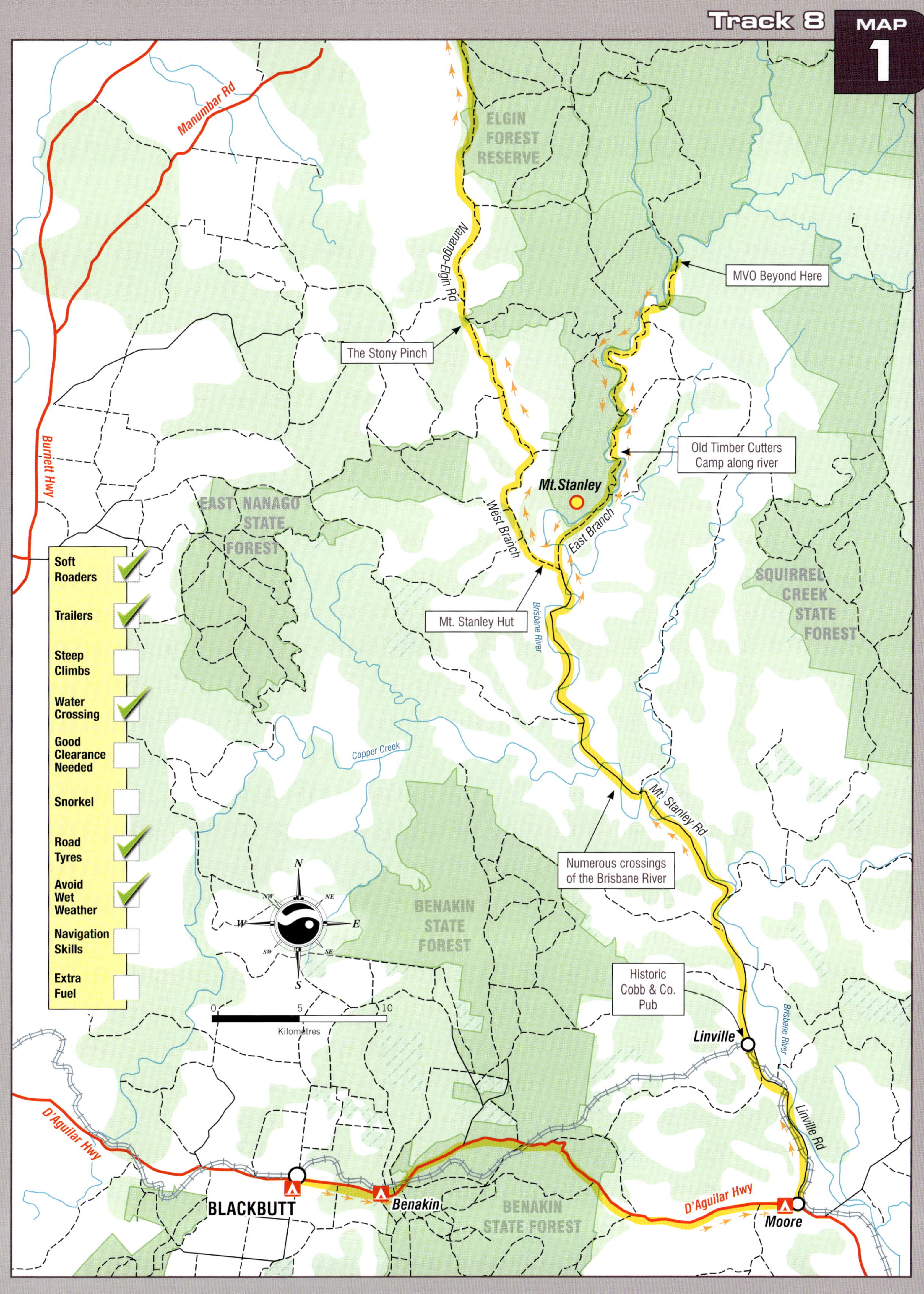

Manumbar Rd
Burnett Hwy
ELGIN FOREST RESERVE
Nanango-Elgin Rd
MVO Beyond Here
The Stony Pinch
Old Timber Cutters Camp along river
Mt.Stanley
West Branch
East Branch
EAST NANAGO STATE FOREST
SQUIRREL CREEK STATE FOREST
Mt. Stanley Hut
Brisbane River
Copper Creek
Mt. Stanley Rd
Numerous crossings of the Brisbane River
BENAKIN STATE FOREST
Historic Cobb & Co. Pub
Linville
Linville Rd
D'Aguilar Hwy
BLACKBUTT
Benakin
Moore
Kilometres
0
5
10
N
NE
E
SE
S
SW
W
NW
Soft Roaders
Trailers
Steep Climbs
Water Crossing
Good Clearance Needed
Snorkel
Road Tyres
Avoid Wet Weather
Navigation Skills
Extra Fuel

Veer right some 13 kilometres north of the Brisbane's east – west divide, and onto the **Nanango – Elgin Vale Road.** The first river crossing is followed by the **"Stony Pinch"** - a distinct and loose spur climb and descent past **Spean HS** and some curious forest festooned with lichen strings. You will cross **Dunlops Creek** on a climb to the Brisbane River headwaters, and a watershed divide.

Bonnevue HS marks a tee intersection on bitumen where you will turn right (watch for traffic – it is a blind corner). Keep right at **Johnstown Road**, to run past **Elgin Vale HS.** Continue straight past Elgin Vale Road and **Porters Road,** before swinging left on the **Kilcoy - Murgon Road.**

You will follow undulating grazing land with skyline views across **Gap Creek,** before turning right onto **Pei Road,** some nine kilometres later.
A plaque erected at the new bridge over **Barambah Creek,** acknowledges the efforts of local participants in a private endeavour who constructed the original bridge here.

Turn right at a tee junction and follow **Kinbombi Road** for approximately 11 kilometres. Then turn left onto gravel and enter **Wrattens National Park** some 2 kilometres later. Keep straight onto A Flat Road.

Approximately 5 kilometres later, veer left onto **Widgee Mountain Road**. You will reach a tee intersection after 3 kilometres where you veer left onto better road (Blacksnake Road). After approximately 8 kilometres a management vehicle road only leads to **Mount Mia Observation Point**.

Walk the rutted climb over a saddle (good views either side), to a dead end trig point on the summit.

At 580 metres, **Mount Mia** is only modest in altitude, but with a steep drop off on the west side, it allows careful visitors to appreciate some expansive views over the **Coast Range.** A thick forest of grass trees blankets the summit and its gentler eastern slopes.

Return from the summit to the main road, turning left for the final run through Wrattens NP. You will leave the national park at the **Shamrock Mine**, on **Black Snake Road.** The **D'Aguilar Gold Mine Company** is currently working this extensive site (no access), and there are numerous mining relics lying in the bush at the foot of **Mount Coora** from the pioneering days.

Above:
Old Stockyards

Below:
Mount Stanley Hut

A patchwork of sealed and gravel road paves the way northward for 18 kilometres, before reaching the **Wide Bay Highway.** Turn right for the final run into **Kilkivan.**

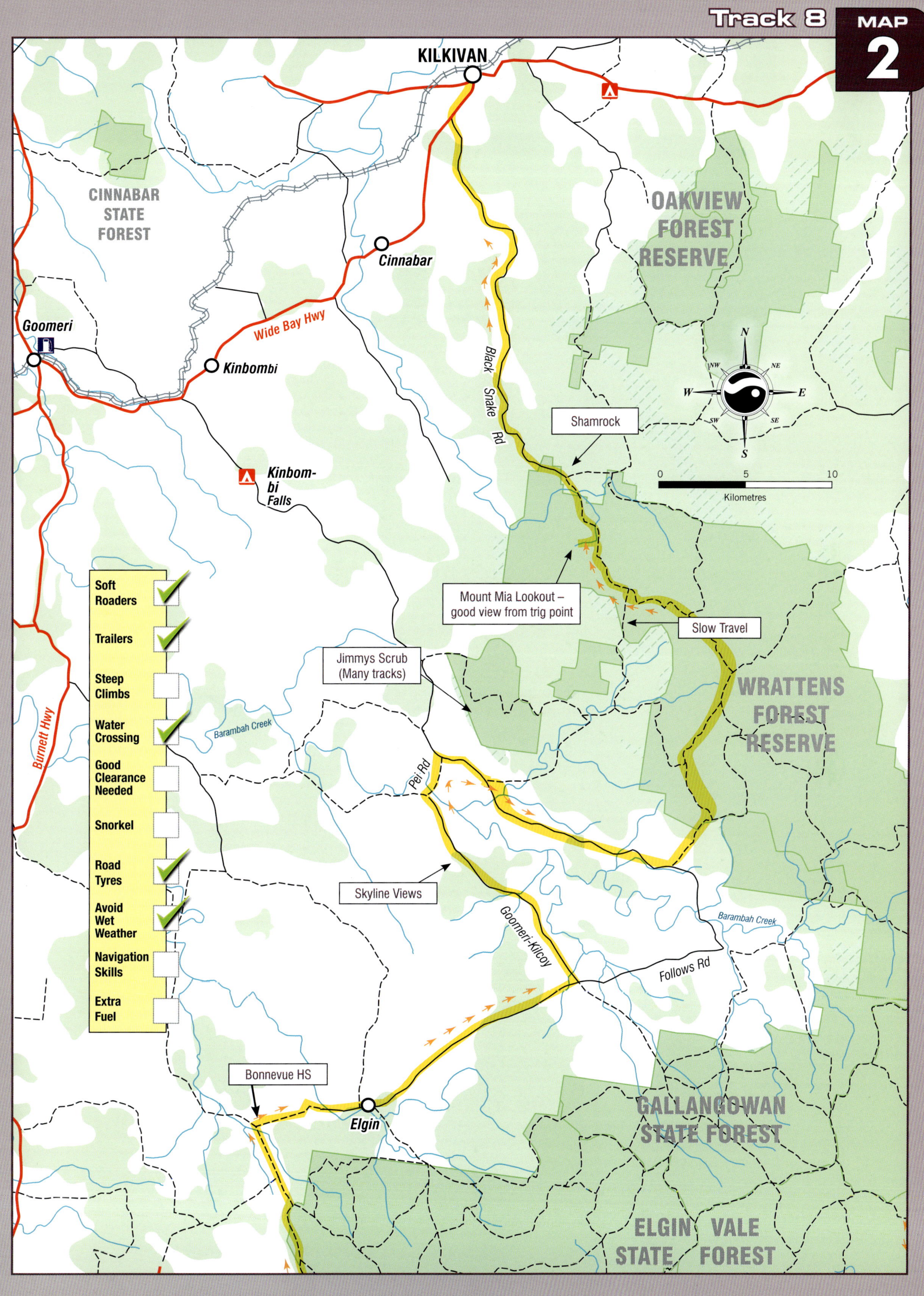
KILKIVAN
CINNABAR STATE FOREST
Cinnabar
OAKVIEW FOREST RESERVE
Goomeri
Wide Bay Hwy
Kinbombi
Black Snake Rd
N
NW
NE
W
E
SW
SE
S
Shamrock
0
5
10
Kilometres
Kinbom-bi Falls
Soft Roaders
Trailers
Steep Climbs
Water Crossing
Good Clearance Needed
Snorkel
Road Tyres
Avoid Wet Weather
Navigation Skills
Extra Fuel
Mount Mia Lookout – good view from trig point
Slow Travel
Jimmys Scrub (Many tracks)
WRATTENS FOREST RESERVE
Burnett Hwy
Barambah Creek
Pei Rd
Skyline Views
Goomeri-Kilcoy
Barambah Creek
Follows Rd
Bonnevue HS
Elgin
GALLANGOWAN STATE FOREST
ELGIN VALE STATE FOREST

TRACK
9

Mary Headwaters

SE QUEENSLAND

Marodian Causeway

Track Snapshot

TOUR ROUTE:
Kilkivan to Musket Flat via the Mary River headwaters.

DURATION AND DISTANCE:
This 90 kilometre run would make an ideal day trip.

TRACK DETAILS:
Soft Roaders and trailers will find the terrain relatively easy, with firm tracks and routine creek crossings.

WHEN TO GO:
All year round, although very wet weather will fill the creeks and compromise the unsealed tracks.

CAMPING:
Kilkivan Bush Camping Park (Rossmore Road, just out of town) has all facilities, while unserviced camping is available at Musket Flat.

FUEL AND SUPPLIES:
Leave Kilkivan with a full fuel tank and plenty of supplies. There is no store at Musket Flat, but you are now within 60 kilometres of towns to the north, east and west.

MAPS:
Sunmap: SE Queensland, but for more detail travel with the Natmap: Maryborough1:250K.

OTHER INFORMATION:
Lovely drive in the warmer weather, with shady forest and trickling water never far away.

*This tour from **Kilkivan** to **Musket Flat** follows an easy pathway through scenic country making up the **Mary River's** western catchment. Travellers will be treated to some superb wetlands on a leisurely amble through state forest and rural communities.*

You will leave Kilkivan via the showgrounds at **Bridge Street,** taking **Mudlo Road** north for just over one kilometre. Turn right onto **Running Creek Road** to follow single lane bitumen and narrow gauge rail on your right. Small rural holdings dot the cleared valley with **Mount Mudlo** and modest range country in the distance.

A series of grids and gates mark the transition to gravel for a string of creek crossings to come. You will cross **Running Creek** and its tributaries initially on concrete causeways, then later at unsurfaced fords.

If water levels are low, it is a relatively easy drive, but following rain there may be some tricky sections – check out the current situation at Kilkivan prior to setting out. In any case you will be presented with some picturesque country, where reeds and coloured grasses are sheltered under paperbarks and dangling bottlebrush.

Some crossings are quite wide and would make a great stop on a hot day – just be aware that this is private grazing land, and santa gertrudis cattle roam the unfenced country. Keep right at the **Archer Road** intersection, some 20 kilometres out of Kilkivan, to stay on Running Creek Road. You will cross the creek on a concrete bridge, before reaching a tee intersection on the **Brooweena – Woolooga Road.**

Turn left onto good gravel to cross Running Creek at a timber bridge.

You then reach a clearing on the downstream side which would make and ideal rest or lunch stop with plenty of shade and trickling water.

Continue northward past **Mount Kola** on the left then over **Sandy Creek Bridge.** Keep right at **Calgoa Road** passing a set of modern timber yards on the left,

Running Creek

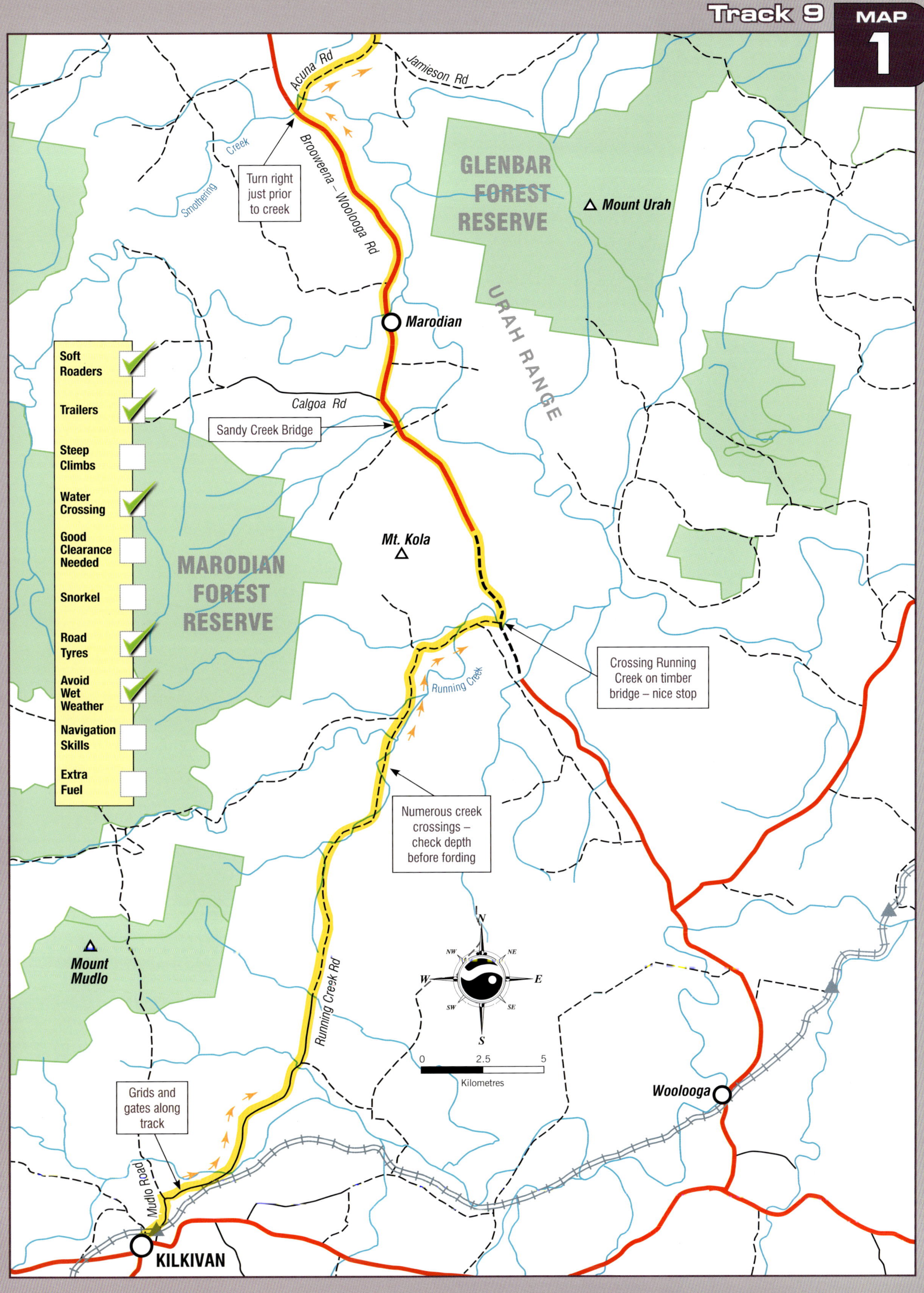
Acuna Rd
Jamieson Rd
Smothering Creek
Turn right just prior to creek
Brooweena – Woolooga Rd
GLENBAR FOREST RESERVE
Mount Urah
URAH RANGE
Marodian
Soft Roaders
Trailers
Steep Climbs
Water Crossing
Good Clearance Needed
Snorkel
Road Tyres
Avoid Wet Weather
Navigation Skills
Extra Fuel
Calgoa Rd
Sandy Creek Bridge
Mt. Kola
MARODIAN FOREST RESERVE
Crossing Running Creek on timber bridge – nice stop
Running Creek
Numerous creek crossings – check depth before fording
Mount Mudlo
Running Creek Rd
N
NW
NE
W
E
SW
SE
S
0
2.5
5
Kilometres
Grids and gates along track
Mudlo Road
Woolooga
KILKIVAN

then the lofty timber bridge over Calgoa Creek. Mount Urah dominates the **Urah Range** in the east, with dense bushland cloaking much of the **Glenbar Forest Reserve.**

You will cross **Lilly Pilly Creek,** before reaching **Smothering Creek,** some 16 kilometres from Running Creek Bridge. Turn right onto **Acuna Road** just prior to this creek, to reach a causeway shortly after. There is a beautiful pool of water here, with a network of trickling feeder creeks, but as it is on private property, just take a peek and move on.

Swing left three kilometres later avoiding **Jamieson Road,** and keeping straight away from **Myona HS** further on. You will reach **Pine Hill HS** next with its park like forest of tall, almost branchless trees and short green grass. A superb wetland surrounds the Queenslander style homestead with windmill and cattle completing the setting.

A short section of sealed road continues beyond Pine Hill, taking visitors through a pocket of rainforest where views toward the **Coast Range** are broken by vines and a tangled mass of greenery. You will cross a final causeway, before reaching a tee intersection. The right option leads to the community of **Tiaro,** but we swing left to **Glenbar HS,** turning right onto **Glenbar Road,** 1.5 kilometres from the tee.

Above: *Aramara Rail Bridge*

Right: *Grasstrees*

Proceed north following the boundary of state forest to the rustic looking homestead of **Sunny Glen. Munna Creek** and the **Teebar Creek** headwaters combine to form a wetland just north of the homestead, as a series of smaller land holdings punctuate the run north.

Continue past **Ellerslie Road** and **Walkers Flat Road** with occasional views of **Stoney Range** on the right. The community of **Aramara** marks the **Maryborough – Biggenden Road,** where you turn left at the tee, and swing right almost immediately to pass under a timber trestle rail bridge.

You will climb through a pocket of **Wongi SF** which forms the watershed between those creeks flowing eastward to the **Mary River,** and those running northward to the **Burrum** and **Burnett Rivers.** A community hall marks the locality of **North Aramara,** where a character pavilion is seen on the footy oval and the Doongal Stock Route passes through town.

Cross **Doongal Creek,** keeping right at **Nahrang Road** toward signposted **"Musket Flat". Cockatoo Creek** is notable for its towering forest and jungle like appearance, before you reach an open area crossed by overhead power distribution cables.

You will reach the hamlet of Musket Flat some 16 kilometres from Aramara, in the shadow of **Musket Flat Mountain.** The town's diminutive size is more than compensated by its obvious pride. The houses are neat and tidy, and there is a picnic/camping area (although without facilities) on the outskirts.

Options beyond Musket Flat include tackling the slightly more demanding **Wongi SF** trek, or continuing east over a series of bridges and causeways. Those choosing the latter will exit state forest on the **Biggenden Road** just 13 kilometres out of **Maryborough.**

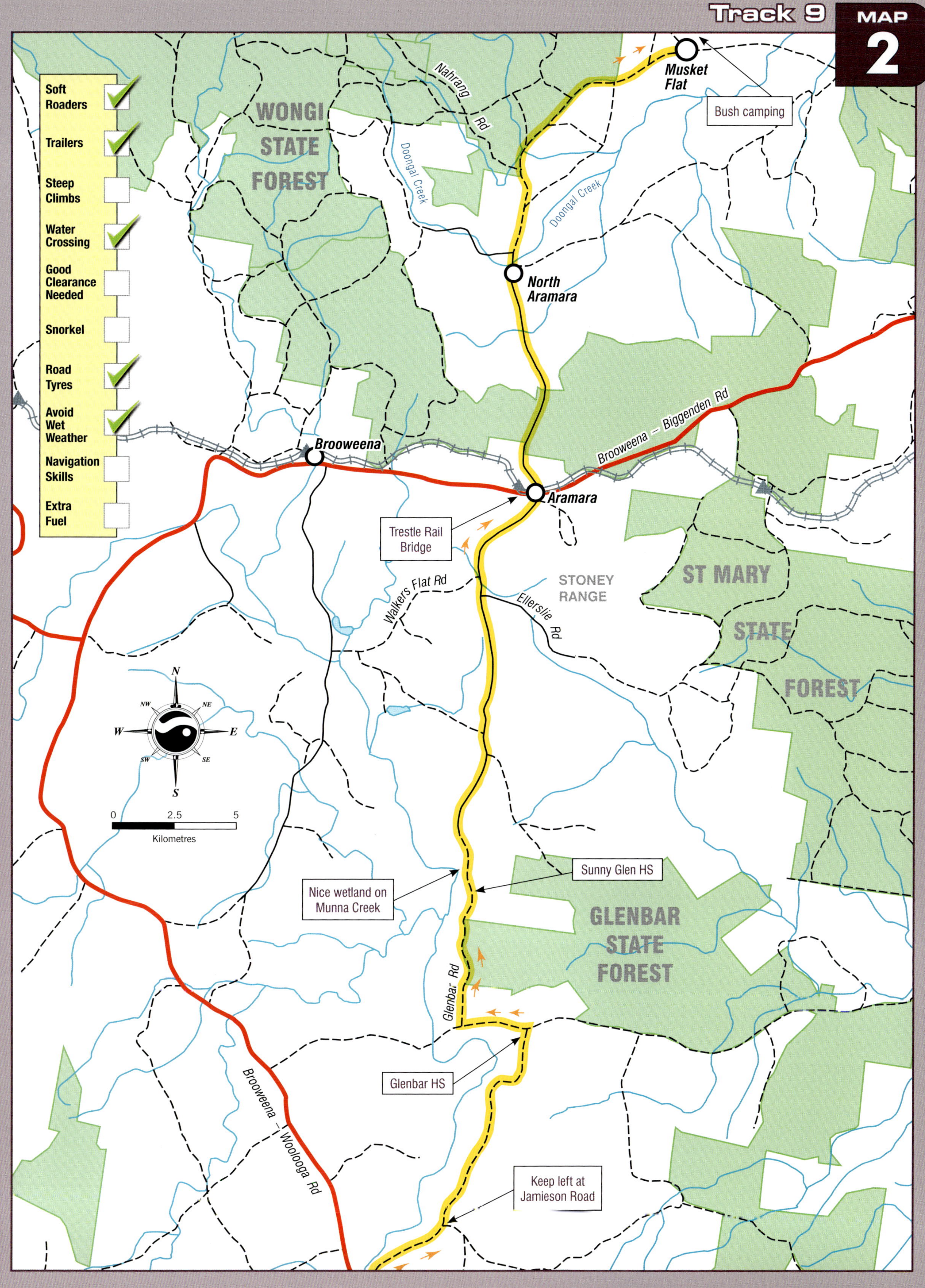
Soft Roaders
Trailers
Steep Climbs
Water Crossing
Good Clearance Needed
Snorkel
Road Tyres
Avoid Wet Weather
Navigation Skills
Extra Fuel
WONGI STATE FOREST
Nahrang Rd
Doongal Creek
Doongal Creek
Musket Flat
Bush camping
North Aramara
Brooweena
Aramara
Brooweena – Biggenden Rd
Trestle Rail Bridge
Walkers Flat Rd
Ellerslie Rd
STONEY RANGE
ST MARY STATE FOREST
N
NW
NE
W
E
SW
SE
S
0
2.5
5
Kilometres
Nice wetland on Munna Creek
Sunny Glen HS
GLENBAR STATE FOREST
Glenbar Rd
Glenbar HS
Brooweena – Woolooga Rd
Keep left at Jamieson Road

TRACK 10 WONGI

SE QUEENSLAND

Oaky Creek Swamp

*This short trek through **Wongi SF** follows an historic wagon route over the **Sea View Range,** before crossing the clear waters of **Agnes Vale** and **Oaky Creeks.** It is a relatively easy drive in dry weather, but will require some navigational skills.*

You will leave **Musket Flat** at the back of the picnic / camping area via a drop gate, directed rather ambitiously via a signpost declaring "Cooktown"! It is true that this stretch of track forms part of the Bicentennial National Trail, but few travellers will be looking to go that far at this stage.

Anyway, once you have managed to reattach the gate, you will find another one 100 metres later (practice makes perfect...) You will pass by an old fingerboard and plaque that directs travellers from here to the port at **Maryborough.** (Musket Flat was first settled in the 1860s as a staging post for wagons heading from inland selections to ships docked on the **Mary River.**)

The track you are following is rather narrow at the beginning, but widens beyond high voltage powerlines and a horse rider's camp, just a few kilometres out of Musket Flat. You will follow the boundary of state forest past eroded sections of track to a signpost pointing to **Mount Doongul.**

The summit track is just over one kilometre long, and once gave access to a fire spotter's tower. The tower no longer exists, and visitors will need to stand on the roofs of their vehicles to see beyond the rim of summit trees.

Return from the summit and continue westward over a creek, turning right on **Warrah Road** one kilometre from the Mount Doongul turn off. Turn left almost immediately to signposted **"Agnes Vale",** following the red and orange diamond National Trail markers.

You will descend to an old timber bridge of dubious quality, passing a weather station at the foot of the **Robinson Range**. A signpost indicating the **Brooweena Section** of Wongi NP flags a road junction, where you follow the main road to the right.

Keep right as you crest the **Seaview Range,** some four kilometres from the bridge, as you follow an old "Convict Road" believed to have been constructed by chain gang labour in the 1860s. You will reach the main **Brooweena – Childers Road** at a tee, turning right at signposted **"Agnes Vale".**

If the weather has been dry you will kick up bulldust along this track, but if rain has fallen recently be wary of greasy sections (any significant rain would make this entire trek a no-go). A couple of creek crossings punctuate the northern run, with flood damage and rocky exits combining to slow progress.

You will pass a horse rider's camp (no facilities) before reaching **Agnes Vale Station** on the boundary of **Wongi SF.** Swing right at the tee junction (left track goes to homestead), then left 1.5 kilometres later, away from the signposted **"Brooweena"** option (this track heads back to Musket Flat).

Pass an old timber mill on the right, then turn left again 1.7 kilometres from the last junction. You will reach **Agnes Vale Creek** after two kilometres, at a stand of enormous leafy trees. This is a lovely place to explore with the infant creek headwaters oozing from the **Sea View Range.**

You will cross the main creek, then a secondary branch via a log bridge, turning left away from the creek, soon after the bridge. Follow this track through to the **Childers – Agnes Vale Road** (noting that it may not be marked on some maps), then turn right at the tee.

Head north on better road, keeping right at **Sawmill Road** to leave state forest 1.5 kilometres later. **Oaky Creek** marks the boundary of Wongi SF, with generous trees shading the concrete causeway. Paperbarks line swampland at the creek fringes before you emerge into grazing country for the final push north.

You reach a tee intersection on the **Isis Highway** for a six kilometre run into **Childers.** Travellers will find all services at the large **Bruce Highway** township. Options beyond here include Fraser Island, Cooloola, or the much closer beach run along the Burrum Coast.

Track Snapshot

TOUR ROUTE:
Musket Flat to Childers via Wongi SF.

DURATION AND DISTANCE:
A nice day trip of 60 kilometres.

TRACK DETAILS:
Easy driving in the main, with a few rough creek crossings thrown in. Trailers OK but some Soft Roaders may struggle.

WHEN TO GO:
All year round if the weather has been dry.

CAMPING:
Unserviced camping at Musket Flat, but a range of options at Childers.

FUEL AND SUPPLIES:
Nothing available enroute, but restock at Childers.

MAPS:
Natmap: Maryborough 1:250K is advisable, but the maze of tracks through Wongi is shown in better detail on the Natmap: Childers 1:100K.

OTHER INFORMATION:
Navigation can be challenging on this tour – travel with the recommended maps, and preferably a vehicle mounted GPS.

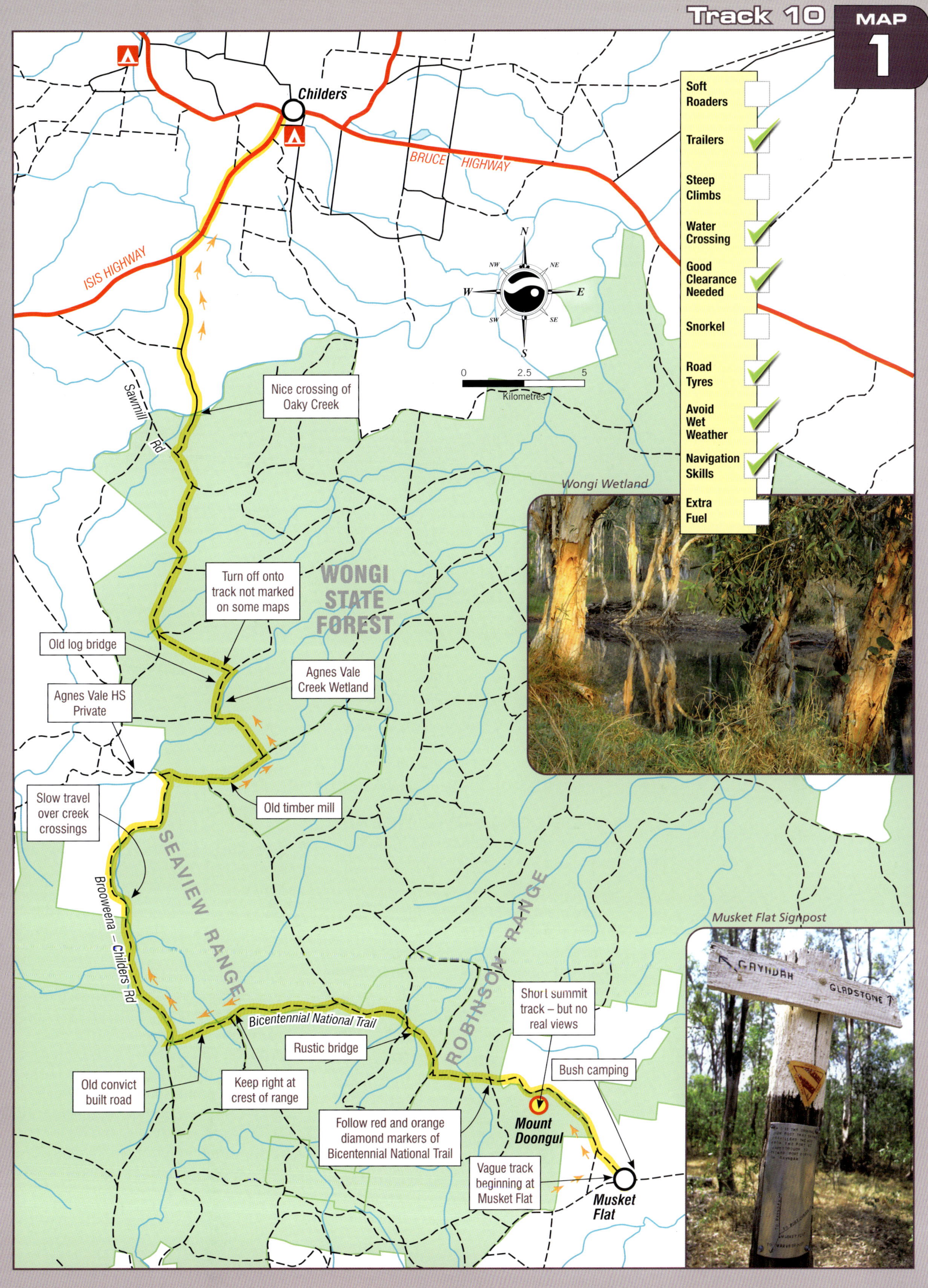

Wongi Wetland

Musket Flat Signpost

TRACK 11

Burrum Coast

SE QUEENSLAND

Theodolite Creek mangroves

Track Snapshot

TOUR ROUTE:
Childers to Childers via the Burrum Coast.

DISTANCE AND DURATION:
This 160 kilometre round trek can be done as a day trip, but it is much more enjoyable with at least one night camped on the beach.

TRACK DETAILS:
Access to and from the Burrum Coast is easy, but travel through the national park is sand and beach driving. Hot weather and/or heavy use will make some sections difficult, and Soft Roaders or those towing trailers will require an experienced hand at the wheel.

WHEN TO GO:
All year round, but avoid the school holiday periods if you are looking for quiet times.

CAMPING:
Excellent beach front camping (without facilities) will be found in the Kinkuna Section, and basic facilities are on offer at Burrum Point. There are a range of accommodation options at Childers.

FUEL AND SUPPLIES:
Stock up in Childers.

MAPS:
Natmap: Maryborough 1:250K, but for more detail you will need Natmap 1:100K Bundaberg, Childers, and Pialba (it is really only the Pialba map that is most useful for the Burrum Point and coastal Kinkuna tracks).

OTHER INFORMATION:
A quiet destination (out of school holidays) with superb coastal heath.

*Beach driving is one of the thrills that 4WD newcomers can't wait to have a crack at. Fortunately Queensland has a number of beaches available for this activity, with **Fraser Island** and **Cooloola** being the most popular. **The Burrum Coast** is another option just north of **Hervey Bay,** and provides a great introduction for those looking to experience a beach run.*

*The sand track network is located within the 23 000 hectares of **Burrum Coast NP,** and is spread over three blocks: the largest sector, **Kinkuna** is found in the north, there is a central **Woodgate section**, and the southern **Burrum River** zone. Kinkuna and Woodgate offer the most possibilities for 4WDing, and will be the focus for this tour.*

Childers is a good starting point for travellers, with all supplies and services available (Woodgate Beach is another option mid trip, although much more limited in range). Head toward **Gladstone** on the ***Bruce Highway,*** taking the **ISIS Highway** turn off six kilometres later.

You will head through the volcanic soils around Cordalba where farmers irrigate mango plantations, together with vegetables and other tropical produce. Turn right some 16 kilometres from the highway interchange, onto **Foley Road,** to follow single lane bitumen through substantial sugar cane fields.

Keep right at **Newlands Road** to view the open channel system, then cross a sugar cane rail line (give way – no lights or gates). The scrub of **Bingera NP** appears on your left, before reaching a tee intersection. Turn left at the tee onto **Goodwood Road** for a busier run past the abandoned rail siding of **Gotlow.**

The main road follows a dog leg path under the rail bridge here, where you need to turn right onto **Coonar Road** almost immediately beyond the bridge. Riverine jungle and the **Elliot River** trace a parallel path eastward, as you cross the rail and reach **Palmbeach Road**, about eight kilometres from the dogleg.

Turn right at this intersection to leave sealed road, and begin a 60 kph zone into **Kinkuna NP.** Keep right 4.6 kilometres later (left option goes to private property) to follow a new track alignment on the boundary of national park. At some point here it would pay to air down your tyres, as softer sand is imminent.

Continue to follow a corridor of scrub to a tee intersection and turn left (the right option follows a narrow inland path with low hanging tree branches that will parallel our prefered route via the coast).

You will immediately enter a coastal camping strip with superb beach front clearings among the foredunes. Coastal casuarinas shade the potential camps, although you will need to be totally self contained if you choose to stop here. Fires are permitted using clean milled timber, but despite the appealing waters of **Hervey Bay** virtually lapping at your feet, swimming is not recommended, and mosquitoes and sand flies can be a menace.

The beach side track meanders past the informal campsites, with bypass tracks

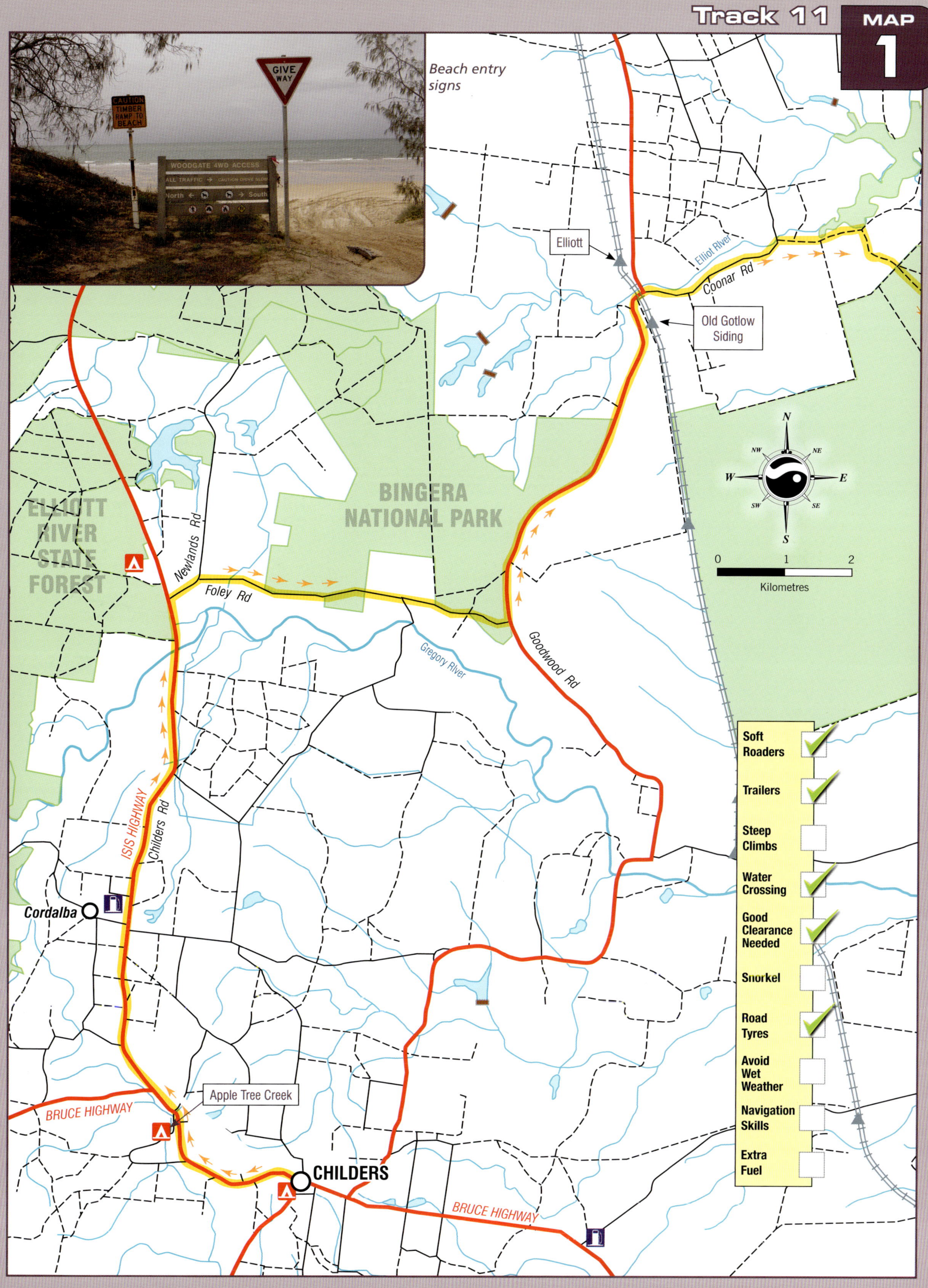
CAUTION TIMBER RAMP TO BEACH
GIVE WAY
WOODGATE 4WD ACCESS
ALL TRAFFIC → CAUTION DRIVE SLOW
North ← → South
Beach entry signs
Elliott
Old Gotlow Siding
Elliot River
Coonar Rd
BINGERA NATIONAL PARK
ELLIOTT RIVER STATE FOREST
Newlands Rd
Foley Rd
Goodwood Rd
Gregory River
N
NE
E
SE
S
SW
W
NW
0
1
2
Kilometres
ISIS HIGHWAY
Childers Rd
Cordalba
Apple Tree Creek
BRUCE HIGHWAY
CHILDERS
BRUCE HIGHWAY
Soft Roaders
Trailers
Steep Climbs
Water Crossing
Good Clearance Needed
Snorkel
Road Tyres
Avoid Wet Weather
Navigation Skills
Extra Fuel

Theodolite track

Follow a southerly path to a national park information board at the main **Woodgate – Childers Road.** Turn left onto bitumen following a straight run into **Woodgate Beach** (you may wish to put some air into your tyres prior to turning if you prefer, otherwise keep your speed down and avoid any sudden swerving for the short run into the village – we will continue to follow the beach past Woodgate).

Once at Woodgate, turn left into Second Avenue, then right toward **Walkers Point.** You will find toilets and shelter shed here, together with a lovely beach (same casuarina lined outlook as Kinkuna, but now with houses aplenty and hordes of people).

Follow the strip housing to the town's southern limits, turning right into 12th Avenue and left onto **Walkers Point Road** to the signposted "Beach Access". Swing hard left through a clump of trees to reach the beach proper shortly after. Turn right at the surf to begin a beach run toward **Burrum Point.**

Try to time this run with low tide (or at least well into a receding tide) as you will negotiate a lagoon and some especially soft sand near the mouth of the **Burrum River.**

A national park sign points the way into Burrum Point Campground almost six kilometres later, where you will find basic facilities, and our exit to the community of Walkers Point. Turn left past a paperbark and fern swampland, before leaving national park, and following bitumen into Walkers Point. You will leave the Burrum via a sealed road back to Woodgate Beach and a signposted run back to Childers.

allowing local travel if the area is busy (the school holiday periods are especially popular, although off peak times are remarkably quiet). Four kilometres later you will reach the end of Kinkuna's beach run and need to swing right at the signposted **"Woodgate"** exit.

Keep left 200 m later (right track is the inland option back to Elliot River), to pass a cabbage palm lined creek on your left. **Theodolite Creek Track** is reached shortly after, where you can turn left to follow a dead end track to an inlet fringed with red mangrove.

This track is especially narrow and winding (trailers will be a problem) so keep your speed down and look out for oncoming vehicles. It is however a section alive with colour – flowering heath, bush peas, and a range of orchids explode in the warmer months following winter. You will reach the South Branch of **Theodolite Creek** after about five kilometres, where a small carpark, table and chairs mark the track's end.

Retrace your steps when you are ready, and turn left back onto the main **Woodgate track.** Swampy country marks travel south through mahogany gums and paperbark. This poorly drained sandy soil is a characteristic of wallum heathland, with moisture retaining leaf litter being an ideal bed for lillies, boronia and bushpeas. Some eroded sections of track have been topped up with road base through here, although the conditions are very much dependent on recent weather.

You will pass a couple of MVO tracks before reaching a tee, seven kilometres from Theodolite Creek Track. Turn left at the tee to arrive at another tee shortly after. Turn right to a crossroads, again turning right onto **Woopis Road,** signposted "Woodgate".

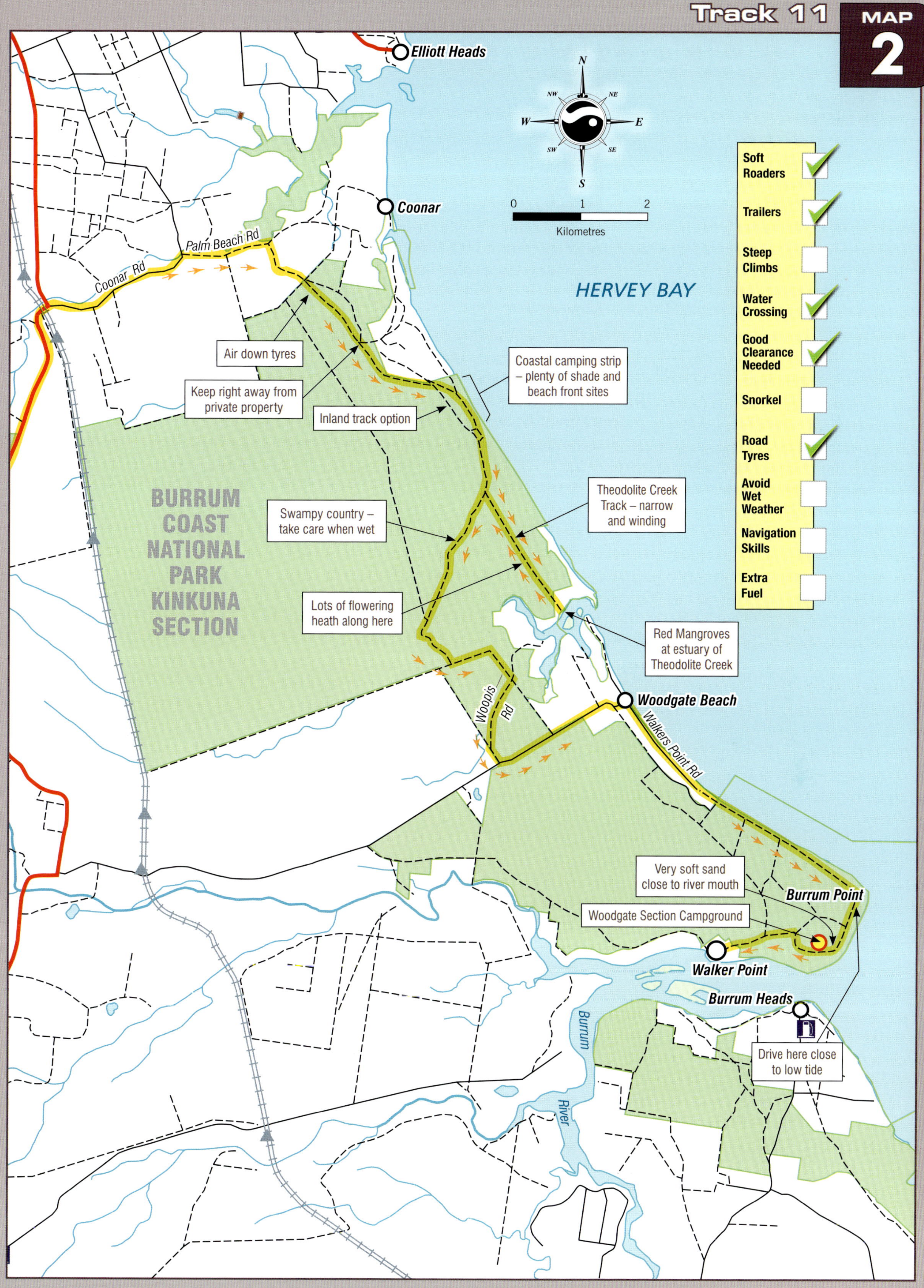

Elliott Heads
Coonar
N
NE
E
SE
S
SW
W
NW
0
1
2
Kilometres
HERVEY BAY
Palm Beach Rd
Coonar Rd
Air down tyres
Keep right away from private property
Inland track option
Coastal camping strip – plenty of shade and beach front sites
BURRUM COAST NATIONAL PARK KINKUNA SECTION
Swampy country – take care when wet
Theodolite Creek Track – narrow and winding
Lots of flowering heath along here
Red Mangroves at estuary of Theodolite Creek
Woodgate Beach
Walkers Point Rd
Woopis Rd
Very soft sand close to river mouth
Burrum Point
Woodgate Section Campground
Walker Point
Burrum Heads
Burrum River
Drive here close to low tide
Soft Roaders
Trailers
Steep Climbs
Water Crossing
Good Clearance Needed
Snorkel
Road Tyres
Avoid Wet Weather
Navigation Skills
Extra Fuel

TRACK 12 COOLOOLA

SE QUEENSLAND

*Visitors to the **Cooloola Coast** will enjoy a **Fraser Island** type experience with the advantage of enjoying the picturesque **Noosa River,** but without the cost and inconvenience of a barge trip. Beach camping, tannin stained lakes and rainforest pockets are all part of the journey, with upmarket accommodation available for those who desire it.*

Tewantin, located just inland from **Noosa Heads** on the **Cooroy Road** is the start point for this trek. Head north out of town via **Moorindil Street**. You will cross the **Noosa River** by ferry (always running during daylight and early evening hours), then reach a tee intersection two kilometres later. Turn right onto **Beach Road** to pass the **Noosa North Shore caravan park** and begin the beach run.

You will need to air down your tyres here, to pass a couple of access tracks on the left, then an access track to the private residences at **Teewah.** Keep straight to reach national park, 14 kilometres from the ferry. Camping is not permitted for the next 14 kilometres, as you pass the Teewah coloured sands, and look out for dolphins and whales along the Coral Sea coast.

A 50 kph speed limit marks the transition to the camping permitted zone as you reach **Red Canyon,** about five kilometres later. You can walk to the foot of these iron oxide stained cliffs, but climbing the formations is not permitted.

Continue northward past **Kings Bore Road** (no entry) for a colourful run to **Little Freshwater Creek,** some nine kilometres from Red Canyon. No camping is permitted north of **Little Freshwater,** but there are good sheltered opportunities in this area.

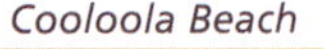

Cooloola Beach

Track Snapshot

TOUR ROUTE:
Tewantin to Elanda Point via Rainbow Beach and Harrys Hut.

DURATION AND DISTANCE:
With 160 kilometres to cover, this trek would be best done as a three or four day undertaking.

TRACK DETAILS:
A range of sandy tracks will be encountered, ranging from the surf beach, to soft access trails to firm inland tracks. Soft Roaders can undertake the trek with experienced drivers, while trailers will need a powerful tow vehicle.

WHEN TO GO:
All year round, although the Cooloola Way and Harrys Hut Road are regularly closed by wet weather.

CAMPING:
Unserviced beach front camping in designated areas is popular, while good facilities feature at Freshwater Camp. Private parks at Rainbow Beach, Tewantin and Elanda Point are complemented by bush camping at Harrys Hut.

FUEL AND SUPPLIES:
Tewantin, Rainbow Beach.

MAPS:
Sunmap: Cooloola Region.

OTHER INFORMATION:
With rainforest walks, canoeing on the Noosa River and one of the longest beaches in Australia, the Cooloola Coast offers something for everyone.

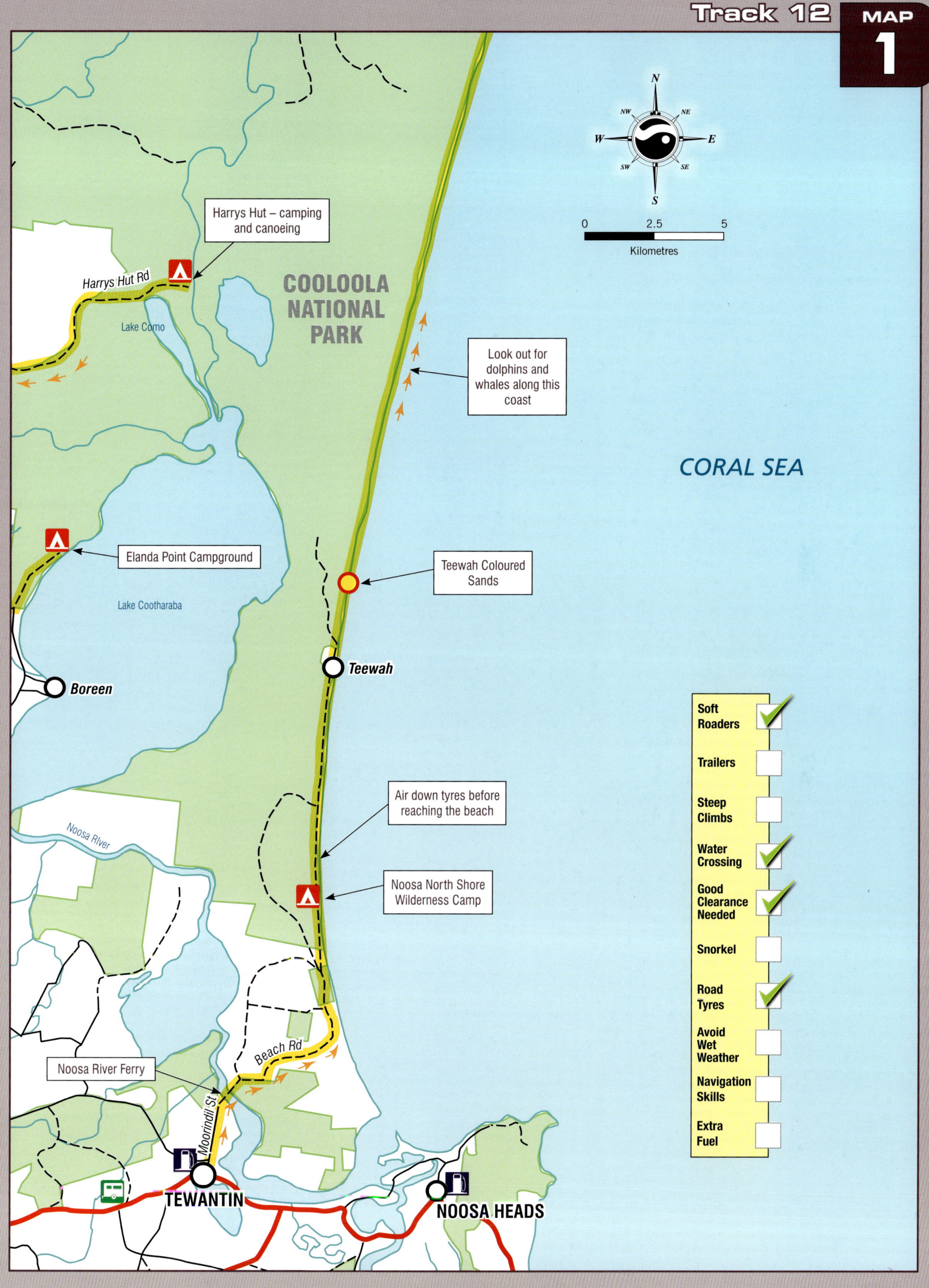

N
NE
E
SE
S
SW
W
NW
0
2.5
5
Kilometres
Harrys Hut – camping and canoeing
Harrys Hut Rd
Lake Como
COOLOOLA NATIONAL PARK
Look out for dolphins and whales along this coast
CORAL SEA
Elanda Point Campground
Lake Cootharaba
Teewah Coloured Sands
Teewah
Boreen
Soft Roaders
Trailers
Steep Climbs
Water Crossing
Good Clearance Needed
Snorkel
Road Tyres
Avoid Wet Weather
Navigation Skills
Extra Fuel
Air down tyres before reaching the beach
Noosa River
Noosa North Shore Wilderness Camp
Beach Rd
Noosa River Ferry
Moorindil St
TEWANTIN
NOOSA HEADS

You will reach **Freshwater Creek Camping Area** three kilometres later where basic facilities are provided in a shaded setting, just inland from the beach. Electric BBQs and coin operated hot showers are welcome features of the camp and fires are permitted in fireplaces with clean milled timber.

Take note of this camp as **Freshwater Road** will be our exit from national park on the return journey. Continue north past the site of the Cherry Venture (a Swedish freighter that was caught in heavy seas in 1973, and remained beached as a rusting hulk until recently). Soft sand is a feature of the run toward **Double Island Point** (named by Captain Cook in 1770, and the site of a lighthouse built 110 years later), but you will swing left at Leisha Track. Sections of boarded corduroy pave part of the climb across this narrow neck of land, taking 4WDers from the **Coral Sea** to **Wide Bay**.

A toilet and picnic area is reached on the sheltered waters west of Double Island Point, and there is a scenic coastal cove at the foot of the twin hummock point. Walkers can get a closer look at the diminutive lighthouse, just 12 metres tall and accessed via a foot track. Visitors may even spot humpback whales on their migratory run between August and October. Anglers could toss in a line for a feed of kingfish or mackeral.

Right: *The Everglades*

Below: *Freshwater Lake*

It is possible to continue east to **Rainbow Beach** via **Wide Bay** but it is only suitable for experienced drivers at the wheel of a capable vehicle. The beach run is routine (just some washed up trees to negotiate), but travel around Mudlo Rocks can be hazardous. The drive is only really feasible at dead low tide, as you weave around the more prominent rocks, and use the smaller ones as stepping stones.

Retrace your steps to **Freshwater Road** and turn inland to follow the 20 kph zone west to a tee intersection at Freshwater Lake. Turn left into a carpark

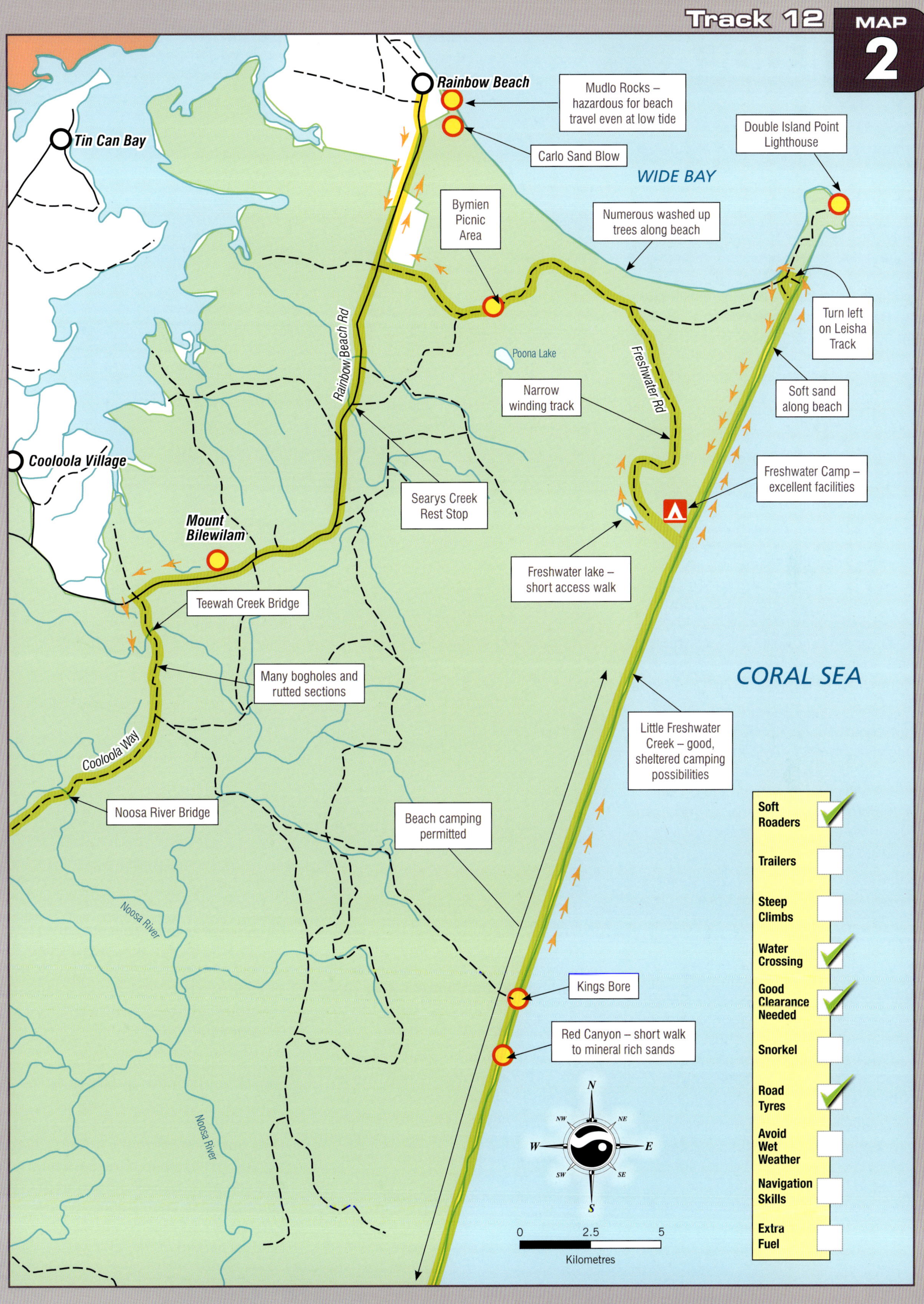
Rainbow Beach
Tin Can Bay
Mudlo Rocks – hazardous for beach travel even at low tide
Carlo Sand Blow
Double Island Point Lighthouse
WIDE BAY
Bymien Picnic Area
Numerous washed up trees along beach
Turn left on Leisha Track
Soft sand along beach
Poona Lake
Freshwater Rd
Rainbow Beach Rd
Narrow winding track
Cooloola Village
Searys Creek Rest Stop
Freshwater Camp – excellent facilities
Mount Bilewilam
Freshwater lake – short access walk
Teewah Creek Bridge
Many bogholes and rutted sections
CORAL SEA
Little Freshwater Creek – good, sheltered camping possibilities
Cooloola Way
Noosa River Bridge
Beach camping permitted
Noosa River
Kings Bore
Red Canyon – short walk to mineral rich sands
Noosa River
N
NE
E
SE
S
SW
W
NW
0
2.5
5
Kilometres
Soft Roaders
Trailers
Steep Climbs
Water Crossing
Good Clearance Needed
Snorkel
Road Tyres
Avoid Wet Weather
Navigation Skills
Extra Fuel

to undertake the 150 metre walk to this small lake. Swimming is popular here if water levels are adequate, but the surrounding forest makes it a worthwhile stop anyway.

Beyond the lake you will negotiate some inland dunes on a narrow winding path punctuated with rough patches. The tree cover becomes increasingly denser closer to **Bymien Picnic Area,** where a carpark and toilets are provided. There is a nice walk from here to the tannin stained waters of **Poona Lake** for those who feel energetic enough for a 4.2 kilometre return walk over undulating ground. It is well worth the effort though with rainforest vegetation shading most of the hike.

You will reach bitumen on the **Rainbow Beach Road** a few kilometres from the lake, so pump up tyres here and turn right to **Rainbow Beach.** This relaxed township is a good place to top up on fuel or supplies, with the **Carlo Sand Blow** accessible via **Cooloola Drive.** Kids can go sand surfing here, while less energetic adults will enjoy the commanding views.

Follow **Rainbow Beach Road** out of town past **Searys Creek rest stop** (lovely melaleuca wetland) and the modest peak of **Mount Bilewilam.** Turn left onto the signposted "Cooloola Way", 17 kilometres south of Rainbow Beach, and begin an unsealed drive.

A bridge spans **Teewah Creek** as you climb past Coops Corner, with potentially rutted and boggy sections marking the Noosa River catchment. You will drop down through scribbly gum and banksia to a timber bridge over the infant **Noosa River,** then climb out reaching the Cooloola Wilderness Trail (a lengthy walking track from Rainbow Beach Road to Harrys Hut, although those hikers up to the challenge may spot the rare ground parrot or the last of coastal Queensland's emu population).

Four kilometres later you will climb to the boundary of national park, keeping left at a track junction and avoiding forestry trails on the right. Follow the main **Pomona Road (Cooloola Way)** past a block of **private property (Tarangau)** as you reach Harrys Hut Road on the left.

Beach access track

Swing left here to follow a dead end track back into national park. Wet weather will close access, but in the dry you will cross Lake Como's feeder creek and several walking tracks enroute to the camping area at **Harrys Hut.**

Timber workers constructed this hut in the 1950s as a cutter's camp, but it was leased to a local chemist for over 40 years as logging operations ceased. Today the site is popular with canoeists who paddle the tranquil Noosa both upstream to informal campsites, and downstream to The Everglades.

Return to the Cooloola Way, keeping straight past **McCrae Road,** to the main **Kin Kin Road** tee intersection. Turn left, taking a steep, winding descent past the Doggrell Forest Trail. Bitumen flags the crossing of **Kin Kin Creek** and Wahpunga Park (nice rest stop), before you turn left onto **Dr Pages Road,** signposted "Boreen Point" and a return to gravel.

Turn left at the **Kinmond Creek Rd** tee intersection through cattle grazing country, to **Lake Flat Road** 2.5 kilometres later. Swing left onto the bitumen here, turning left again at a tee back into national park. Follow the shores of **Lake Cootharaba** to **Elanda Point**, where a national parks office and a private caravan park mark the end of the road.

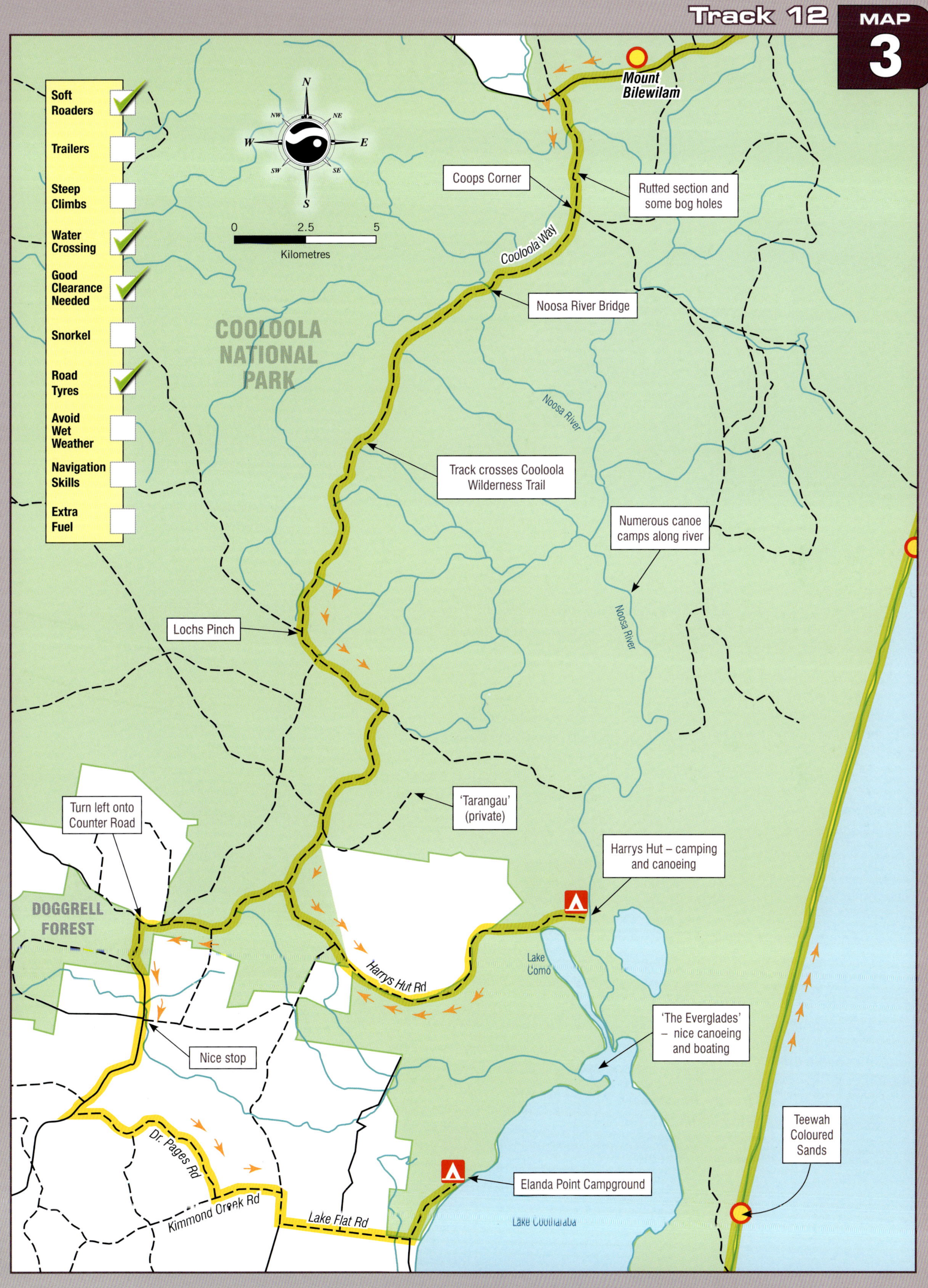

Soft Roaders
Trailers
Steep Climbs
Water Crossing
Good Clearance Needed
Snorkel
Road Tyres
Avoid Wet Weather
Navigation Skills
Extra Fuel
N
NE
E
SE
S
SW
W
NW
0
2.5
5
Kilometres
Mount Bilewilam
Coops Corner
Rutted section and some bog holes
Cooloola Way
Noosa River Bridge
COOLOOLA NATIONAL PARK
Noosa River
Track crosses Cooloola Wilderness Trail
Numerous canoe camps along river
Noosa River
Lochs Pinch
'Tarangau' (private)
Turn left onto Counter Road
Harrys Hut – camping and canoeing
DOGGRELL FOREST
Lake Como
Harrys Hut Rd
Nice stop
'The Everglades' – nice canoeing and boating
Teewah Coloured Sands
Dr. Pages Rd
Elanda Point Campground
Kimmond Creek Rd
Lake Flat Rd
Lake Cootharaba

TRACK 13

Fraser Island

SE QUEENSLAND

Birrabeen Road

__Fraser Island__ is on everyone's wish list, and its attraction is obvious once you arrive. This sandy playground combines exhilarating 4WDing opportunities with great fishing and quiet moments relaxing by the shore of the most scenic lakes you will ever find.

Unfortunately this destination's secret was revealed many years ago, and increasing numbers of visitors are putting enormous pressure on what remains a fragile ecosystem. Rubbish and waste disposal, together with fire use and track degradation has restricted visitor activity to particular areas, and put the brakes on some unsustainable habits.

While the limitations may seem harsh (no more vehicle based camping at __Lake McKenzie__ for example), the longer term outcome will mean that future visitors will also be able to enjoy this four wheelers paradise.

Access to the island is limited to registered 4WD vehicles – including those towing a camper trailer or boat – with barge services operating from __River Heads (near Hervey Bay)__ and __Inskip Point (via Rainbow Beach).__ Bookings are necessary for those leaving via River Heads, to either __Kingfisher Bay Resort__ or __Wanggoolba Creek,__ but the two ferry companies operating from __Inskip Point__ will transport on demand during the daylight hours.

Prior to leaving the mainland you will need to arrange a vehicle permit, and camping permits for areas controlled by the Queensland's Department of Environment and Science. The vehicle permits can be purchased at __River Heads,__ but camping permits can only be organised via the internet www.qld.gov.au/camping or phoning 13 7468 (24 hour service).

Private camping and accommodation is available at a number of resorts on the Fraser coastline, and these would need to be booked in advance also. The summer period and school holiday breaks are particularly busy on Fraser, so organise travel to the island at these times well in advance.

There are numerous 4WD hire outlets on the island and mainland, but if you are travelling with your own vehicle, it would be a good idea to give the underbody a protective spray at one of the coin operated booths on the mainland. It is especially important to visit one of these centres on your return though, to thoroughly wash the accumulated salt spray from the chassis and hidden corners of your vehicle.

Once you have attended to the vital preliminaries, bookings and protective spray, stock up on food and fuel – it is understandably more expensive on the island – then head to the barge departure point. We have chosen Inskip Point as the preferred venue, as you can then follow our suggested itinerary from the island's south to the northern tip in a continuous link, before returning to pick up other destinations of interest.

Track Snapshot

TOUR ROUTE:
Fraser Island, Hook Point to Sandy Cape and return.

DURATION AND DISTANCE:
The 350 kilometres will probably take about six days, allowing for plenty of stops.

TRACK DETAILS:
Sand driving only on the island, varying from firm beach travel at low tide, to more powdery sand on the beach access tracks. The inland tracks are variable, but generally routine if you have reasonable clearances. Trailers can be towed by vehicles with sufficient power, and Soft Roaders are a possibility with care.

WHEN TO GO:
Queensland school holidays are particularly busy, and summer is often hot and wet, although rain will not close sandy tracks like it can on the mainland.

CAMPING:
Dispersed beach camping (no facilities) is permitted in marked zones. Basic facilities are provided at a number of camping areas across the island, with only limited opportunities for camp fires.

FUEL AND SUPPLIES:
Arrive on the island with a full fuel tank(s) and plenty of supplies. Food and fuel is available at the built up villages, albeit at a premium price.

MAPS:
Hema: Fraser Island, Sunmap: Fraser Island.

OTHER INFORMATION:
Be prepared for heavier than usual fuel consumption in the soft sand, and organise your vehicle and camping permits in advance.

Departing from **Inskip** throws you in the deep end however, as the barge access track usually crosses soft sand and will require a reduction in tyre pressures. We suggest a starting point of around 18 p.s.i., and only dropping further if you strike very soft sand, or are bogged alone with an incoming tide.

While travel in company is good insurance for any 4WD run, the added security of additional vehicles is almost essential in sand. Recovery procedures are quicker and simpler, requiring little more than a snatch strap. However as mentioned earlier, Fraser is a popular destination and passing traffic is frequent, so don't be too concerned about travelling solo.

Travellers tempted to tow a camper or boat though, must be well experienced

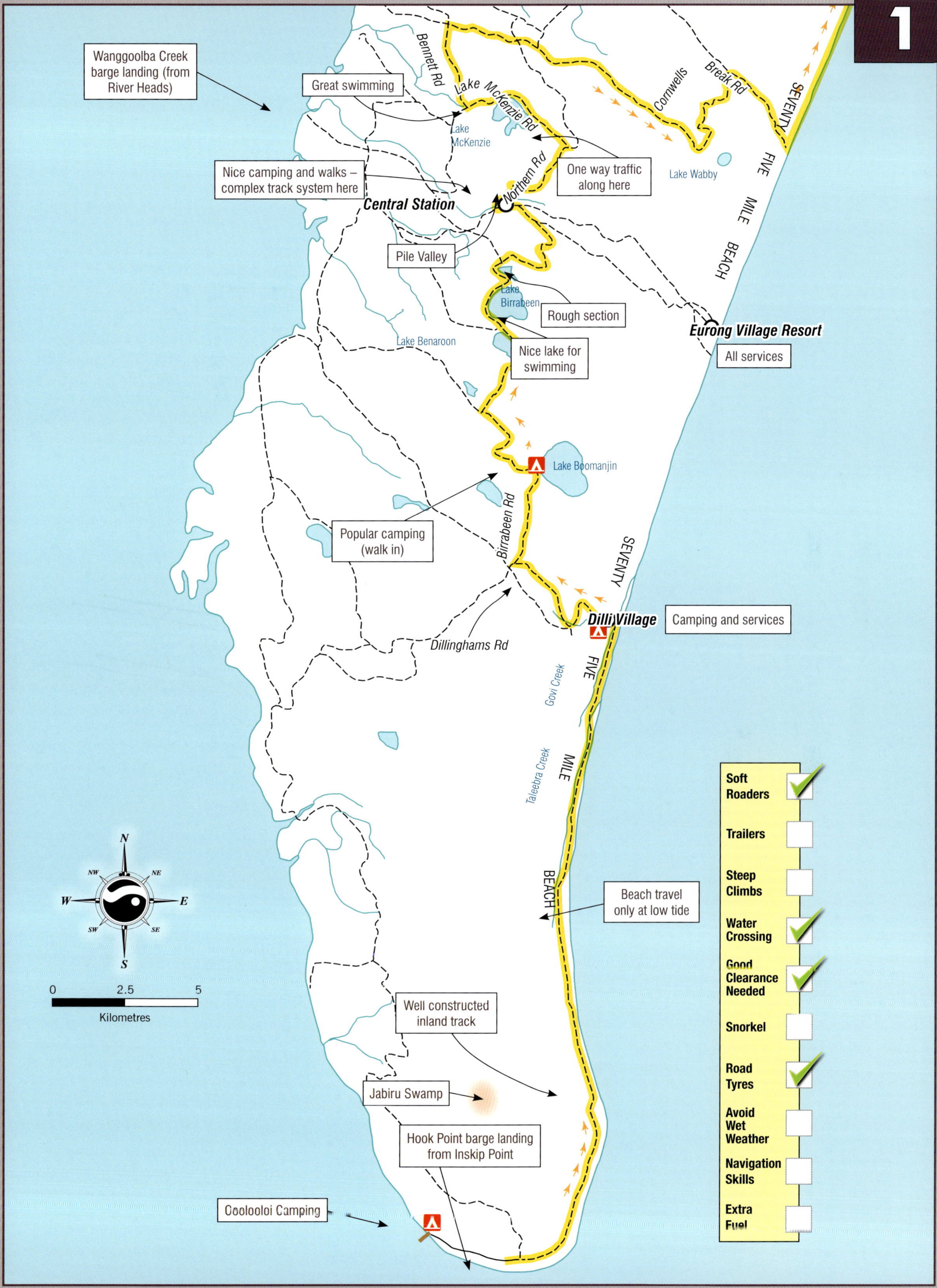

Wanggoolba Creek barge landing (from River Heads)

Great swimming

Bennett Rd

Lake McKenzie Rd

Lake McKenzie

Cornwells Break Rd

One way traffic along here

Lake Wabby

SEVENTY FIVE MILE BEACH

Nice camping and walks – complex track system here

Central Station

Northern Rd

Pile Valley

Lake Birrabeen

Rough section

Eurong Village Resort

All services

Lake Benaroon

Nice lake for swimming

Lake Boomanjin

Popular camping (walk in)

Birrabeen Rd

Dillinghams Rd

Dilli Village

Camping and services

Govi Creek

Taleebra Creek

Beach travel only at low tide

N NE E SE S SW W NW

0 2.5 5

Kilometres

Well constructed inland track

Jabiru Swamp

Hook Point barge landing from Inskip Point

Coolooloi Camping

Soft Roaders	✓
Trailers	
Steep Climbs	
Water Crossing	✓
Good Clearance Needed	✓
Snorkel	
Road Tyres	✓
Avoid Wet Weather	
Navigation Skills	
Extra Fuel	

Lake Boomanjin

in sand driving, and preferably be travelling with others. You will need a powerful vehicle (and an auto transmission is best) and avoid the narrow winding inland tracks, where passing opportunities are limited.

Once aboard the barge you will make a quick trip to **Hook Point** and depart the ferry via a hinged steel ramp. It will probably pay to exit in low range on bagged tyres as the beach can be soft and there is an uphill climb from the ramp.

You have now reached the southern tip of the island with **Seventy Five Mile Beach** extending from here to the northern tip some 123 kilometres away. Most of this extended run follows the beach with the best access to be found at low tide. However the majority of the coast run is negotiable by 4WDs to within a couple of hours either side of high tide, and especially on an outgoing tide.

The southern beach can be difficult at times other than low tide. You can choose to follow the bypass track for 19 kilometres to a drop down onto the beach proper. This bypass is uncharacteristically wide and well surfaced, so remain in 2WD for its passage, and keep speeds down if travelling on aired down tyres.

There is a 50 kph speed limit in place along here anyway, and this together with the usual road rules are enforced by police across Fraser. Travel northward follows low growing heathland flanking **Jabiru Swamp,** where banksia forests crowd colourful displays of spring wildflowers.

Camping areas are located east of the bypass road, but offer no luxuries, and self contained toilet facilities are required. Once you reach the end of the bypass engage 4WD and continue through the dune system to reach the shores of the Coral Sea.

You will cross **Taleebra Creek** a couple of kilometres later, then cruise the firm sand into **Dilli Village,** just two kilometres further on. **Govi Creek** marks access to Dilli and its private facilities. Dingo proof fences are built around most of the serviced camping areas on the island, and Dilli is no exception. Continue westward through the small village, following Dillinghams Roads past views of **Jabiru Swamp** on a winding journey to a tee intersection some seven kilometres from Dilli Village.

Turn right onto **Birrabeen Road** for a further four kilometres before reaching Fraser Island's largest lake. At almost 200 hectares, **Lake Boomanjin** is the world's largest perched lake (the term "perched" applies to many lakes across Fraser where accumulated humus and leaf litter has lined the sandy bottom of dune undulations, allowing rain water and run off to collect in the now water tight basin).

Camping is popular here, as the morning light colours this broad expanse of water, fringed with paperbarks, and stained orange by leeching tannins. Facilities include toilets and cold showers, but vehicle based tourers must carry all of their gear into the fenced camping area.

Continue along Birrabeen Road through some swampy area to a pair of timber bridges about five kilometres away. You will skirt the southern shore of **Lake Benaroon,** before reaching a carpark at Lake Birrabeen some five kilometres beyond the second bridge.

A short walk brings you to the white sandy beach ringing Birrabeen. Unlike Boomanjin, this lake is a window lake; formed as the natural water table has risen above a depression in the sandy topography. Stunning clear water invites

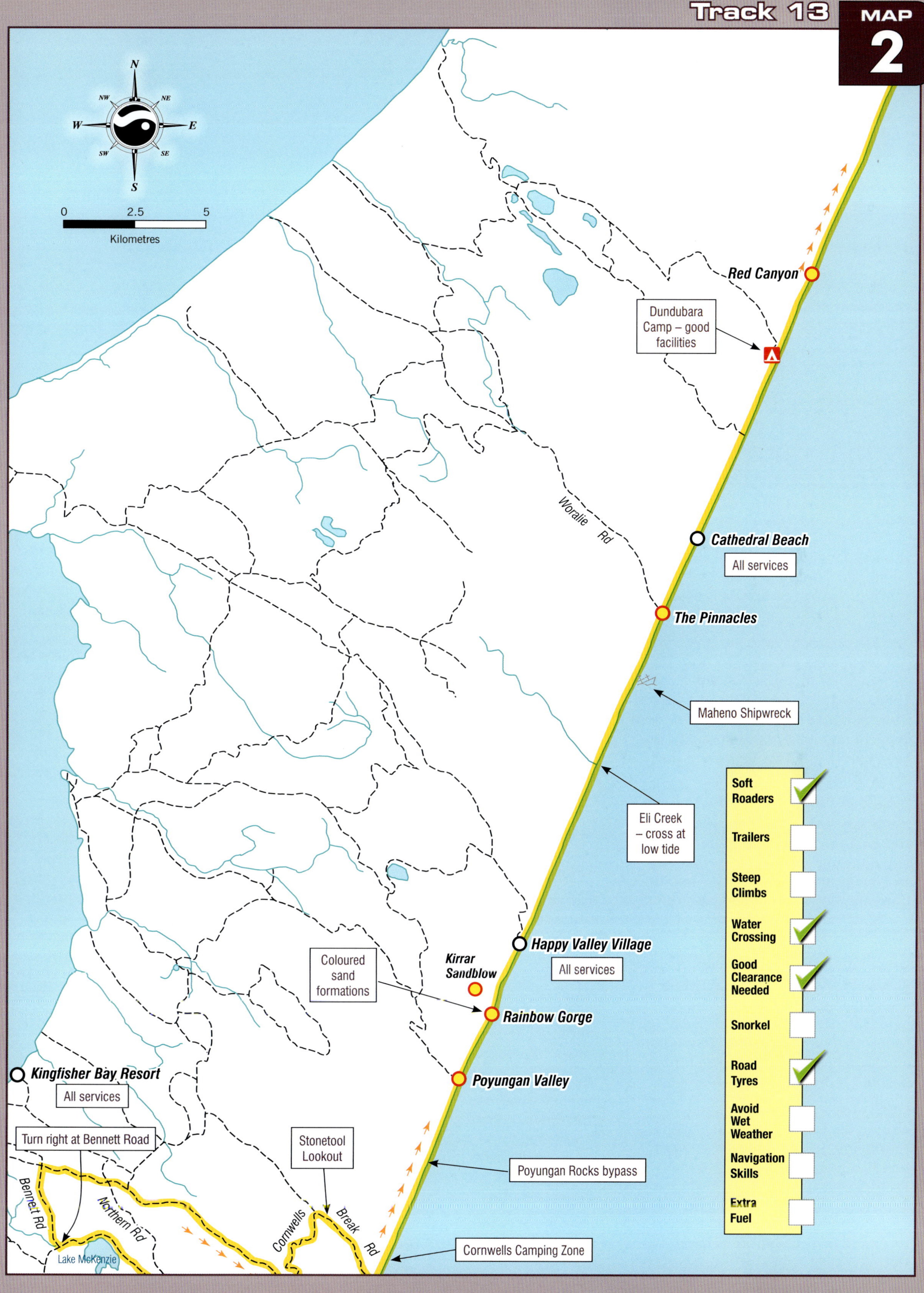
N
NW
NE
W
E
SW
SE
S
0
2.5
5
Kilometres
Red Canyon
Dundubara Camp – good facilities
Woralie Rd
Cathedral Beach
All services
The Pinnacles
Maheno Shipwreck
Eli Creek – cross at low tide
Happy Valley Village
All services
Kirrar Sandblow
Coloured sand formations
Rainbow Gorge
Poyungan Valley
Kingfisher Bay Resort
All services
Turn right at Bennett Road
Stonetool Lookout
Poyungan Rocks bypass
Bennett Rd
Northern Rd
Cornwells Break Rd
Lake McKenzie
Cornwells Camping Zone
Soft Roaders
Trailers
Steep Climbs
Water Crossing
Good Clearance Needed
Snorkel
Road Tyres
Avoid Wet Weather
Navigation Skills
Extra Fuel

East coastline

visitors to swim here, and if conditions are suitable, do so, as the popular alternative, **Lake McKenzie** is often very busy.

Two kilometres beyond Birrabeen you will reach a tee intersection. Turn right here and follow a nasty downhill section punctuated with tree roots and rugged steps. Hold the vehicle back in the lower gears to negotiate these obstacles, and keep an eye open for oncoming traffic in the tortuous conditions.

Dimly lit rainforest marks the transition into tall timber country as you approach Central Station. The popular campground here is reached six kilometres from Birrabeen, and the location is ideal for a good base camp.

Two large camping areas are found within a fenced compound and there is ample room for camper trailers or large groups. Coin operated hot showers are available, but open fires are not permitted (open fires are only allowed in group facilities provided at **Dundubara** and **Waddy Point** using milled timber brought in from the mainland only).

Some excellent walks originate around Central Station with lengthy possibilities in addition to the "must do" **Wanggoolba Creek boardwalk.** Visitors here follow a short section of the impossibly clear waters, flowing quietly under a canopy of rainforest timbers, vines and huge Angiopteris ferns.

Relics from the earlier wood cutting days stand nearby, testament to the resource boom days when timber harvesting (and some sand mining) was a lucrative industry. Massive satinay trees – also known as turpentine – were felled and used as rot resistant wharf timbers in exotic locations as far away as London.

The track system around **Central Station** is rather complex, and travellers should carry an up to date map to negotiate the network of one way and loop sections. From the camping area at Central Station you can head west toward the barge landing at Wanggoolba Creek, or head east (after a tight U turn) to **Eurong Village** on the coast.

Eurong is one of the larger private centres on the island, with camping and accommodation, together with a mini supermarket and fuel availability. Fill up with fuel whenever possible on your Fraser travels as the sand driving will increase your usual fuel consumption, and supplies cannot be guaranteed at smaller outlets across the island.

We will leave Central Station via the main **Eurong Road,** but swing left onto the Northern Road about one kilometre later. Huge brush box and satinay trees usher the descent into **Pile Valley,** as you reach **Lake McKenzie Road** a few kilometres later.

Turn left onto the one way road and trace the lake's northern fringe to a carpark some five kilometres later. This is a very popular site and is best seen out of the peak travelling season, or at least by avoiding the midday crush, when tourist buses are at their most numerous.

It is only a short walk to the crystal clear lake with its white sandy beaches and tempting waters. The most popular swimming beach is found closest to the carpark, but if you walk to the north just a few hundred metres, you will find a quieter bathing location, hidden from the sometimes noisy crowds.

Continue the one way drive away from McKenzie and turn right at **Bennett Road,** just a kilometre later. Follow this track northward, before swinging east to again meet the **Northern Road** at a four way junction. Maintain your easterly path across the intersection as you head through banksia, grasstree and some open country to the **Lake Wabby** turn off, about eight kilometres from the junction.

Turn right to reach a small carpark near Lake Wabby, from where a steep walking track will take you to the lake. Formed by a sandblow that has naturally dammed a creek, Wabby is the deepest of Fraser's lakes at 11 metres.

Energetic visitors can reach the lake lookout via a short walk (one kilometre, 30 minute return) or continue to the lake shore itself – a more strenuous three kilometre (90 minute) return hike.

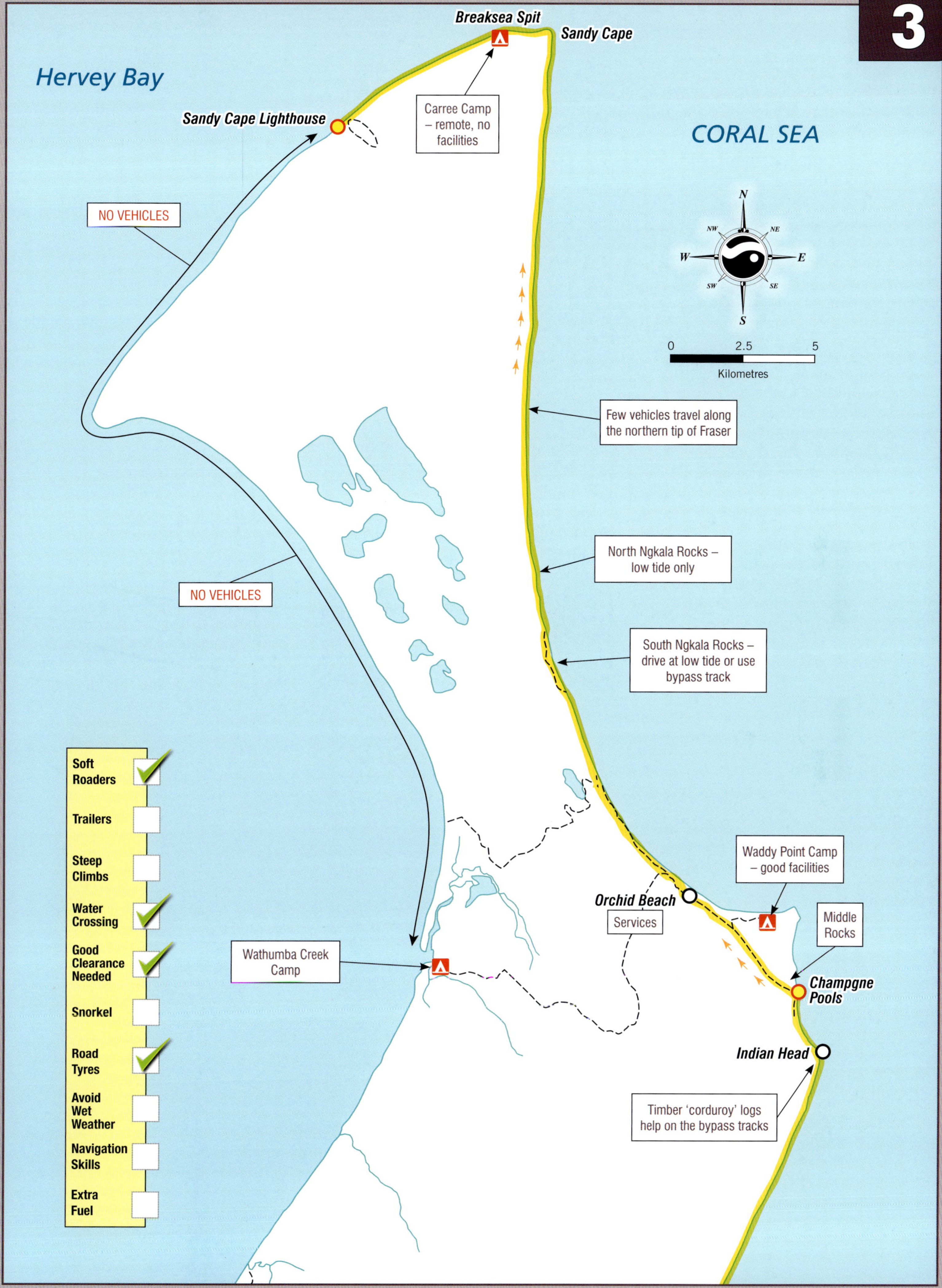

Breaksea Spit
Sandy Cape
Hervey Bay
Sandy Cape Lighthouse
Carree Camp – remote, no facilities
CORAL SEA
N
NW
NE
W
E
SW
SE
S
0
2.5
5
Kilometres
NO VEHICLES
Few vehicles travel along the northern tip of Fraser
North Ngkala Rocks – low tide only
NO VEHICLES
South Ngkala Rocks – drive at low tide or use bypass track
Soft Roaders
Trailers
Steep Climbs
Water Crossing
Good Clearance Needed
Snorkel
Road Tyres
Avoid Wet Weather
Navigation Skills
Extra Fuel
Waddy Point Camp – good facilities
Orchid Beach
Services
Middle Rocks
Wathumba Creek Camp
Champgne Pools
Indian Head
Timber 'corduroy' logs help on the bypass tracks

Those willing to make the effort will be rewarded with some superb views of the lake and probably get to see the resident tortoises and catfish.

Return to the carpark turn off junction and turn right through a cycad forest to the **Cornwells Break Road** junction a few kilometres later. Swing right again at this intersection and drive for a kilometre to Stonetool Lookout. The roadside vantage point takes in one of the many areas of mobile dune across the island.

You will descend from the lookout via a corduroy of parallel timber poles laid perpendicular to the track. Many of Fraser's more difficult inland trails feature this type of traction aid, while other sections are paved with a more contemporary version, where plastic honeycomb has been embedded in the sand.

Travel beyond the corduroy enters a superb stand of scribbly gums, where white and creamy trunked trees are stained brown and decorated with countless crazy scribbles. Follow a winding route through the forest and back onto the beach at **Cornwells Camping Zone**.

There are numerous camping zones dotted along the eastern coast; each clearly signposted, but none offering any facilities at all. Self sufficient campers will find some picturesque sites just inland from the foreshore, but still at the mercy of the prevailing winds.

From **Cornwells Break Road** head north along the beach for about five kilometres to the **Poyungan Rocks Bypass,** then a further three kilometres to **Poyungan Valley. Rainbow Gorge** lies a couple of kilometres further on, and it is worth stopping here to make the easy two kilometre return walk through these coloured sand formations.

Visitors will skirt the Kirrar Sandblow, and walk through some coastal forest of native pine and paperbark. However the coloured sands are most spectacular with iron oxides having leeched a spectrum of tones into the ancient formations.

Beyond the gorge, vehicles again head inland to bypass Yidney Rocks, and bounce up to the **Happy Valley** turn off. This wilderness retreat offers most services within a section of land excised from the national park.

If you continue straight, you will again return to the beach and follow the surf for seven kilometres to **Eli Creek.** This freshwater crossing has earned a formidable reputation for vehicle destruction over the years, but conservative driving will see you safely across. Tackle the crossing as close to low tide as possible, perhaps walking the route first if previous vehicles have not left an obvious path.

The creek pushes out up to four million litres of water per hour, and a substantial step will have formed at the river bank. There is a popular camping zone just south of the crossing, so stop here if the tidal conditions are worrying.

Once committed to the crossing select low second and push across at your predetermined entry and exit points. In general (as with other river crossings) it is usually best to exit the river from further downstream than your entry point so that you experience less drag from the body of water.

A short boardwalk allows visitors to explore the lower reaches of **Eli Creek** on the northern side of the crossing. Three kilometres further on you will stretch your legs again as the **Maheno Wreck** comes into view. There is no access onto the rusting hulk, but it is well worth

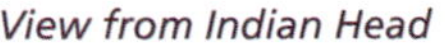

View from Indian Head

stopping to appreciate what is left of this once grand vessel.

Coloured cliffs adorn the drive beyond here as you pass **Woralie Road,** and reach **The Pinnacles** shortly after that. A popular stretch of coast for surf fishing marks the remaining few kilometres into **Cathedral Beach,** where the usual services can be found.

Dundubara Camping Area is located six kilometres north of Cathedral and offers excellent bush camping within a dingo fenced enclosure. Vehicle based camping is possible here, with hot showers, flushing toilets and gas BBQs. Several inland walks originate at the camp, and while the dingo fence detracts somewhat from the wilderness experience, these enclosures will help to break the link that has developed, where the dingo population associates humans with food availability.

Heading north from **Dundubara** you will pass more coloured sands at **Red Canyon** a few kilometres on, then begin a relatively lengthy run to **Indian Head** 14 kilometres later. The imposing bluff at Indian Head is bypassed via some patches of soft sand and sections of corduroy.

You will return to the beach for three kilometres, then begin a longer bypass around Middle Rocks and **Waddy Point. Champagne Pools** is reached from a small carpark located on top of the bypass, and is worth a look especially if the tide has receded, leaving a pair of rocky pools to hold the foaming seawater.

Champagne Pools

Follow a one way sand track for five kilometres to the Waddy Point turn off. Beach front camping is possible here, just two kilometres from the junction. However we continue straight onto a two way track past the airstrip at **Orchid Beach,** before reaching the Hotel / Store.

Beach travel is still possible beyond Orchid Beach, but it is much less popular than what you have done so far. You will drop down to the beach via a right fork in the track (one way) and travel past a sand blow to the **Ocean Lake** turn off.

It is only a kilometre drive inland, and a short walk meanders through paperbarks to excellent views of the lake's inky waters. Return to the beach and follow it for a few kilometres to **South Ngkala Rocks.** If the tide is dead low you may skirt these rocks by weaving through the maze of black boulders strewn on the seaward side.

If recent tidal influences make it impossible to tackle the ocean route, then follow a bypass track inland for about a kilometre. This option can be very soft in the warmer months and perhaps impassable to some vehicles. Travel with caution via either route, and preferably travel in company.

North Ngkala Rocks lie a couple of kilometres further north and must be tackled at low tide, but once clear you will have a relatively easy run for about 20 kilometres to the very tip at **Sandy Cape.**

The Breaksea Spit extends for some 30 kilometres further north of here, taming the South Pacific Ocean with a sheltered piece of water to the west. You will round the cape to reach the Carree Camping Zone, and perhaps have to negotiate some fallen trees on the foreshore.

This northern most camping zone is especially attractive, with some sheltered sites overlooking the emerald waters of Hervey Bay. You may only drive a further seven kilometres to **Sandy Cape lighthouse,** as a substantial vehicle exclusion zone extends down the west coast, but self contained campers will find few more appealing areas on Fraser than this northern refuge.

Visitors will need to retrace their steps south to leave the island, with any number of inland options possible on the return journey.

Chapter 3
CENTRAL QUEENSLAND

◀ *Salvator Rosa NP*

TRACK 14

Salvator Rosa

CENTRAL QUEENSLAND

Above: *Station relic*

*The **Salvator Rosa** Section of Carnarvon NP marks the western reaches of this stunning sandstone belt, and while a lot fewer visitors make the journey out here, those who do will see that as a bonus. This trek takes in the highlights of Salvator Rosa, and continues southward to visit the Warrego River wetlands, then exit through the Chesterton Range.*

We begin the journey at **Tambo** on the **Landsborough Highway,** 60 kilometres east of **Blackall. Tambo** is recognised as the oldest town in central west Queensland, having been settled in 1863. Stock up on fuel and supplies here, because there is nothing else available enroute.

Turn left over the infant **Barcoo River** at signposted **"Springsure"** onto the **Dawson Developmental Road** (also known as the **Wilderness Way**). A prominent sign indicates the road status ahead – take heed as wet weather will put an end to any vehicle travel.

A couple of homesteads mark a sustained climb through the **Dingo Fence** to skirt around **Mount Blunt** on your right. Numerous bottle trees mark **Highland Station** before you cross **Windeyere Creek** – a significant waterway about 30 kilometres from **Tambo.**

Track Snapshot

TOUR ROUTE:
Tambo to Mitchell via Salvator Rosa NP and the Warrego River.

DURATION AND DISTANCE:
This 600 kilometre trek will take the best part of three days – or more if you choose to stop for a while to enjoy the features of Salvator Rosa.

TRACK DETAILS:
Routine station country tracks feature in the main, which will be closed in the wet, but suitable for all vehicles and trailers when dry. A short section of the Spyglass Peak track will need good clearances.

WHEN TO GO:
Avoid wet weather and the heat of summer.

CAMPING:
Bush camping with basic facilities at Salvator Rosa, with commercial parks at Tambo and Mungalala (next to the pub).

FUEL AND SUPPLIES:
No fuel or supplies available enroute; Tambo and Mungallala are the only outlets.

MAPS:
Hema: Queenslands Outback, Sunmap: Outback Queensland. Natmap: Eddystone 1:250K may prove useful for the maze of tracks around Bogarella Station.

OTHER INFORMATION:
Travellers to this area of Central Queensland need to be competent navigators, as the road signs are limited; a vehicle mounted GPS would be useful.

Below: *Spyglass Peak*

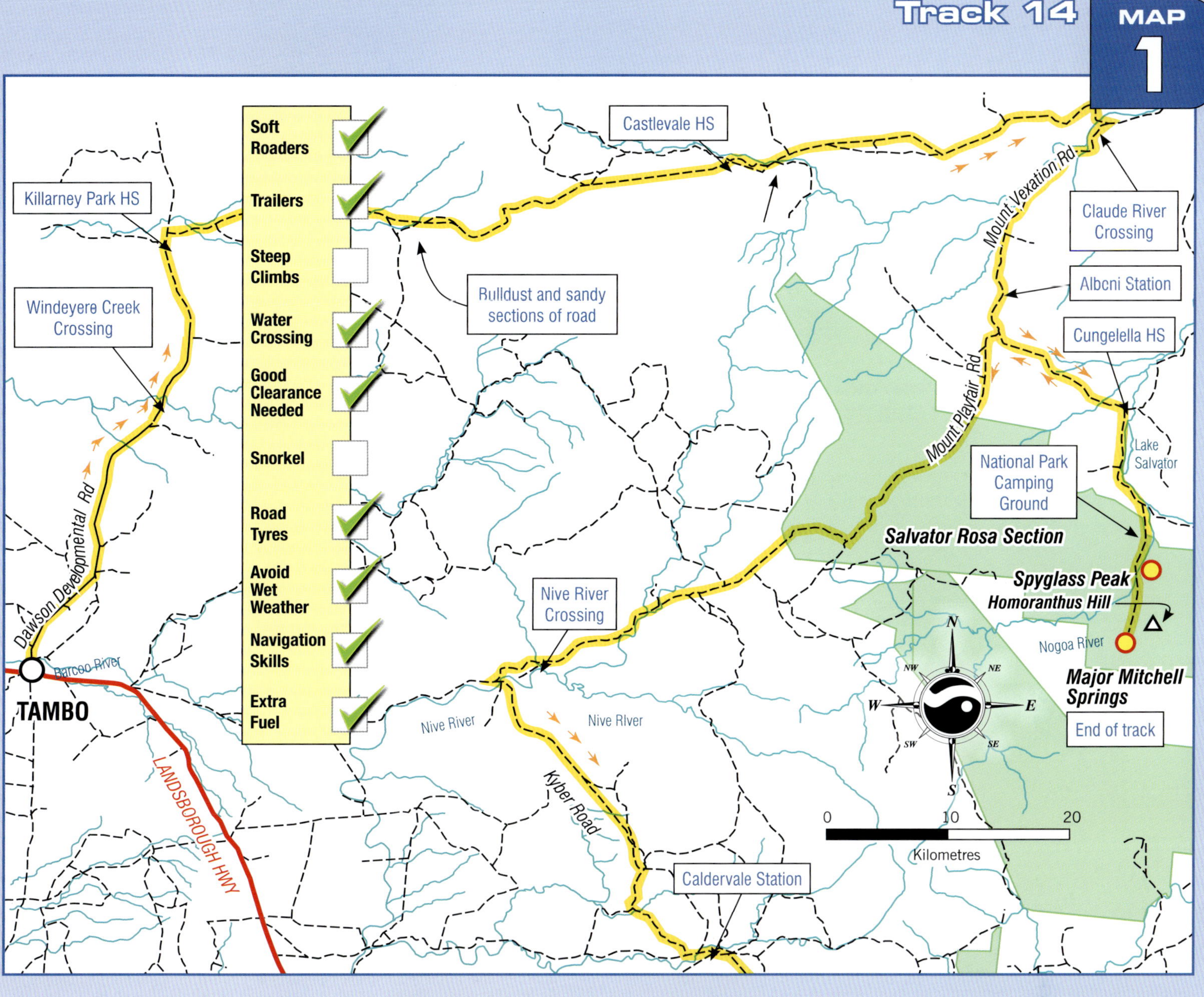

Unsealed road begins at **Killarney Park,** where you turn right at signposted **"Springsure",** 46 kilometres out of **Tambo.** Yards, tank and windmill mark the major junction, and from there a deterioration in road quality with patches of bulldust and sandy sections.

Native pine cloaks the bushland below **Sugarloaf Peak,** before you reach the **Castlevale Nature Reserve.** A steep descent on corrugated gravel paves the way past stunning range views, with sheer cliff faces and domed sandstone formations. Glimpses of the **Carnarvon Range** continue to **Castlevale HS,** where you begin a descent to the **Claude River** (a major tributary of the Nogoa – to be visited later in the trek).

You will climb out into cleared land with great views, before again crossing the **Claude,** and turning right immediately after onto **Mount Vexation Road,** about 130 kilometres from **Tambo.** A winding piece of road passes **Albeni Station** on the left, to a tee intersection six kilometres later. **Mount Playfair Road** branches to the right (take note of this junction, as it will be our exit through **Salvator Rosa**), but you will keep left here to head into the range.

Pass **Lake Salvator HS** on the right, to a junction on **Mount Vexation Road,** some 14 kilometres from the **Mount Playfair** intersection. An old grave site marks the turn right onto **narrow track** at **Cungelella Station,** where travellers now follow a broad arm of **Lake Salvator** to the boundary of **national park.**

The **Nogoa River** camping area is reached three kilometres later, where basic facilities are located within a fairly large area. Camping within **Salvator Rosa** is only permitted here, as flash floods make river side camping dangerous. Camping permits and fees apply. A tag with your booking number must be displayed at your campsite.

Rougher road heads south from the camping area, with a major crossing of the **Nogoa River** being the first obstacle. A timber corduroy base offers some assistance to negotiate the wide sandy river, although at the time of our most recent visit it had washed downstream.

The track continues to follow some superb stretches of the **Nogoa** as it weaves through roof high grasses and hidden bogholes. **Spyglass Peak** comes into view within a couple of kilometres, and a parking bay is found soon after. There is a 400 metre walk to the sandstone formation, where the forces of erosion have punched a 10 metre diameter hole into one of the sandstone peaks.

Nearby **Louisa Creek** flows into the **Nogoa River** at more than 100 litres per second. Underground springs feed the constant flow, which meets the Nogoa at a picturesque confluence, coloured with white sands, reeds and crystal clear waters.

Continue the drive past **Homoranthus Hill** for outstanding views, to a locked gate at **Major Mitchell Springs**. Back in 1846, an exploration party headed by Mitchell, camped here to recuperate and survey the potential grazing lands nearby. Today walkers can follow the marshy area to an old set of yards constructed in the 1940s.

You will now need to retrace your steps, first to the camping area, then return to the **Mount Playfair Road** junction, some 40 kilometres from the **springs.** Once back at the turn off, swing left (west) past **Goodliff HS,** and into what is termed the **Goodliff Section** of **Carnarvon NP.**

Begin a winding climb past crumbly orange lichen stained sandstone to a plateau, before desending out of **NP,** following the **Tambo** signs through native pines. Cross a grid into **Malta Station** for a crossing of the **Nive River,** then a winding run to a tee intersection.

Tambo is some 43 kilometres to the right at this junction, and those with limited time can exit the range via this option. Travellers who swing left here will continue via a series of stations, with limited signage and road realignments that may not correspond with some maps – press on if you are adventurous and a reasonable navigator.

Proceed past the **Malta HS** turn off to some open country with range views. Turn left at a tee intersection on **Kyber Road,** to pass **Calderville HS** on the lower earthen track option, then swing right three kilometres from the homestead. Nice Jump Up country and bottle trees precede an especially scenic run through lime green trees, grasslands and dark red range country.

Warrego River

Turn left onto a **sealed intersection** at a bottle tree some 20 kilometres from **Caldervale HS.** The views continue to the goat breeding station of **Mount Lindsay,** where steel stockyards mark another tee intersection. Swing right here, with the **Warrego River** tracing your drive south, just 200 metres away on the left. You will cross the river at a causeway, four kilometres prior to the **Bogarella HS,** then make your way through the **Dog Fence** 27 kilometres after the homestead.

Hoganthulla Creek is crossed just prior to a tee intersection where you will turn left to closely follow this waterway eastward. Cross through the **Dog Fence** again to parallel intricate channels and waterways, with a prominent pinnacle dominating the local ranges.

You again reach a tee intersection on **Hoganthulla Creek**, where you turn left to pass **Wetlands HS** on your right. Turn right onto signposted **"Mitchell Road",** eight kilometres beyond **Wetlands** to again cross **Hoganthulla Creek** at a steepish ford. Native pines colour the way past **Taylors Plains,** where a large waterhole marks the homestead (no access).

Keep right at a fork four kilometres later, passing **Redford** and **Muldoon** homesteads. **Resurfaced road** from here offers better drainage and good travelling through the **Chesterton Range** foothills, with glimpses of **Mount Hotspur** to be seen on the right.

Umberil and **Bangor** stations usher the final kilometres into **Mungallala,** where a hotel and adjoining campground await your arrival. This small cypress milling town grew from its original roots as a **Cobb and Co** changing station. Those looking for more facilities will find them at **Mitchell,** just 45 kilometres by bitumen to the east. **Mitchell's** artesian spa baths are a popular venue on the banks of the **Maranoa River**.

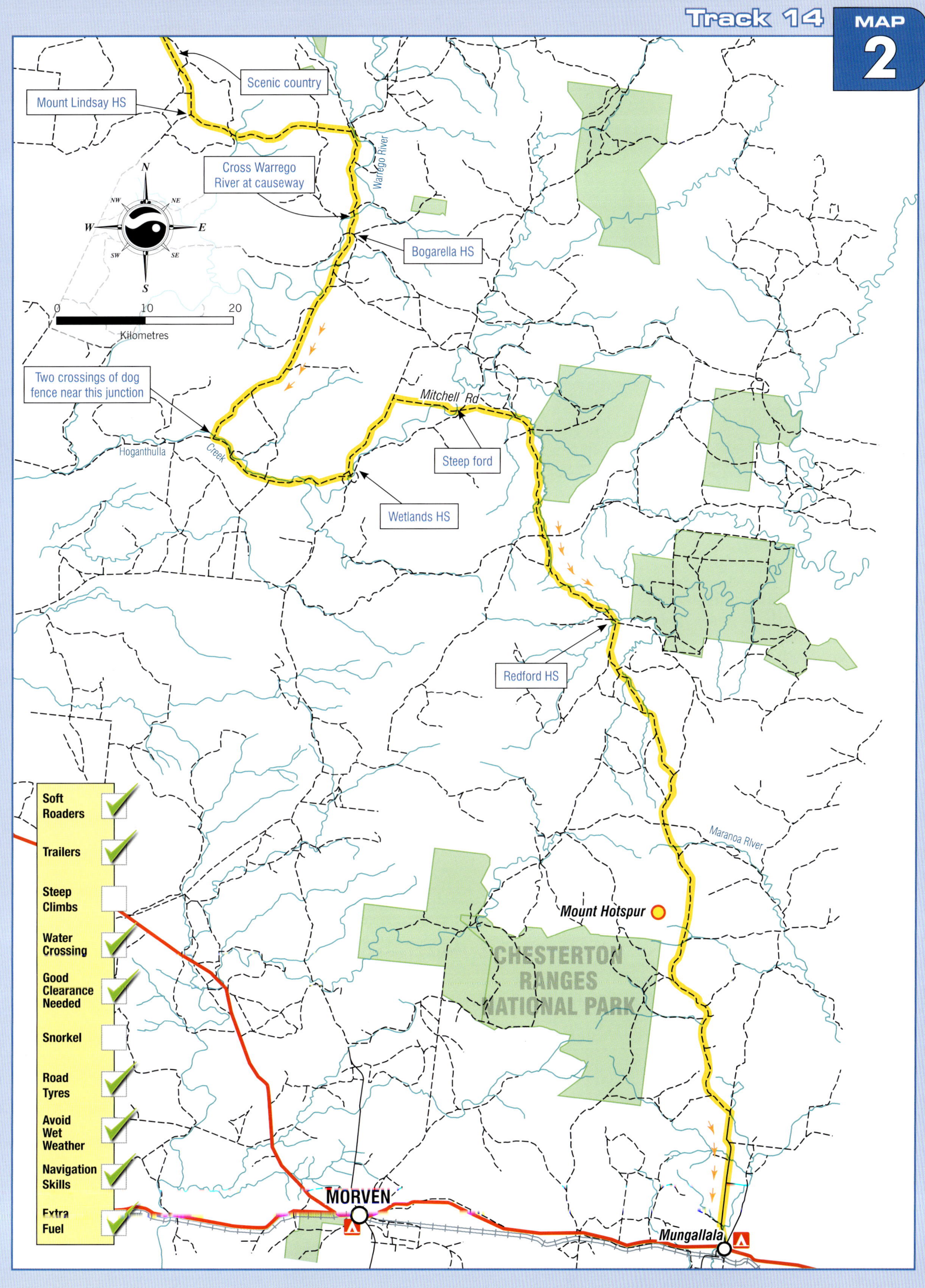
Scenic country
Mount Lindsay HS
Cross Warrego River at causeway
Warrego River
Bogarella HS
N
NE
E
SE
S
SW
W
NW
0
10
20
Kilometres
Two crossings of dog fence near this junction
Mitchell Rd
Steep ford
Hoganthulla
Creek
Wetlands HS
Redford HS
Maranoa River
Mount Hotspur
CHESTERTON RANGES NATIONAL PARK
MORVEN
Mungallala
Soft Roaders
Trailers
Steep Climbs
Water Crossing
Good Clearance Needed
Snorkel
Road Tyres
Avoid Wet Weather
Navigation Skills
Extra Fuel

TRACK 15 MITCHELL TO CULGOA

CENTRAL QUEENSLAND

Neabul Creek

*This relatively easy trek through grazing and cropping country picks up a couple of Queensland's lesser visited national parks (**Thrushton** and **Culgoa Floodplain**) with a superb outback town based camp on **Wallam Creek** to break the journey.*

The action begins on the **Warrego Highway** at **Mitchell,** where you head west toward **Charleville,** turning south to **Bollon** after two kilometres. Historic **Mitchell Downs Station** (established 1860) is passed as the unsealed road penetrates grazing lands, then the more forested areas along **Wallam Creek.** A series of floodways marks the approach to **Abbieglassie** (and its imaginative mail box), before a number of homestead turn offs flag the passing of **Tongy** and **Kenilworth.**

A cross road some 172 kilometres from **Mitchell** marks the turn off to **Homeboin HS.** Swing left at the junction, keeping to the right of the homestead itself, to cross **Wallam Creek.** Continue to follow a southerly direction, away from a station track to the east, before reaching **Shannendoah Station.**

Veer left away from the homestead on the main road to reach **Thrushton NP,** 18 kilometres from the **Homeboin** turn off. You will follow the boundary fence on your right, to cross **Neabul Creek** at a concrete causeway. Proceed a further five kilometres to an easily missed junction where a single grader scrape has cut access into the national park at a set of old yards.

Only a couple of minor tracks allow access into **Thrushton** (all other tracks are formed alongside the fencelines) but **Neabul Creek** access is a possible stop to camp or stretch your legs.

Follow the main track east along the netting fence to a farm house marking the corner of **Thrushton's** two separate blocks. Turn right here, then head straight, through a number of gates and potentially boggy patches.

You will reach the **Balonne Highway** bitumen at a tee intersection, where you turn right for 15 kilometres into **Bollon.** This small grazing township offers a pub, store and fuel outlet, together with a very pleasant weir side camp. Free camping with grassy, shaded sites front **Wallam Creek** and its resident koalas, with toilets and fireplaces available, and it is just a short stroll into the main street.

Head south to leave town via the **Fernlee Road,** west of the community, just opposite the main **Mitchell Road.** You will pass **Heather HS** before turning left onto the signposted **"Runnymede" road.** The blacktop is left behind as you pass a large dam on the left, then **Runnymede Station** and its collection of outbuildings, 34 kilometres from **Bollon.**

Fenceline on the left marks the old telegraph line that mostly still stands on substantial posts of rail line. This impressive piece of pioneering infrastructure continues for 30 kilometres, linking a series of stations to Bollon and beyond (regular inundation would make travel unviable here at times, so the telegraph line was a vital link to the outside world).

You will follow **Mungallala Creek** south past a lovely Queenslander style homestead, with shearing shed and other outbuildings at **Wilgamah,** to **Kanowna HS,** where improvised timber poles have taken over from the rail poles. Scrubby forest cloaks the country to a tee intersection, where you turn right to signposted **"Coomburra".**

Travellers cross the **Mungallala Creek wetlands,** then swing immediately to the left onto the **Mulga Downs Road.** Stockyards are passed near the junction, but there is a transition to cropping as you head further south.

You again cross the **Mungallala,** then reach a junction 60 kilometres into the **Mulga Downs Road.** Keep right at the junction, passing broad acres of floodplain land, with grain sheds and silos dotting the landscape.

Turn right onto **Byra Road,** keeping right away from **Tara HS,** for a short run into **Culgoa Floodplain NP.** The national park was established in 1994 following the surrender of **Byra Station** and some adjoining sheep properties. An information centre at **Byra Lagoon** will help visitors to identify the broad range of plant and animal species found within the **national park**; especially the colourful parrot family, including major mitchell cockatoos.

Flooding of the **Culgoa** occurs periodically, allowing black box woodlands to flourish at their most northern limits. Native grasses are home to a robust kangaroo population, and natural artesian springs form their own unique ecosystem in the park.

Camping is permitted at **Byra Lagoon,** although visitors must be self sufficient in everything including firewood. A network of old station country tracks criss cross the park, but it is the main road heading across the NSW border that takes you into **Culgoa NP** and **Weilmoringle.**

Track Snapshot

TOUR ROUTE:
Mitchell to Culgoa River via Thrushton NP.

DURATION AND DISTANCE:
Two days with an overnight stop at Bollon would be a good choice for this 400 kilometre trek.

TRACK DETAILS:
Easy driving in the dry, with station tracks and sections of bitumen. Suitable for all vehicles and trailers.

WHEN TO GO:
Dry weather outside of hot summer months would be most suitable, especially within the flood prone Culgoa area.

CAMPING:
Excellent camping at Bollon (basic facilities) with bush camping at Culgoa Floodplain NP (ph: 07 4622 4266 for details), and commercial parks at Mitchell.

FUEL AND SUPPLIES:
Fuel and supplies at Bollon and the larger centre of Mitchell.

MAPS:
Hema: Outback Queensland, Sunmap: Outback Queensland.

OTHER INFORMATION:
With few tourists likely to use these roads, you will appreciate the variety of Queensland station country at a leisurely pace.

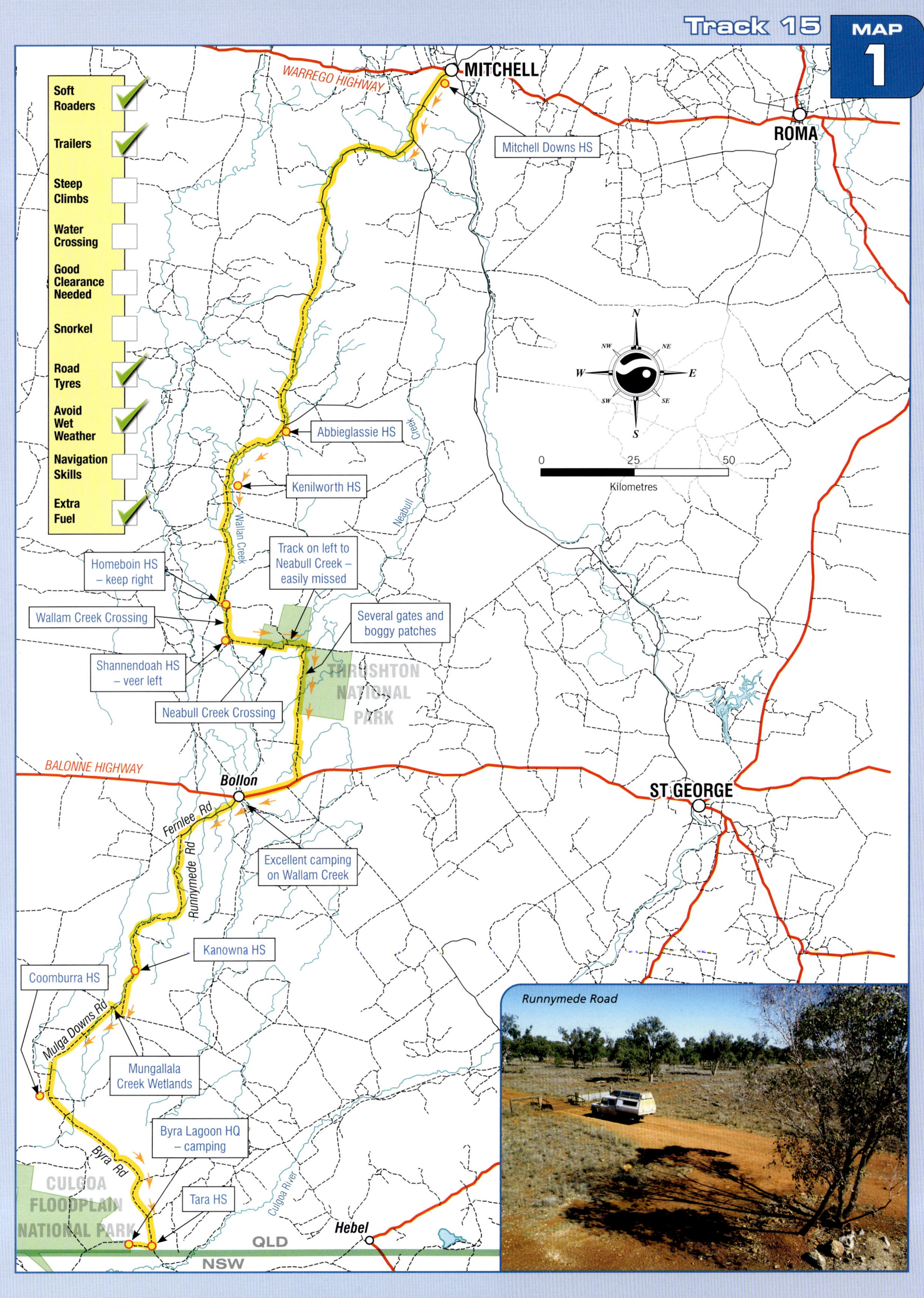

Runnymede Road

TRACK 16

Carnarvon Gorge

CENTRAL QUEENSLAND

Dargonelly Rockhole

Track Snapshot

TOUR ROUTE:
Injune to Rolleston via Mount Moffat and Carnarvon Gorge.

DURATION AND DISTANCE:
Allow about five days for the 680 kilometre jouney.

TRACK DETAILS:
Routine station tracks and a minor section of tougher track at Mount Moffat allow full size 4WDs and trailers to undertake the trek. Soft Roaders driven with care can also complete the tour, but all vehicles are limited to dry weather.

WHEN TO GO:
April to November is the best time to avoid summer rains, but be prepared for cold weather at Mount Moffat. School holidays are popular and bookings are required.

CAMPING:
Bush camping with basic faclities at Carnarvon Gorge, Mount Moffat (several locations) and Takarakka Bush Resort (www.takarakka.com.au).

FUEL AND SUPPLIES:
Injune and Rolleston offer most services and supplies.

MAPS:
Hema: Outback Queensland, Sunmap: Central Queensland.

OTHER INFORMATION:
The Carnarvon Gorge walk is lengthy but well worthwhile. Carry plenty of water and head out early in the day.

*The waters of **Carnarvon Creek** begin to trickle from an elevated sandstone belt in central Queensland, before flowing along one of the most scenic gorges to be found in the state. Centuries of erosion has sliced through the **Carnarvon Range,** leaving some towering formations in its wake, and fostered a unique micro climate where ancient flora thrives. The main gorge extends for about 30 kilometres, and with walls rising up to 200 metres, it presents an imposing spectacle.*

*This tour visits the region's more popular sections, **Carnarvon Gorge** and **Mount Moffat;** each linked by **Carnarvon Creek**, but each quite different in character and appeal. The gorge area is outstandingly rich in scenic attraction, while visitors to **Mount Moffatt** will enter an elevated plateau of rugged features, with some routine 4WD challenges thrown in for good measure.*

We begin this journey at **Injune** on the **Carnarvon Development Road,** about 80 kilometres north of **Roma.** This small township will be your last chance to top up on supplies (including drinking water) until you return here for the second leg of the trek which will take in **Carnarvon Gorge.** Unfortunately there is no vehicle access from the **Mount Moffat Section** to the gorge area, even though they lie within hiking distance.

There are two possibilities for travel to **Mount Moffatt** out of Injune, and we will take one option on the way in, and the other on our exit. The conventional route via **Womblebank Station** is the easier route, but travellers heading in via **Merivale Station** will enjoy a scenic alternative. If you are to follow our suggested route, take the **Merivale** option first, as any subsequent wet weather is more likely to close this road before the other.

Head north from Injune past a left turn (signposted Mount Moffat) just a couple of hundred metres up the road. This road leads to **Womblebank** via a sawmill and will be your return route to Injune. Instead look for the second road which veers left about one kilometre later. It will be signposted **"Westgrove Road"**, and this narrow strip of bitumen pierces through scrub and grassland, where grazing cattle can be a hazard for careless motorists.

Logging trucks also share the road, so slow down especially on the crests and bends as you head into some plantation forests. Keep right at the **Rockvale** turn off, as you descend to a concrete bridge over Hutton Creek, about 27 kilometres from Injune. Native pines mark the transition to State Forest about 12 kilometres later as you pass **Westgrove Station** on the right, then hit gravel eight kilometres later.

You will enjoy some open country around **South Westgrove Station** for a while, before again reaching State Forest just prior to **Merivale Station**, 60 kilometres from Injune. Three kilometres later you will reach a major signpost and junction – keep left at this intersection until you reach a set of stockyards about one kilometre beyond that. You will now veer right back into **State Forest** for a winding and corrugated journey to a concrete causeway over the **Merivale River's east branch,** eight kilometres from the yards.

Loose stone and thicker sand patches pave the way past some minor station tracks (keep straight ahead) to the **Merivale River's west branch.** This major branch is more likely to hold water, but with a rock and concrete fording, should pose no real problems in the dry. There is a small clearing on the eastern side where you may stop to appreciate

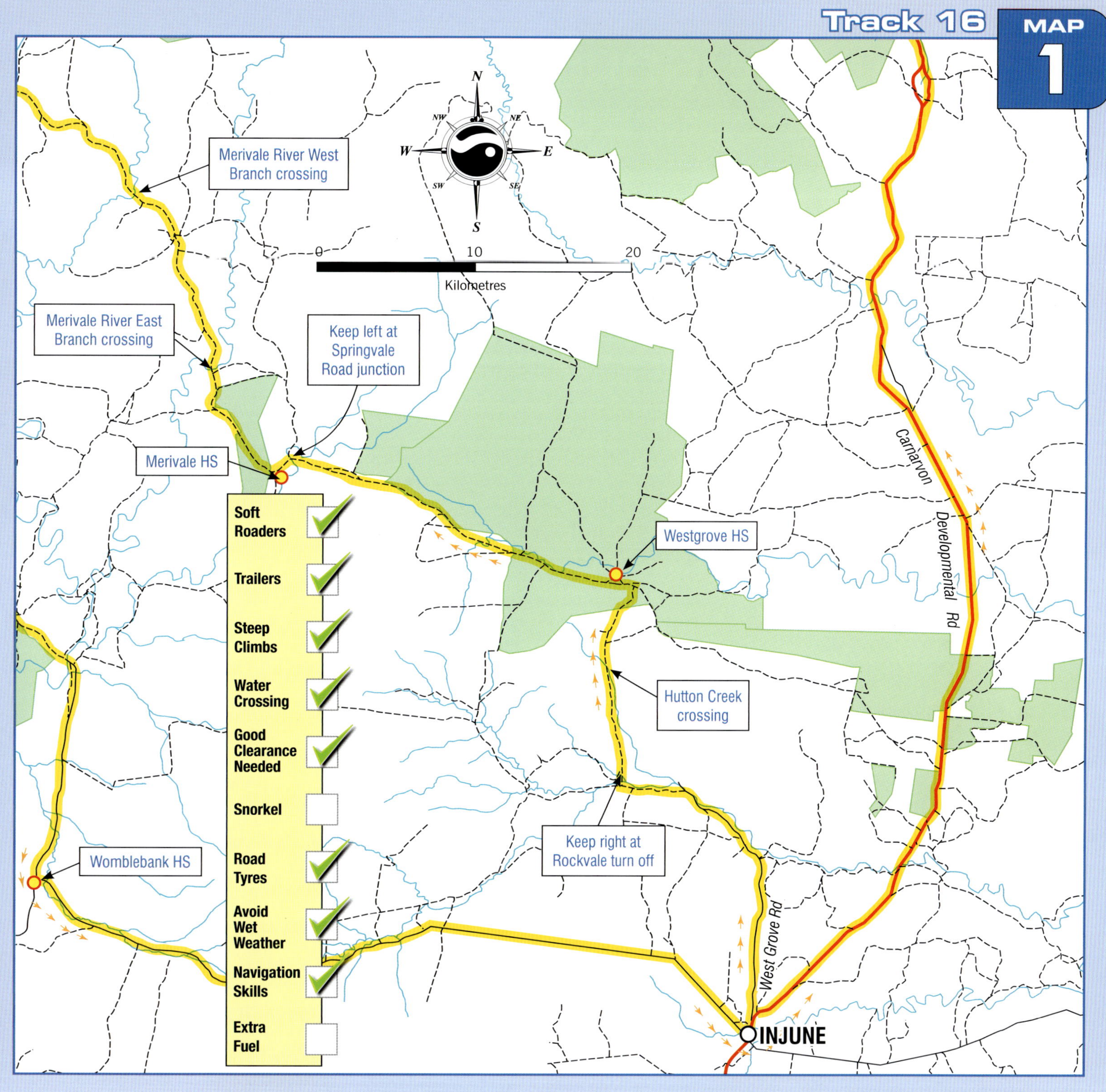

the potential power of this waterway – flood debris hangs from the trees, while in peaceful times a metallic tinge colours the water.

Most of this region's rain falls in the December – March quarter when the access roads can be cut for days at a time. However storms occur at anytime of the year, so always carry additional food and water as a safeguard for any unplanned delays.

Beyond the **Merivale** you will negotiate a couple of creeks (take extra care with any sharp ruts and gutters here) before reaching a tee intersection, some 11 kilometres from the river.

Turn right onto a wider road, taking note of the location, as you now meet the **Womblebank** option junction, and following a common section of road into the **Mount Moffatt** sector. **Macrozamias** and superb wattle forests colour the descent to a minor branch of the **Maranoa River,** where keen eyed visitors will spot a lonely bush grave site.

Just beyond the major gully, you will reach a slab hut and old stockyards located at the foot of an orange sandstone escarpment. The renovated two roomed timber dwelling is well worth a stop, and good views can be made from a nearby peak, although there is no defined walking track. This hut was originally the living quarters for stockmen working at the larger **Warrong HS,** but that dwelling was destroyed by fire many years ago.

You are nearing national park now, and visitors who wish to have a campfire

CARNARVON GORGE

should collect fallen timber over the next 10 kilometres or so. Nights can be very cold at **Mount Moffatt** over winter and firewood collection is not permitted within the national park, so consider your situation carefully before entering the park.

Smooth barked apple and grasstrees usher your passage into the park with Cathedral Rock heralding an information board and the beginnings of a six kilometre circuit walk. Energetic visitors should undertake this hike, as it reveals the essential elements that are typical of the **Mount Moffatt Section,** and there is little other designated walking within this sector.

Formations to be seen on the hike include The Looking Glass and The Chimneys (both are the result of continuous wind and water erosion), and The Tombs – a fascinating glimpse into a rarely seen **Aboriginal burial procedure.** Visitors to the latter site will also appreciate a gallery of indigenous artwork, adorning a rock overhang.

Vehicles heading north from the information board can turn right onto a lesser used track, some seven kilometres further on. Follow this sandy trail past the **Top Moffatt Camp junction** (rugged 15 kilometre trek to camping area at the foot of **Mount Moffatt**), then veer left through some verdant riverine forest, as you parallel **Long Gully.**

You will reach a set of stockyards just prior to what was the old homestead (now the Ranger's residence) and find a small visitor's centre. Campers should register and pay here, bearing in mind that prebooking may be required at **Mount Moffatt** especially during school holiday periods.

Continue north from the information centre for seven kilometres on a gradual

Slab hut

climb to the **West Branch Camp** turn off. Keep left at this junction for another kilometre or so, then turn right through a gate. Rougher road greets you as the Dividing Range looms closer, and you climb abruptly through ironbark forest to the **Rotary Shelter Shed Camp** and its surprising views.

A small number of potential camp sites overlook the **Maranoa Valley** with **Mount Moffatt** peaking on the horizon. A long drop toilet together with tables and seats round out this excellent camping possibility, but be warned that at about 1000 metres of altitude, frosts and cold nights are all but certain here over winter.

Beyond the camp you will drop into low range for a fairly routine climb over erosion control mounds to the Top Shelter Shed some three kilometres later. The views are even more impressive here as you absorb the broad landscape sculpted by ancient volcanic activity.

Travel through denser forest coloured with happy wanderer to **Peawaddy Gorge** on your left, three kilometres later, then meander across the undulating range backbone. **Mahogany** gums stand tall as you enter the dominant **Consuelo Tablelands,** where bluegums flourish and parrots whisk around the tree tops.

The track finishes at the headwaters of **Carnarvon Creek** and while experienced bushwalkers can hike through untracked country into the gorge from here, it is a difficult expedition, and the Rangers must be informed of your intentions.

Four wheel drives can now return via the route they have come by until they reach the 4WD gate about 18 kilometres away. Once through the gate, veer right for two kilometres, and turn right again onto the **Marlong Plain Track.**

A short drive later will bring you to a parking area on the fringe of natural grassland, surrounded with sandstone escarpment. Old watertanks and fencelines stand as reminders of the pastoral heritage here dating from the 1860s. Bluegrass plains and trickling waters were welcome resources to the pioneering graziers, but the remote and rugged country certainly tested the mettle of those drawn here.

Continue to follow **Marlong Creek** past **Lot's Wife** and **Marlong Arch** (the latter is an amazing sandstone formation

Lot's Wife

and will be worth the short walk in) to the **Dargonelly Rock Hole** turn off. Swing left here and drive for less than a kilometre to a camping area on **Marlong Creek.** This broad grassed location is ideal for larger groups, with fireplaces, toilet and permanent rock pools.

From the camp turn off it is three kilometres further before you return to the main **Mount Moffatt Road,** and retrace your steps to the **Westgrove junction.** A windmill and tank mark this intersection, where you keep right on the return leg and emerge into open country.

Crystal Brook is passed 21 kilometres beyond the **Westgrove junction,** as skyline views typify this elevated grazing country. **Blacktop** begins on **Farmleigh Station,** and you will turn left 19 kilometres later at **"Womblebank"** – a cluster of buildings dominating a high point on the range. A sustained descent marks the remaining 45 odd kilometres back to Injune, and completion of the **Mount Moffatt leg.**

By way of contrast the **Carnarvon Gorge** leg involves no 4WDing (assuming dry roads), but rain will quickly affect the unsealed sections that you use. Again top up on fuel and food at Injune, as your next supply point is Rolleston, some 260 kilometres and several days away.

Campsite bookings for **Carnarvon Gorge** are essential within the national park, and note that they are only available during the non-summer Queensland school holidays; ring 13 7468, or book online www.qld.gov.au/camping. These campsites are located right in the gorge

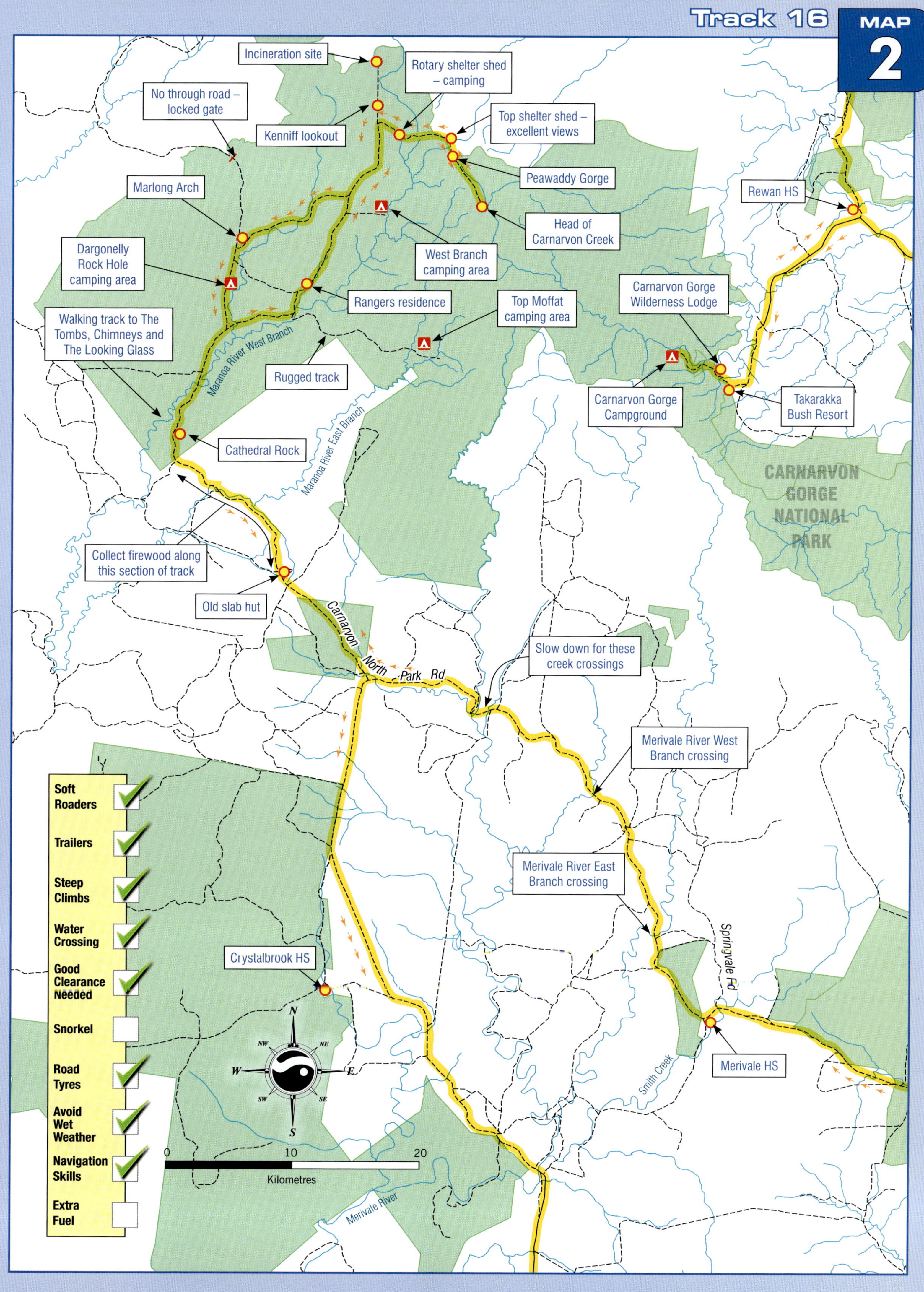
Incineration site
Rotary shelter shed – camping
No through road – locked gate
Kenniff lookout
Top shelter shed – excellent views
Peawaddy Gorge
Marlong Arch
Head of Carnarvon Creek
Rewan HS
West Branch camping area
Dargonelly Rock Hole camping area
Rangers residence
Top Moffat camping area
Carnarvon Gorge Wilderness Lodge
Walking track to The Tombs, Chimneys and The Looking Glass
Maranoa River West Branch
Rugged track
Carnarvon Gorge Campground
Takarakka Bush Resort
Cathedral Rock
Maranoa River East Branch
CARNARVON GORGE NATIONAL PARK
Collect firewood along this section of track
Old slab hut
Carnarvon North Park Rd
Slow down for these creek crossings
Merivale River West Branch crossing
Merivale River East Branch crossing
Springvale Rd
Crystalbrook HS
Merivale HS
Smith Creek
Merivale River
N
NE
E
SE
S
SW
W
NW
0
10
20
Kilometres
Soft Roaders
Trailers
Steep Climbs
Water Crossing
Good Clearance Needed
Snorkel
Road Tyres
Avoid Wet Weather
Navigation Skills
Extra Fuel

area, but are very popular and no fires are permitted.

An alternative campground, **Takarakka Bush Resort** ph 07 4984 4535, is found four kilometres from the gorge and provides shady powered sites, basic supplies and communal fireplaces. **Carnarvon Gorge Wilderness Lodge** is another option for visitors (ph 07 4984 4503), with cabins available and tavern facilities. The lodge is located three kilometres from the gorge itself, and is open all year round.

Once booked in, follow the blacktop along the **Carnarvon Developmental Road** for about 110 kilometres, then take the signposted turn off to the gorge section, although you will need to be on the lookout for this sign, as it is rather small and appears quickly at bitumen speeds.

The turn off is sealed initially, but deteriorates into gravel some 25 kilometres later. Dips and floodways mark the drive into national park as you pass the signposted turn to Takarakka (on a bend in Carnarvon Creek), and later, the **Wilderness Lodge.**

Short walks to **Rock Pool** and **Baloon Cave** are found off the main road, which itself finishes at the gorge visitor area. Most travellers to the gorge will wish to undertake a walk along the main creek, where rock pavers allow visitors to criss cross the waterway as they head upstream. Gleaming white cliffs overlook the perpetually flowing creek, with a gorge width that varies from 40 metres at its narrowest, to almost half of a kilometre.

Many tributary ravines radiate from the main gorge, some of which can be up to 60 metres high and only a couple of metres wide. These narrow side gorges may see direct sunlight for only an hour per day, and their shaded sandstone walls are dripping with ferns and mosses.

The delicate plant life of the tributary gorges contrast with the hardier vegetation of the main gorge and exposed ridge tops. Harsh sunlight is reflected from the shiny fronds of the cabbage palm. These palms grow rampantly throughout the area, and often to towering heights. **Macrozamia palms,** which are actually a very slow growing cycad thrive in large numbers – some very old specimens reach to six metres in height.

To undertake all of the gorge marked track system will involve about 27 kilometres of trail and a lengthy day. Fortunately the main gorge is relatively flat and easy going, so many people undertake this hike to their furtherest planned destination, then return and take in the side attractions as time and energy permit. Always carry adequate water for these walks as the creek water should not be consumed untreated. If the weather is very hot, you may prefer to stash a container of water somewhere on the outgoing journey, and pick it up on your return, saving some weight on the hike.

Carnarvon Gorge

We would recommend **Ward's Canyon** and **The Art Gallery** as two must see locations, although **The Amphitheatre** is also an amazing experience. Ward's Canyon takes in a superb waterfall (flowing all year round) and brings you into an almost prehistoric garden of king ferns.

The Art Gallery presents an enormous white sandstone wall, adorned with over 2000 Aboriginal engravings and paintings. Dating from a relatively recent 3500 years ago, this artwork is simply amazing, with vibrant stencil works depicting a multitude of hands, boomerangs and animal motifs.

Those comfortable with ladders will find **The Amphitheatre** to be a rewarding destination. Visitors will enter via a narrow rock corridor, before arriving at an enormous slab sided chamber, still being etched away by flowing waters. Some vegetation grows on the cavern floor, where a dusty surface remains unaltered by the windless environment in this remarkably silent chasm.

Of course many other attractions are worthy contenders on your travels, and it really just depends on the group's fitness as to what can be seen. Our advice is to leave early on the walk, and plan to see as much as practicable, making sure to keep the next day as a rest day.

Vehicles need to exit **Carnarvon Gorge** via the same way as they entered, although an alternative option will bypass some bitumen. Some 24 kilometres east of the gorge you will reach a signpost on your left marked **"Rewan Road".**

You can follow this gravel station track past **Rewan HS** on a scenic run toward **Consuelo HS.** The trail follows a branch of the **Comet River,** and wetlands are evident from the road. Watch out for rough grids on the northern run, before you reach bitumen about 50 kilometres later. Veer left onto the blacktop and follow it into **Rolleston,** with multiple choices for travel beyond here.

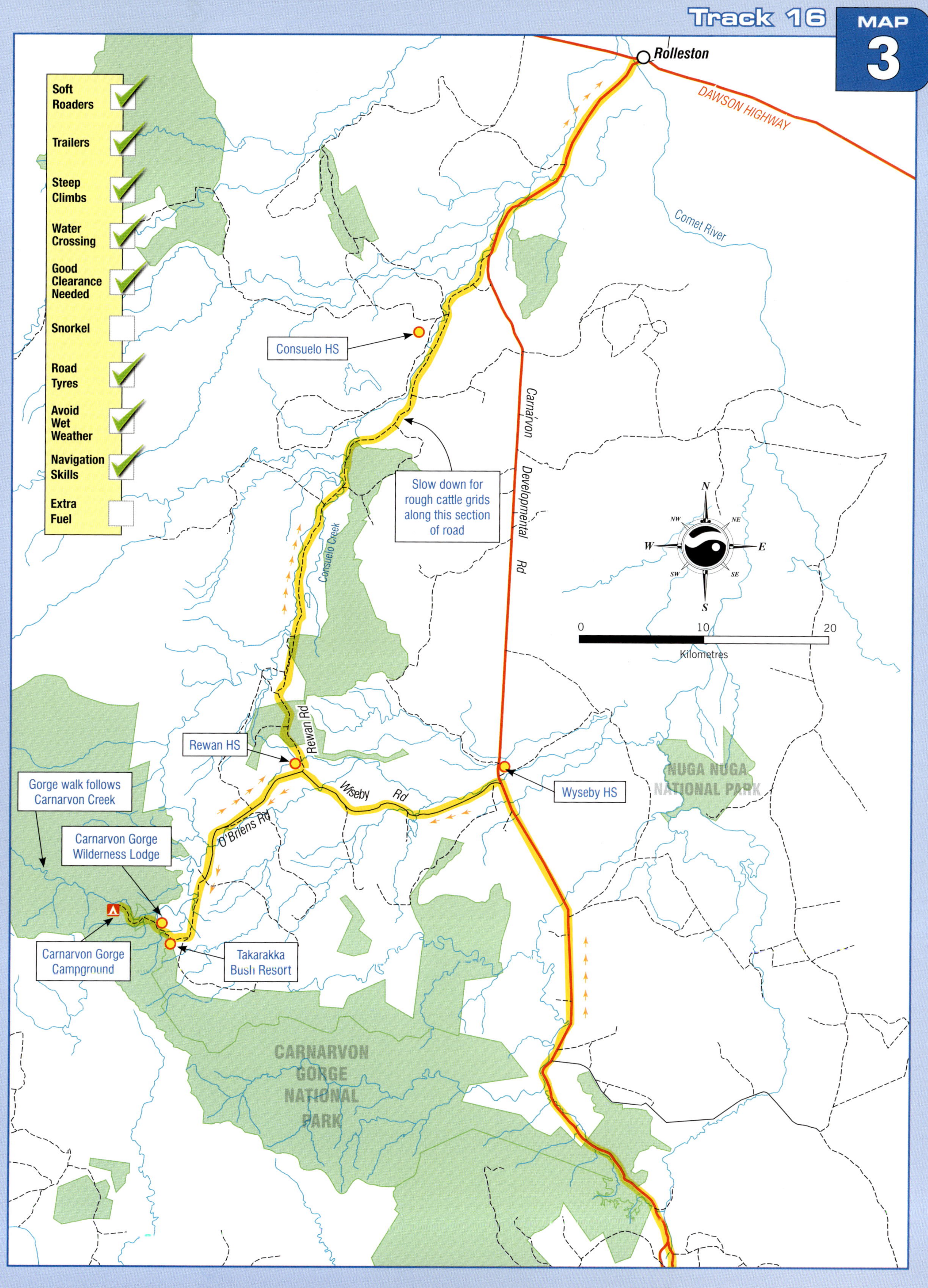
Soft Roaders
Trailers
Steep Climbs
Water Crossing
Good Clearance Needed
Snorkel
Road Tyres
Avoid Wet Weather
Navigation Skills
Extra Fuel
Rolleston
DAWSON HIGHWAY
Comet River
Consuelo HS
Carnarvon Developmental Rd
Slow down for rough cattle grids along this section of road
Consuelo Creek
N
NW
NE
W
E
SW
SE
S
0
10
20
Kilometres
Rewan Rd
Rewan HS
Wyseby HS
Wiseby Rd
NUGA NUGA NATIONAL PARK
Gorge walk follows Carnarvon Creek
O'Briens Rd
Carnarvon Gorge Wilderness Lodge
Carnarvon Gorge Campground
Takarakka Bush Resort
CARNARVON GORGE NATIONAL PARK

TRACK 17

Expedition Range

CENTRAL QUEENSLAND

Track Snapshot

TOUR ROUTE:
Theodore to Moura via Isla Gorge and Expedition NP.

DURATION AND DISTANCE:
Two days minimum (more if bushwalking at Robinson Gorge) and 300 kilometres.

TRACK DETAILS:
Dirt roads and rocky creek crossings prevail, limiting travel to full sized 4WDs and robust trailers.

WHEN TO GO:
April to November is best, avoiding sustained wet weather.

CAMPING:
Bush camping at Isla Gorge, Spotted Gum, Lake Murphy and Robinson Gorge. Caravan parks at Theodore and Taroom (17 kilometres off suggested route).

FUEL AND SUPPLIES:
Stock up at Theodore; there is nothing else enroute.

MAPS:
Hema: Outback Queensland, Sunmap: Outback Queensland, Natmap: Taroom 1:250K may be useful.

OTHER INFORMATION:
Like Salvator Rosa in the west, Expedition NP receives few visitors compared with the more popular Carnarvon Gorge section. It is however well worth the effort of getting here.

Robinson Gorge

It was Ludwig Leichhardt who first put European footprints across the ***Expedition Range*** *in 1844. The optimistic explorer located and named* ***Robinson Creek*** *amid the sandstone ramparts of this spectacular area in Central Queensland.*

Settlers followed the next year with modern day ***Taroom*** *offering ideal grazing lands. A coolibah tree bearing into Leichardt's initials stands in the township, not far from the* ***Taroom Hotel*** *(a character building nicknamed the "Pub with no Beer" as it is now used as the Visitor Information Centre).*

Four wheel drivers however will enjoy the remote nature of this trek, and its superb scenic qualities, found where ever you look. There is even a chance to select low range, as you grapple with some rugged country around ***Starkevale Creek.***

We begin the journey at **Theodore** on the **Leichhardt Highway**. Stock up on supplies here as there will be no other opportunities for 300 kilometres and at least a couple of days – perhaps several more if you take a liking to the ample attractions, or unexpected rain hems you in for a while.

Head south on bitumen toward Taroom, passing a series of floodways and **Isla Plains HS**. Some 35 kilometres later you will reach the turn off to **Isla Gorge Lookout**. Swing right here for a short run into a camp ground with basic facilities. There is a lookout adjacent which offers sweeping views over the undulating terrain, although only experienced hikers can proceed into the wilderness, as there are no marked walking trails.

Continue to follow the sealed road south through pockets of state forest, with views toward the **Gilbert Range**. Turn right some 40 kilometres beyond Isla Gorge on the **Fitzroy Developmental Road**, signposted **"Bauhinia Downs"**. Follow the blacktop onto gravel, turning left two kilometres later onto the **Glenhaughton Road**. We now follow Robinson Creek on a scenic run through cropping and grazing country with palms delineating the water course.

You will enter the **Lake Murphy Conservation Park** about 10 kilometres from the **Leichhardt Highway**. This perched lake fringed with red gums only fills when Robinson Creek floods, but when full attracts a multiplicity of birdlife. Camping is permitted here with basic facilities provided. There is a marked four kilometre walking track beginning in the camping area that takes in the natural beauty of Robinson Creek.

Wanui Yards marks your exit from Lake Murphy as you pass a series of homesteads, keeping right at a junction 10 kilometres from the lake. Several floodways together with a jump up, pave the way past the prominent peak of **Round Mountain** on your right.

Fernbrook Creek marks the turn off to **Currajong HS** on the left, some 30 kilometres from the last junction. Keep right at the intersection, following **Currajong Road**, past **Glenhaughton HS** to a track junction about nine kilometres later.

Swing left here for a couple of creek crossings, before beginning a steep rocky descent. You will need to keep

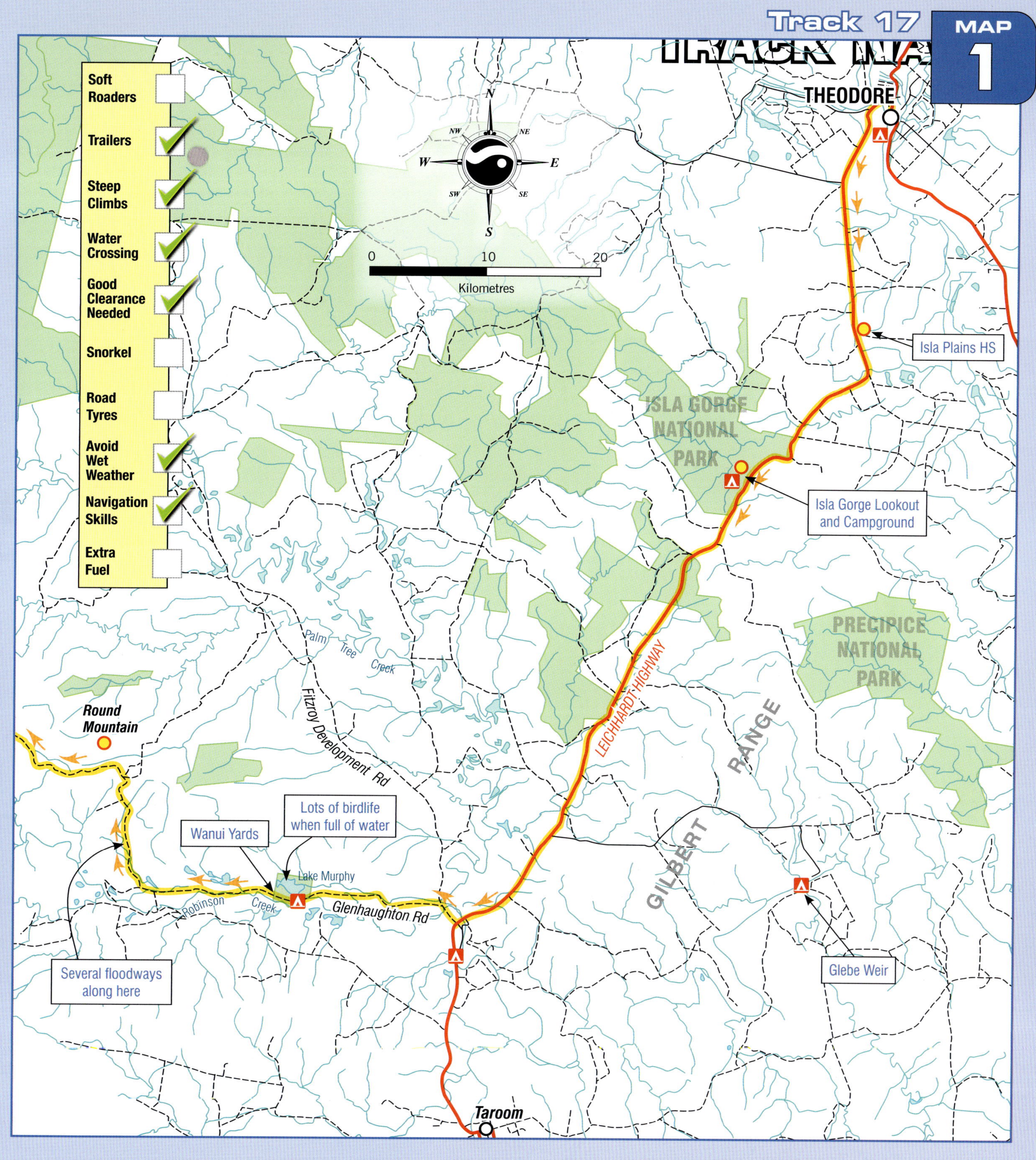

your speed down, and watch your wheel placement to negotiate the eroded beginnings to **Starkevale Creek**.

Shepherds Peak overlooks your progress past **Cattle Dip Track** on the left as you keep right into a camping area shortly after. Basic facilities are provided at the pleasant creek side location, where grassy sites and shady trees are abundant.

You may drive to within 600 metres of **Cattle Dip Lookout** (a viewpoint looking down to a permanent water hole beneath towering cliffs) but other destinations are by foot only. The sandy base of **Robinson Creek** is especially appealing with palms, bottle brush and delicate ferns.

EXPEDITION RANGE

Rough vehicle travel continues north of **Starkevale Camp** as a number of waterways and rocky obstacles slow your travel. You will reach a tee intersection where the left hand option will take you to **Spotted Gum Camp**. This remote camp in the oil bore area is reached at the end of a 12 kilometre dead end track.

There are no facilities provided at Spotted Gum, and while the area lacks the drama of Robinson Gorge, it is located on a plateau at the origin of several creeks. If you choose to visit Spotted Gum you will still need to retrace your steps to the national park boundary, then continue northward.

Further on you will cross **Ruined Castle Creek** before reaching a tee intersection on the main **Glenhaughton – Bauhinia Road**, about seven kilometres from NP boundary. Swing left here for a winding journey over **Spring Creek**, tracing the upper reaches of Ruined Castle Creek.

Mapala HS is reached some 13 kilometres beyond the intersection, as you leave state forest, and follow the main road, avoiding the side tracks. A large bottle tree ushers the way into **Comely Station** for yet more creek crossings, and your arrival at a tee intersection on the sealed **Dawson Highway**. **Bauhinia** is just two kilometres to the left, while the much larger centre of **Moura** is an hour's drive to the east.

Left: *Wainui Yards*

Below: *Taroom grassland*

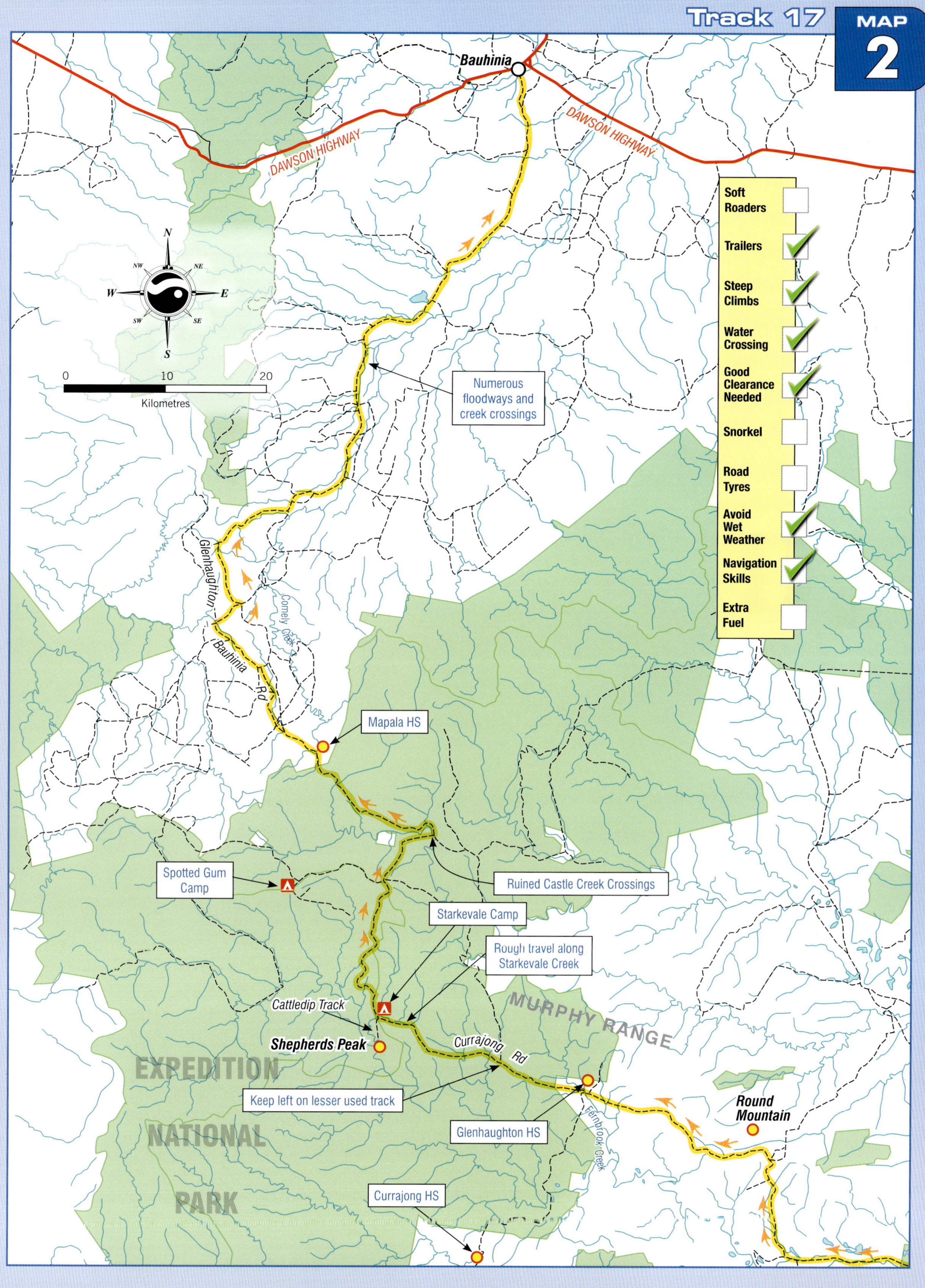

Bauhinia
DAWSON HIGHWAY
DAWSON HIGHWAY
N
NE
E
SE
S
SW
W
NW
0
10
20
Kilometres
Numerous floodways and creek crossings
Soft Roaders
Trailers
Steep Climbs
Water Crossing
Good Clearance Needed
Snorkel
Road Tyres
Avoid Wet Weather
Navigation Skills
Extra Fuel
Glenhaughton
Cornely Creek
Bauhinia
Rd
Mapala HS
Spotted Gum Camp
Ruined Castle Creek Crossings
Starkevale Camp
Rough travel along Starkevale Creek
Cattledip Track
Shepherds Peak
MURPHY RANGE
Currajong Rd
EXPEDITION
NATIONAL
PARK
Keep left on lesser used track
Glenhaughton HS
Fernbrook Creek
Round Mountain
Currajong HS

Chapter 4
CHANNEL COUNTRY

◀ *Red Mulga*

TRACK 18 THE DIAMANTINA

CHANNEL COUNTRY

Hunter's Gorge

Track Snapshot

TOUR ROUTE:
Kynuna to Birdsville following the Diamantina River.

DURATION AND DISTANCE:
Allow five days for the 940 kilometre trek (including the national park loop drive).

TRACK DETAILS:
Gibber, bulldust and sandy tracks dominate, making some Soft Roaders a questionable option, although trailers are no problem.

WHEN TO GO:
Avoid wet weather and the hot summer months.

CAMPING:
Nice river side camping with basic facilities within Diamantina NP (Gum Hole, and the more popular Hunters Gorge), with some bush camping possibilities at Old Cork. Serviced camping at Birdsville, Bedourie and Kynuna.

FUEL AND SUPPLIES:
Most supplies at Birdsville and Bedourie, with fuel and basic supplies at Kynuna.

MAPS:
Hema: NE, Sunmap: Outback Queensland.

OTHER INFORMATION:
Fuel capacity could be a problem for some on this trek. You will need a minimum range of 760 kilometres (Kynuna to Bedourie) and fuel for 840 kilometres if you undertake the national park loop drive.

Queensland's Channel Country is a big destination. It is home to big floods, big droughts, and big station country – but most of all it has big character. Pioneering history literally oozes from the landscape, with tangible links remaining to this day.

Our tour starting point at ***Kynuna*** *is typical of the area. The town's centrepiece* ***"Blue Heeler" Hotel*** *looks as authentic and inviting as it may have more than a century ago, when Cobb & Co. used the establishment as a staging depot. Today ringers and truckies share the bar with recreational travellers, and the evolving walls of outback scrawl provide hours of reading opportunity for all visitors.*

You will leave **Kynuna** via the **Landsborough Highway** and travel east for some 15 kilometres to the signposted **"Combo Waterhole"** turn off. Travel south from here for another 7 kilometres to a fenced off area surrounding the waterhole.

These historic grounds are the closest you can drive on public roads to the **Diamantina River headwaters,** and are reputedly the inspiration for Banjo Paterson's classic work: Waltzing Matilda. A two kilometre walking track allows you to visit the famous billabong, and admire the efforts of local graziers, along the way as they attempted to drought proof their holdings.

Chinese labourers constructed rock retaining walls known as "shotovers", from flat stones arranged in an interlocked pattern. The resulting embankments held water in drier seasons, but still allowed wagons to use the roads following times of flood.

Pastoral use of the land followed quickly behind the footsteps of John McKinlay and his party – the first white people to see the Diamantina. McKinlay was searching for signs of the Burke and Wills expedition after they had failed to return. McKinlay did not return with joy on that front, but had managed to open up some viable grazing country.

From **Combo,** return 1 kilometre to track on right and turn here to steer a path along the Diamantina as it follows the **old Landsborough Highway route** past a series of stations. It is predominately sheep country around the Combo, with brahman cross cattle found here on the cusp of their more typical northern homeland.

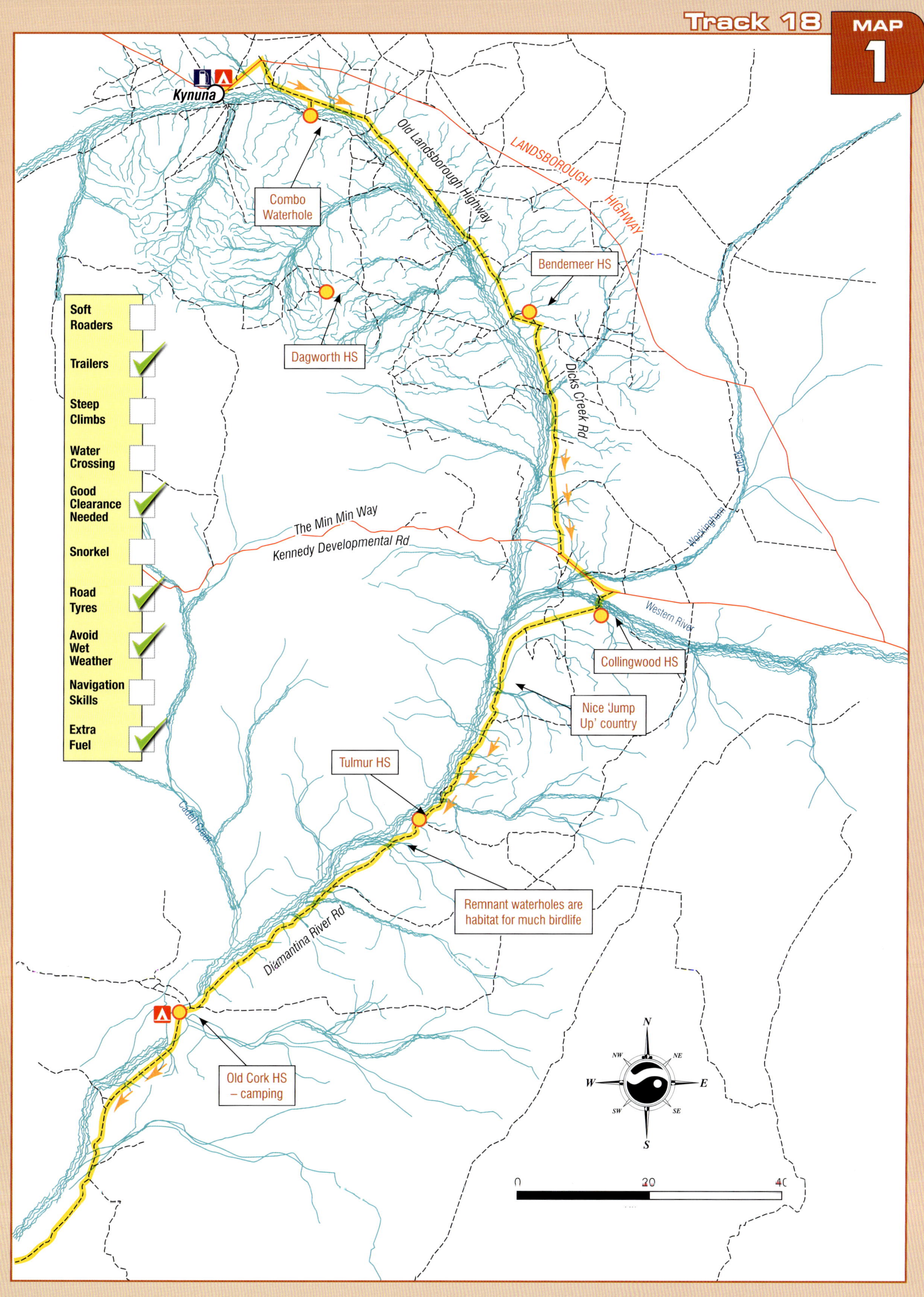
Kynuna
Combo Waterhole
Old Landsborough Highway
LANDSBOROUGH HIGHWAY
Bendemeer HS
Dagworth HS
Dicks Creek Rd
Soft Roaders
Trailers
Steep Climbs
Water Crossing
Good Clearance Needed
Snorkel
Road Tyres
Avoid Wet Weather
Navigation Skills
Extra Fuel
The Min Min Way
Kennedy Developmental Rd
Wockingham Creek
Western River
Collingwood HS
Nice 'Jump Up' country
Tulmur HS
Remnant waterholes are habitat for much birdlife
Diamantina River Rd
Old Cork HS – camping
N
NE
E
SE
S
SW
W
NW
0
20

THE DIAMANTINA

A lonely grave heralds the turn off to **Dagworth Station,** after 16 kilometres flat gibber paved terrain extends to a distant pink range in the west. Ignore the turn off, and continue straight for 36 kilometres. Veer left at an intersection signposted Dagworth and **Cathedral Hills.** Lookout for windmills in the area as they pump hot water to the mitchell grass plains, in a location right on the boundary for artesian water availability.

Continue approximately 5 kilometres, passing **Bendemeer HS** on the left, before turning right onto **Dicks Creek Road,** where you turn right to maintain a southern course along the river. The remains of an old telegraph line flags your arrival 37 kilometres later on the **Kennedy Developmental Road.** Turn left onto bitumen for 11 kilometres, then take the dirt again, as you swing right onto the **Diamantina River Road.**

You will cross the **Western River** (a tributary of the Diamantina) at **Collingwood Station,** then travel through some "jump up" country and channels as the merging waters consolidate. Causeways and porcupine grasses flag some rocky hills around **Tulmur HS,** where seasonal water holes will attract ducks, herons and flocks of cockatoos.

The dusty road will continue to a tee intersection near **Old Cork**, about 105 kilometres from the **Kennedy Developmental Road intersection. New Cork** is located to the left, with signposted **Boulia** to the right. You will need to take the right turn option, but swing left again onto the **Diamantina River Road** after a couple of kilometres.

Right: *Station signage*

Old Cork itself is worth a look around with the now dilapidated residence boasting big shady verandas and quality stonework, but gradually succumbing to the elements. First selected in the 1870s, Old Cork remained viable for more than a century before it was abandoned to the spinifex country. A meathouse and old tanks together with the remains of a chicken run support the remote country feel. An enormous windmill is difficult to overlook, while some camping possibilities can be found nearby.

Beyond Old Cork multiple paths mark the Diamantina's passage as flat grassy plains are encountered periodically. With the south western travel comes a transition to minor sand dune country where prevailing winds have heaped Diamantina sediments into linear mounds. These parallel dunes have been stable for at least 8000 years, unlike the mesa country to the east that is still eroding to this day. You will notice the prominence of these jump ups closer to **Brighton Downs** and the **Mount Windsor junction.**

The old Mayne Hotel is located on the boundary of **Diamantina National Park,**

Below: *Cork ruins*

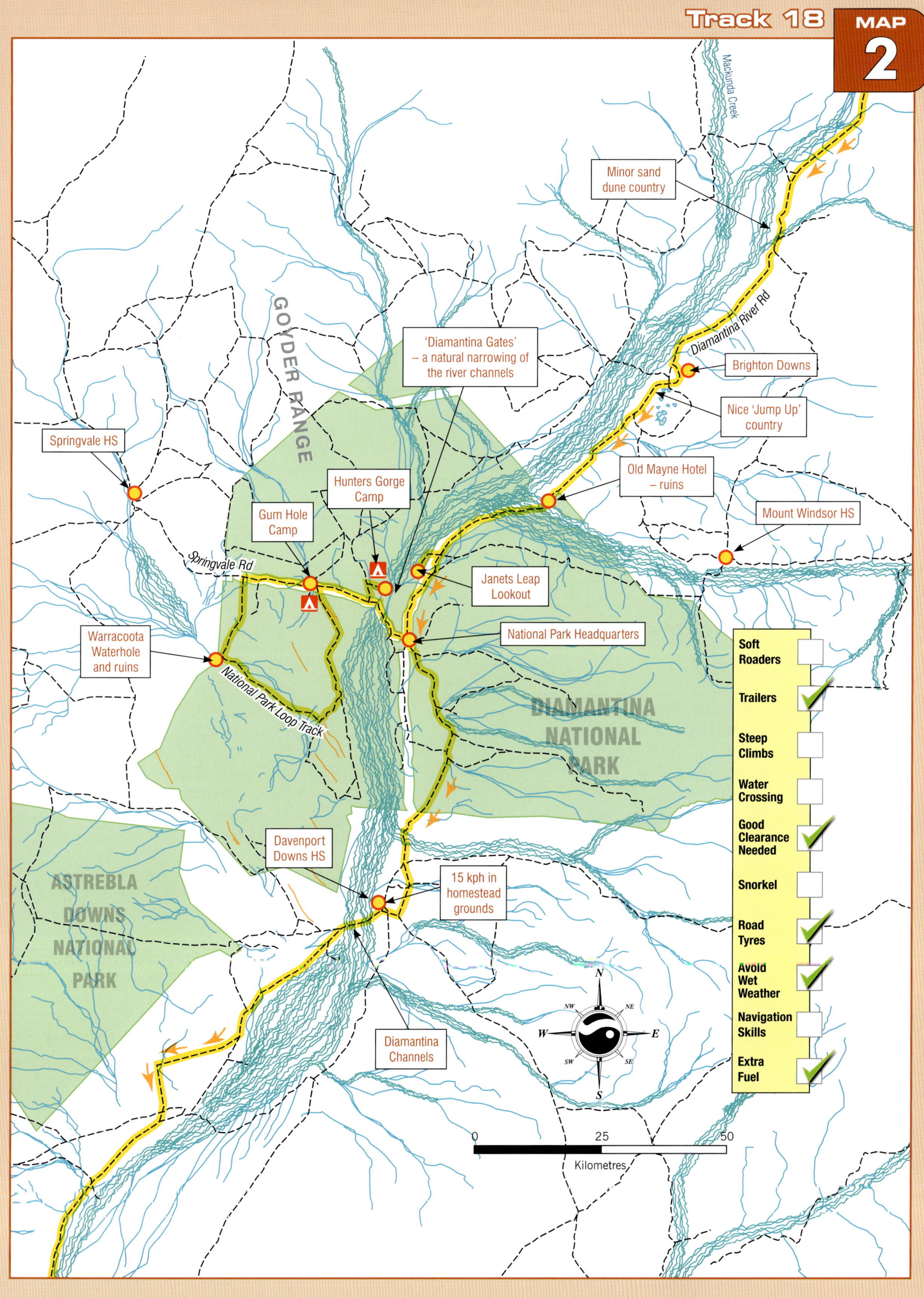
Mackunda Creek
Minor sand dune country
Diamantina River Rd
Brighton Downs
Nice 'Jump Up' country
'Diamantina Gates' – a natural narrowing of the river channels
GOYDER RANGE
Springvale HS
Hunters Gorge Camp
Gum Hole Camp
Old Mayne Hotel – ruins
Mount Windsor HS
Springvale Rd
Janets Leap Lookout
National Park Headquarters
Warracoota Waterhole and ruins
National Park Loop Track
DIAMANTINA NATIONAL PARK
Davenport Downs HS
15 kph in homestead grounds
ASTREBLA DOWNS NATIONAL PARK
Diamantina Channels
N
NE
E
SE
S
SW
W
NW
0
25
50
Kilometres
Soft Roaders
Trailers
Steep Climbs
Water Crossing
Good Clearance Needed
Snorkel
Road Tyres
Avoid Wet Weather
Navigation Skills
Extra Fuel

about 20 kilometres beyond the private road junction leading to **Mount Windsor HS,** and it is well worth a stop. The hotel ceased trading in 1951, and now lies in ruins, but you will still see some structural timbers, and the collapsed underground cellar, where drinks and food could be kept cool during a string of 50 degree days.

An old horseyard still stands, together with fences of homemade mesh wire, and some rusting tanks. Established around 1888, the pub was a popular stop over for travellers, and with its adjacent small cemetery, remains a harsh resting place to this day.

From **Mayne** you will drive 31 kilometres through national park to a right turn signposted **"Janets Leap".** Although fairly rough, this approximately 3 kilometre dead end access track is a must. The view from its lookout takes in the extensive channel country, with a superb vantage point over the **"Diamantina Gates"** - a funneled view of the river as it is squeezed through the Goyder and Hamilton Ranges.

Return to the **Diamantina River Road** and turn right, travelling for eight kilometres to the national park headquarters on the junction of **Springvale Road.**

The scenic Warracoota Circuit Drive begins on Springvale Road near Gum Hole camping area. The drive takes visitors on a 90 kilometre amble through surrended grazing country and natural floodplain features. It is an excellent self paced journey and well worth undertaking to get a good feel for this country. Download the national park brochure before you visit.

There are two bush camping areas within the national park: **Gum Hole** is one possibility on Whistling Duck Creek, but the more popular choice is **Hunters Gorge** at the foot of the **Goyder Range.**

Campers will set up on a **Diamantina waterhole** under some shady coolibahs, with toilets and fire pits provided at both camping areas. Drinking water must be carried for the duration of this tour, and fuel stoves are preferred in this fragile environment. Fishing is permitted at the waterhole, but remember to leave some for the pelicans. Other birdlife includes falcons, ducks, and cormorants, with raucous flocks of corellas cruising up and down the waterway.

This national park protects over 500 000 hectares of channel country since it was sold to the Queensland government in 1992, with native animals enjoying the transition. Other beneficiaries include shrubs and trees struggling for life at their geographical limit. And at least one rare plant – a native fuschia – is found in the park.

You will leave the national park by heading south from the park headquarters along the **Diamantina River Road** for 51 kilometres, to a left junction. Keep right at this turn off as you reach the grounds of **Davenport Downs HS,** a few kilometres later. Now you cross the braided **Diamantina Channels,** an area showing signs of flooding and cattle use when wet. Take it slowly and carefully through this very cut up section.

Cork waterhole

Regular truck use tends to cut up the next 100 kilometres or so of road, so watch out for ruts and bulldust holes as you make your way through gibber plains and other more productive country.

An old cemetery outside of **Monkira Station** illustrates the harsh life of our pioneers. A dozen or so graves date from the 1890s when typhoid fever swept the district. **Monkira HS** also marks the finish of the **Diamantina River Road,** and your turn right onto the **Diamantina Developmental Road.**

While this wider route allows faster speeds it is still unsealed, and the gibber road surface blends easily with the adjacent country of dark purple and black gibber. In fact were it not for the graded spoon drain, you may not know where the road finishes and the station country begins. Some sections of this **Developmental Road** seem more like a moonscape than anything terrestrial!

Avoid several side tracks from the **Developmental Road** and follow it over causeways for about 105 kilometres to No 3 Bore. Artesian Basin water was so important to the development of this land, that many were sunk around the 1890s. This particular bore still has the old steam engine left on site, as it was not financially viable to relocate it once the drilling was completed.

While some bores were sunk to 2000 metres, the average depth was more like 500 metres – still this was an ambitious project in its day, when you consider that the steam engine was carried here in pieces on a bullock dray, then reassembled on site.

An alternate unsealed road heads south from here to Birdsville, or head westward for 28 kilometres to reach the **Eyre Developmental Road.** Head north to **Bedourie** (23 kilometres away) if you urgently need fuel, or turn south toward Birdsville if you can travel another 162 kilometres without filling up.

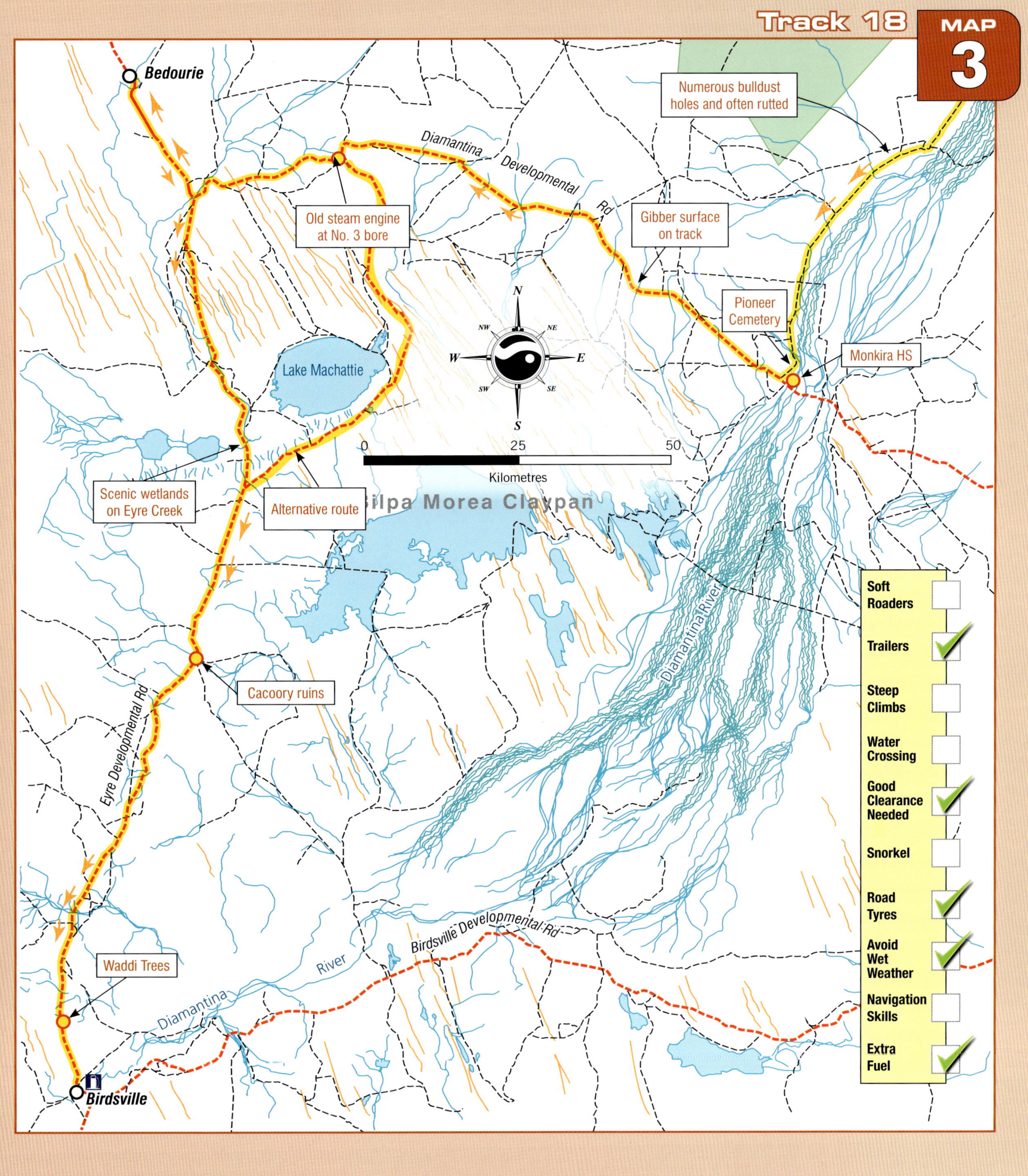

Turn south toward Birdsville on the mostly sealed Developmental Road. This final leg south passes some nice wetland near **Eyre Creek,** (watch out for cattle on road through here), **the Cacoory ruins,** and a curious stand of waddi trees just prior to **Birdsville. The Diamantina** is confined to a single channel as it washes its way through **Birdsville,** before again fanning out on the edge of **Simpson Desert,** and in very wet years, reaching **Lake Eyre.**

TRACK 19 HADDON CORNER

CHANNEL COUNTRY

Birdsville Hotel

Track Snapshot

TOUR ROUTE:
Tibooburra to Birdsville via Noccundra and Haddon Corner.

DURATION AND DISTANCE:
It will take three or four days to drive the 1000 kilometres – more if you choose to visit Innamincka mid trek.

TRACK DETAILS:
Rocky gibber strewn tracks, with sand drifts (dunes on the Haddon Corner access) limits this trek to full size 4WDs. Robust trailers can undertake the journey.

WHEN TO GO:
Avoid the heat of summer and any wet weather.

CAMPING:
Designated camping is available at Tibooburra, Noccundra, the Dig Tree Reserve, Innamincka and Birdsville. Travellers bypassing Innamincka have a long stretch without official camping opportunities. If you choose to camp overnight by the road, ask at the station for permission (try your UHF) or at the very least select a site away from stock watering points, do not light a fire, no shooting, and leave no trace of your stop.

FUEL AND SUPPLIES:
Tibooburra, Innamincka and Birdsville offer all supplies, while Noccundra offers fuel only.

MAPS:
Hema: SE, Sunmap: Outback Queensland.

OTHER INFORMATION:
The optional turn off to Innamincka is well worth the effort, but deserves at least a couple of days. There are waterholes, fishing opportunities and the remnants of early European history at every turn.

*The **Channel Country** of western Queensland is a landscape of sand dunes, gibber plains and ephemeral waterways, where **Haddon Corner** bites a piece out of the sunshine state. A scattering of cattle stations are complemented by very few population centres; in fact you will pass just two lonely pubs on this trek of about 1000 kilometres.*

The journey begins at **Tibooburra,** just 54 kilometres south of the Queensland border in western NSW. Leave the township well stocked with supplies (especially fuel and water). You may choose to top up at **Innamincka** enroute (a 100 kilometre diversion), but if not you will only be able to refuel at **Noccundra**, with 700 kilometres of outback driving ahead of you.

Head north on the **Silver City Highway** to the Queensland border, crossing over at **Warri Gate** on the Dog Fence. Shut the gate and continue north through the **Narranappa Sandhills** to a junction some 40 kilometres later. The left fork offers the shortest option for travel onto **Haddon Corner,** travelling via **Santos Station.** While it is a relatively easy drive, it can be a little tricky to navigate as there are several intersections where oil and gas extraction plant operates, and the main through road may not be the one that sees the most traffic.

So keep right at the junction, and left of the **Tickalara Station** turn off that follows. You will pass **Naryilco HS** to cross the first of countless floodways punctuating the journey north. Continue the drive past the old Huddersfield ruins on the left, as another turn off to Santos is reached some 45 kilometres later.

Keep straight with views of the **Cooper floodplain** visible on the left, past the **old Bransby outstation. Mount Milford** on the right flags the impending crossing of **Grahams Creek.** Follow an undulating run through gidgee and mitchell grasses to the tiny town of **Noccundra.**

Perhaps town is a little over done these days; it is really only a sandstone pub and basic accommodation rooms with a few building ruins dating from the 1880s. A memorial to the Hume expedition recounts the tragedy of those searching for survivors of the Leichardt Expedition, also perishing here. The old police station closed 50 years ago, but you can still get fuel and a feed from the hotel. Camping is available here too, at a waterhole on the nearby **Wilson River.**

Continue north (on bitumen now) for about 20 kilometres to a tee intersection on the **Bulloo Developmental Road,** otherwise known as the Adventure Way. Beginning in **Cunnamulla** to our east, this narrow sealed road crosses most of Queensland's iconic channel rivers. We turn left for seven kilometres, then veer left again at the **Eromanga turn off.**

(It is possible to reach **Haddon Corner** by keeping right here. You will follow a sealed road to **Bundeena HS,** then turn left onto the **Durham Downs Road.** Unsealed road crosses the Cooper channels here, with the main station track heading south on the west bank. The **Cook Road** continues west through

MAP 1

COOPER FLOODPLAIN
Bulloo Developmental Rd
Bulloo Developmental Rd.
Wilson River
Noccundra Hotel and camping
Grahams Creek
Old Bransby Outstation
Mt Milford
Watson Oil Field
Numerous floodways along road
Santos HS
Naryilco HS
Tickalara HS
Bullock Lakes
Keep right at Santos HS turnoff
Narranappa Sandhills
QLD
NSW
Warri Gate in dog fence
SILVER CITY HIGHWAY
Tibooburra
N
NE
E
SE
S
SW
W
NW
0
20
40
Kilometres
Soft Roaders
Trailers
Steep Climbs
Water Crossing
Good Clearance Needed
Snorkel
Road Tyres
Avoid Wet Weather
Navigation Skills
Extra Fuel

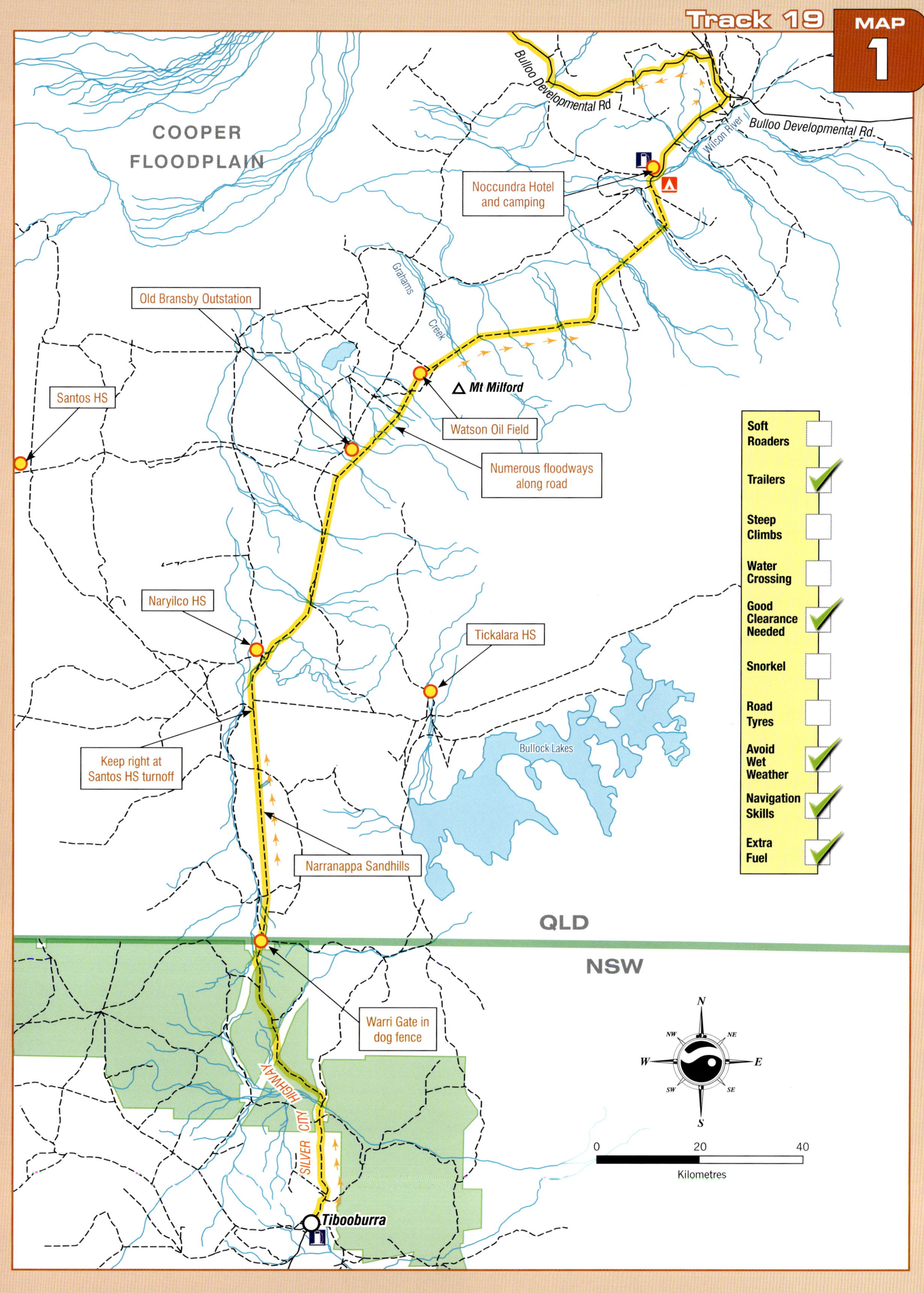

jump up country, where red mulga colours the creek lines. The outpost of Cook encompasses a bore, stockyards and old meathouse. The grader scalloped track heads into dune country, then a shotline maze of tracks before meeting the **Arrabury Road**.)

The above option is remote, rarely used and a navigational challenge; so assuming that you have chosen to remain on the **Adventure Way,** follow the blacktop past the Jackson Oilfield, where beam pumps and control gear dot the gibber plains. There is no access to the equipment here or at the **Naccowlah Oil Field,** some 70 kilometres further west from this junction.

Braided channels of the Cooper begin in earnest now, with the bitumen mostly continuing to the South Australian border. Keep left at the **Durham Downs** turn off, and away from the **Ballera Gas Centre.** Stone and gibber paves the way westward with just drifts of sand as you reach an intersection about 70 kilometres from the gas centre.

The lesser used track to your right is the **Arrabury Road** – and our route to **Haddon Corner** – while the main road on your left continues to Innamincka. Those who continue straight ahead will find the famous Burke and Wills Dig Tree via a 12 kilometre dead end station track.

There is much to do in the Innamincka area, so those with time available can swing left to cross the Cooper at the **Burke and Wills Bridge,** making the 58 kilometre run into the popular outback town. A pub, store and national parks office are the major establishments, and there is great camping on the **Cooper Creek.**

Those turning right at the **Adventure Way** intersection must ensure that they have enough fuel for a further 600 kilometres or so (if not you will be visiting Innamincka regardless). You will beat a path on more stones and gibber through the **Saint Ann Range,** to a series of floodways. The eastern dunes of the **Strzelecki Desert** develop on each side of the track, before you pass the **Arrabury HS** turn off, and reach a tee intersection.

This is the **Innamincka – Windorah Road**; another option north for those who chose to visit **Innamincka.** (Travellers will leave Innamincka via the **Cordillo Downs Road,** following a stock route past numerous bores to the infamous **Cordillo Downs** turn off. A left turn here traces a rock strewn path through **Sturts Stony Desert** to pass a significant woolshed and desolate ruins. Thankful travellers may reach **Birdsville** in the same day – but it is a long day).

We will keep right at **Arrabury** to closely follow the **South Australian border** where sand plains and gibber meet. You will cross floodways draining toward the ephemeral expanse of **Lake Yamma Yamma** in the east, before reaching a left turn signposted **"Haddon Corner",** some 90 kilometres from **Arrabury.**

Swing left for a 14 kilometre winding run over sand hills to a corner post. A few plaques and memorials mark what is really a rather unremarkable piece of

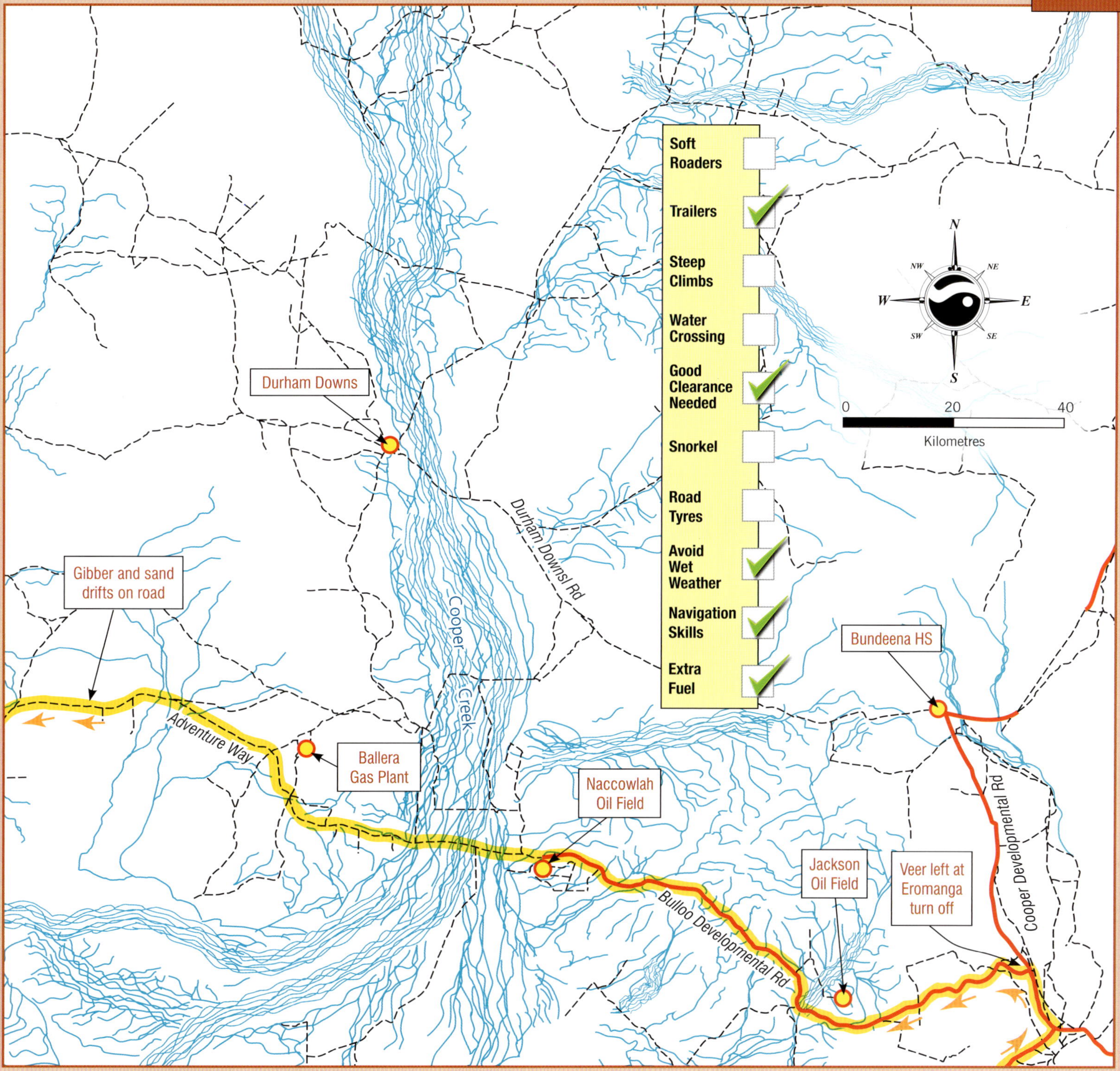

Soft Roaders	
Trailers	✓
Steep Climbs	
Water Crossing	
Good Clearance Needed	✓
Snorkel	
Road Tyres	
Avoid Wet Weather	✓
Navigation Skills	✓
Extra Fuel	✓

N
NW
NE
W
E
SW
SE
S

0 20 40
Kilometres

Durham Downs
Durham Downsl Rd
Cooper Creek
Gibber and sand drifts on road
Adventure Way
Ballera Gas Plant
Naccowlah Oil Field
Bulloo Developmental Rd
Jackson Oil Field
Veer left at Eromanga turn off
Cooper Developmental Rd
Bundeena HS

country, although few people will travel the vast distances of inland Australia without making the final effort to get here.

Retrace your steps to the **Innamincka – Windorah Road,** turning north past **Planet Downs outstation,** and reaching a tee intersection on the **Birdsville Developmental Road.** A right turn here takes you into **Windorah,** but we will swing left to make a run into some minor range country, with table top peaks and gidgee woodland.

Mount Hal flags a turn north into the tiny ghost town of **Betoota.** The 1880s sandstone and iron pub has recently reopened, but no other services are available. Old diesel and water tanks sit behind a fence, with the local airstrip and racetrack coming to life only for the annual race meet.

Continue westward past the **Cordillo Downs** turn off, following a gibber strewn trail to the **Diamantina River floodplain.** You will pass **Durrie HS** turn off, then a shortcut to the **Eyre Developmental Road** (both on your right), before **Roseberth HS** flags the last 35 kilometres into **Birdsville.**

This famous outback town sits on the fringe of the **Simpson Desert** as a last

Haddon Corner

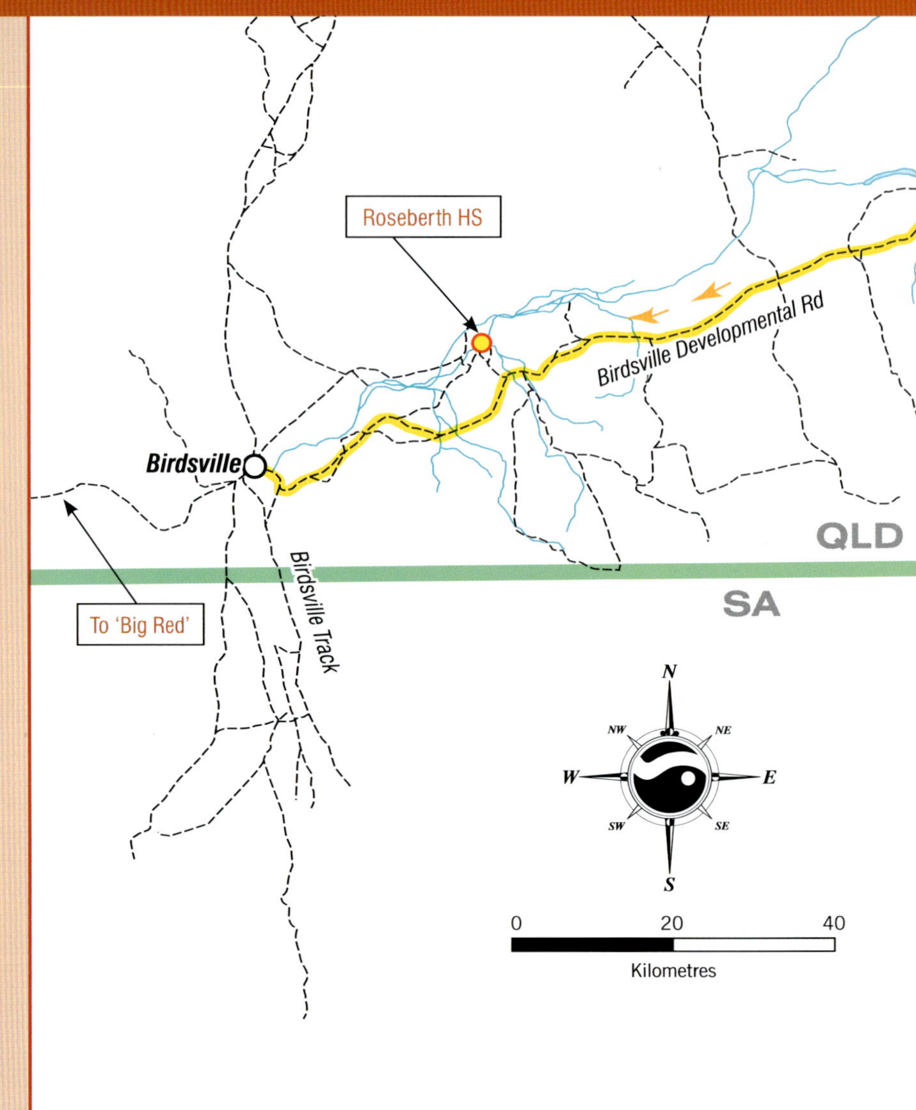

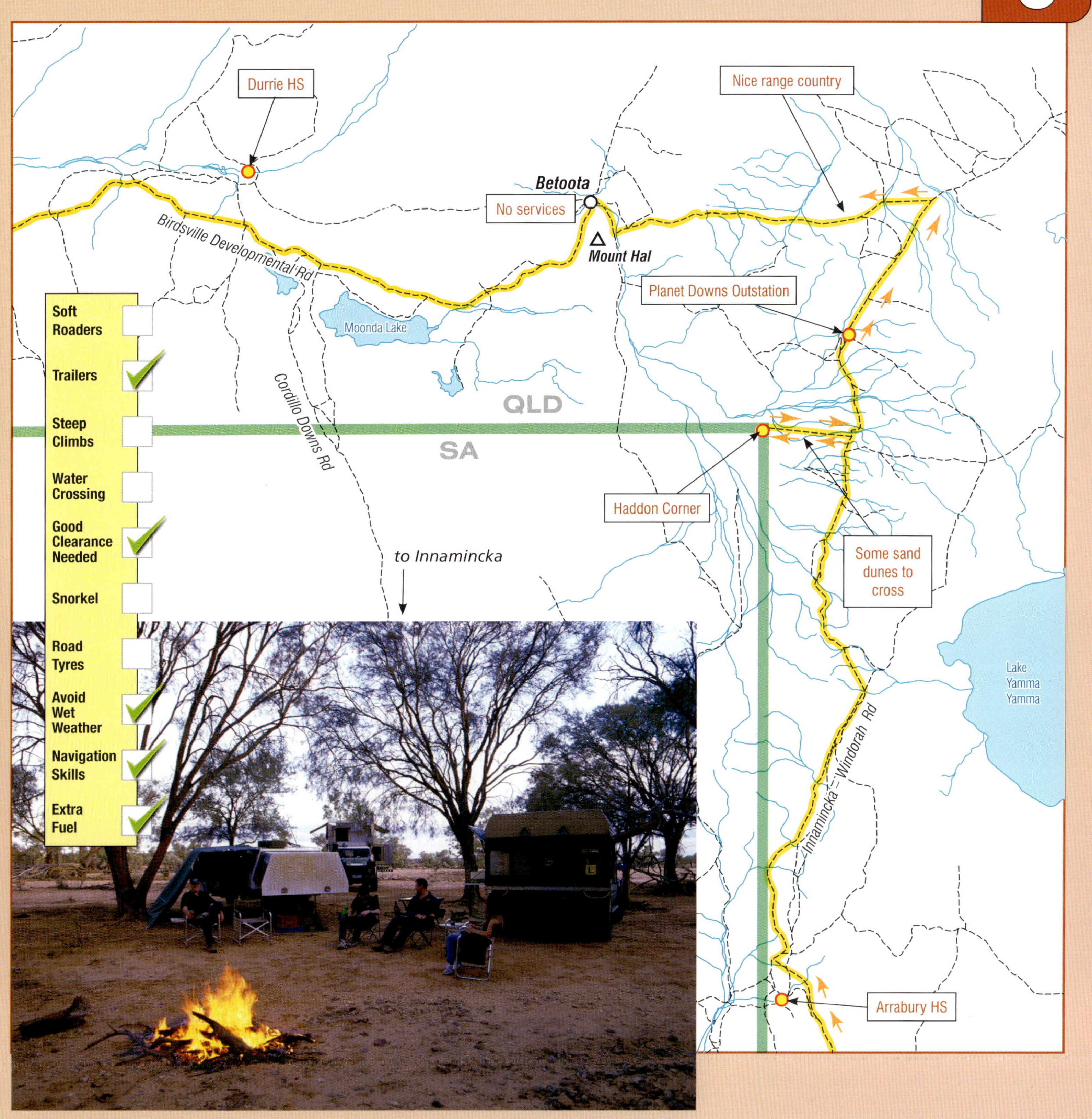

Camped in Channel Country

outpost for supplies in south west Queensland. Its pub and annual horse races are legendary, but there is an excellent visitor centre, bakery and cafe, together with other places of interest.

Many 4WDers find the challenge of Big Red to be irresistible. This dominant dune is found less than 40 kilometres west of **Birdsville**, and is the largest obstacle for **Simpson Desert** travellers to negotiate. You can try to conquor this dune with aired down tyres (15 – 20 psi), UHF radio set to channel 10 (to communicate with others on a similar mission), and a great sense of caution – multiple vehicles, full throttle acceleration and a steep lurching climb are a potentially disastrous combination.

Options beyond **Birdsville** include: west across the **Simpson Desert** (great iconic trip), south along the **Birdsville Track** (also iconic, but substantially easier), or north via the **Eyre and Diamantina Developmental Roads** to **Boulia** (see our Min Min Trek).

TRACK 20

The Georgina

Channel Country

Track Snapshot

TOUR ROUTE:
Boulia to Mount Isa via Urandangi.

DURATION AND DISTANCE:
Two to three days would be suitable for this 540 kilometre trek.

TRACK DETAILS:
Bulldust, floodways and sandy sections pave a mostly routine 4WD path across the Barkly Tablelands. Soft Roaders can undertake the journey with care, and trailers should be robust.

WHEN TO GO:
April – November avoids the monsoonal weather of northern Australia, but any wet weather will close these tracks quickly.

CAMPING
Boulia and Mount Isa have numerous options. There is camping at Tobermorey and Urandangi, and a few possibilities for informal camping near the major rivers.

FUEL AND SUPPLIES:
Boulia, Tobermorey HS, Urandangi and Mount Isa.

MAPS:
Hema: NE, Outback Queensland.

OTHER INFORMATION:
As always, carry plenty of water, fuel and food on these Outback treks. Breakdowns or wet weather can halt travel, and the Tobermorey – Urandangi Road does not see a lot of traffic.

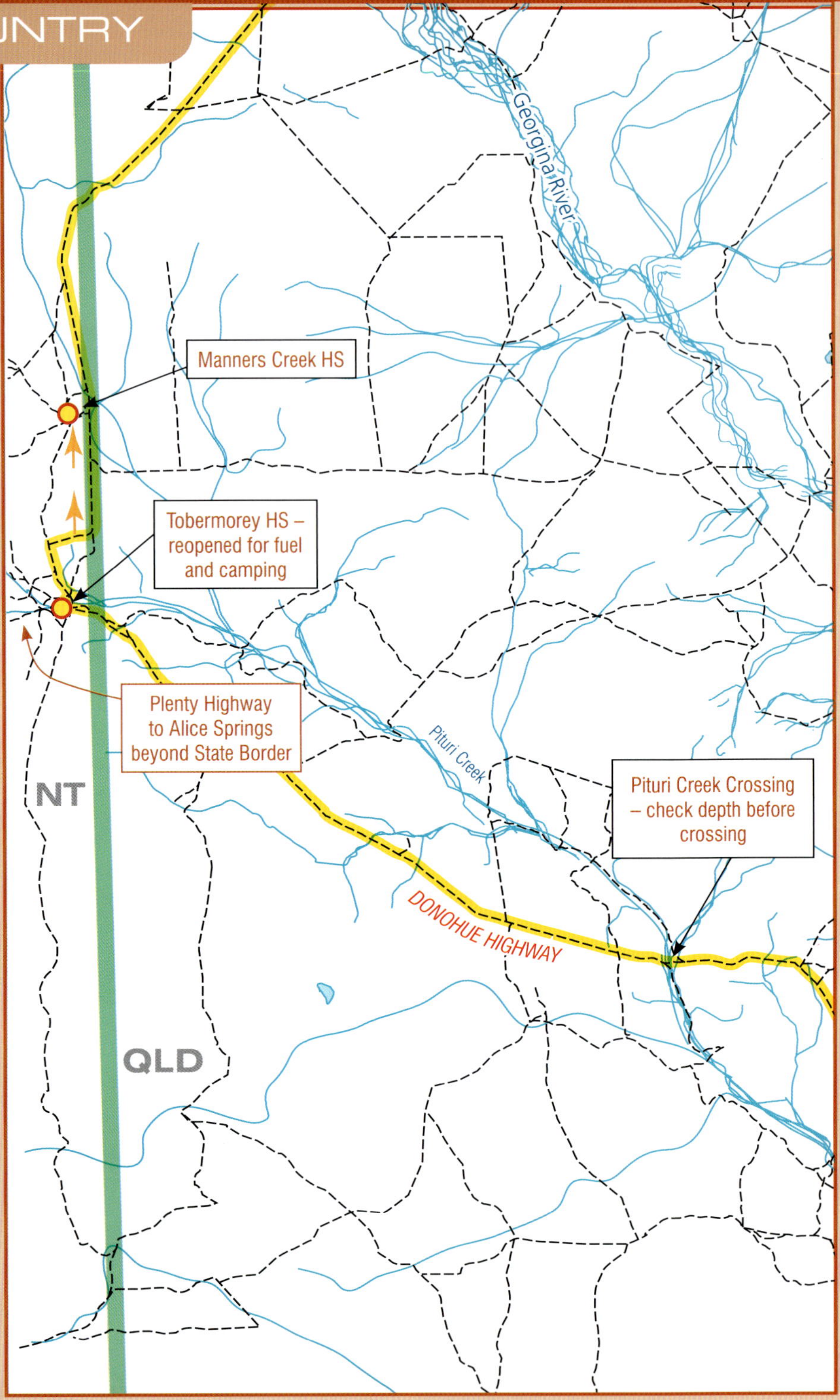

*Travellers heading west from **Boulia** follow in the footsteps of pioneering stockmen who blazed a trail across the northern **Simpson Desert** in search of water. Ridley Williams was one of the first Europeans to locate a series of watering points that would link the **Paroo River** with Alice Springs.*

*Stock were moved along this route from 1884 making use of the surface water within **Queensland's Channel Country,** then smaller water holes and bores in the Northern Territory. Vehicular access improved in the 1960s with the Donohue Highway, and its NT cousin (the Plenty Highway) providing continuity of travel.*

*This trek centres around the **Georgina River,** following the **Donohue** to the NT border, then travelling via **Urandangi** to **Mount Isa.***

You will leave Boulia via the **Diamantina Developmental Road**, taking the bitumen toward Mount Isa. Turn left after eight kilometres onto the **Donohue Highway**, and begin the run west past a number of stations (a couple offer accommodation – details are available from the Boulia Tourist Information Centre).

The sealed surface continues after crossing Gidya Creek, before you pass both **Wirrilyerna** and **Badalia Homesteads**. From here sealed and unsealed road alternates as you cross a grid at the **Dog Fence**, and keep right at the **Herbert Downs** turn off, some 75 kilometres from Boulia.

You will cross **Cottonbush Creek** as sand hills begin to encroach from either side of the road. Continue west to the braided channels of the **Georgina River**, and the **Ken McGuire Bridge**, which spans the major branch. (This crossing together with numerous creeks further west were – and still are - a major reason for traffic diversions on the Donohue during wet weather.)

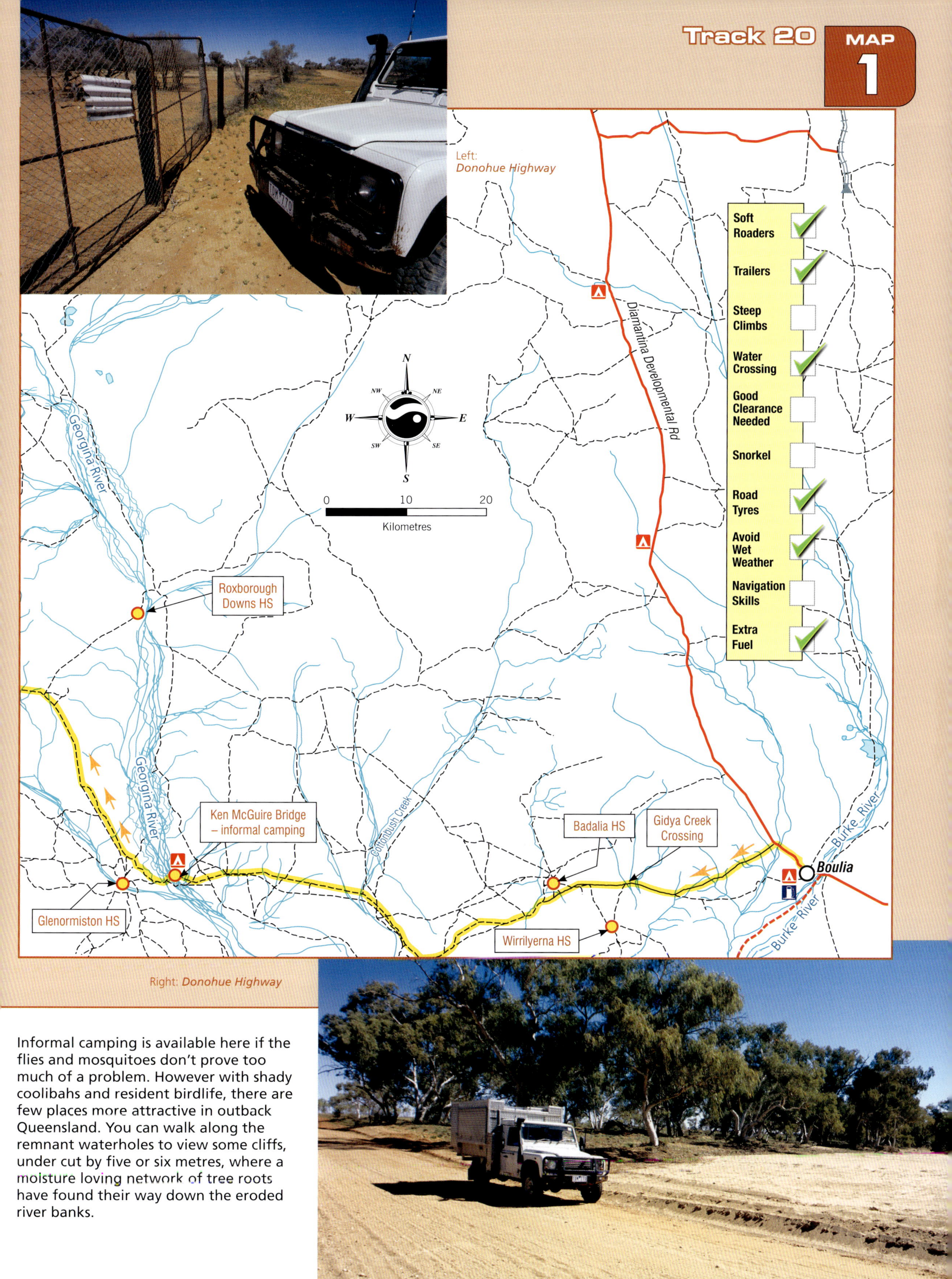

Left: *Donohue Highway*

Right: *Donohue Highway*

Informal camping is available here if the flies and mosquitoes don't prove too much of a problem. However with shady coolibahs and resident birdlife, there are few places more attractive in outback Queensland. You can walk along the remnant waterholes to view some cliffs, under cut by five or six metres, where a moisture loving network of tree roots have found their way down the eroded river banks.

The Georgina

Georgina River

Suitability	
Soft Roaders	✓
Trailers	✓
Steep Climbs	
Water Crossing	✓
Good Clearance Needed	
Snorkel	
Road Tyres	✓
Avoid Wet Weather	✓
Navigation Skills	
Extra Fuel	✓

Templetown Creek
BARKLY TABLELAND
Georgina River
Warwick Downs Outstation
River side camping
NT
QLD
Urandangi
Patches of bulldust in dry conditions
Georgina River

The Georgina is often dry, but can close the road for days and sometimes weeks at a time. Check out its current condition at Boulia prior to departure.

Keep right at the **Glenormiston HS** turn off to follow grassy floodplain to the **Roxborough Downs** turn off, some 38 kilometres later. Keep left at the junction (the track on your right offers a dry weather station country option for reaching **Urandangi**), to cross a series of floodways.

Pituri Creek is encountered about 12 kilometres from the Roxborough Downs turn off, where lignum bush lines several channels. Sealed road now spans this potentially deep crossing.

More causeways punctuate the run west to the NT border, as you reach **Tobermorey HS** shortly after. This large cattle station supports up to 23 000 head of Brahman and Santa Gertrudes cattle, and is open to the travelling public. Tobermorey also marks our turn off to **Urandangi**, rather than continue westward travel via the **Plenty Highway**.

(Those who wish to continue via the Plenty to Alice Springs will still need fuel for a further 215 kilometres – to reach Jervois HS – with an additional 350 kilometres required from there to the Alice. The Plenty offers a scenic run through intermittent range country along a largely unsealed road.)

The Urandangi turn off is reached some nine kilometres from the border, where you will swing north to parallel the state boundary, albeit within NT lands.

Keep right at **Manners Creek HS** to cross a number of causeways, returning to Queensland, some 45 kilometres beyond the Plenty Highway junction.

Rough, rutted sections with frequent bulldust patches mark the next 50 or so kilometres into Urandangi. Wet weather will quickly transform the journey however, with mud and numerous floodways contributing to the list of hazards.

You will cross the **Georgina** a couple of kilometres prior to a tee intersection, where you will turn left into the historic town. **Urandangi** dates from the 1880s when it was established to serve the growing demands of drovers pushing stock across the region. Today its one remaining pub carries on the tradition for locals and travellers alike.

An unusual acacia (Georgina Gidgee) made life difficult for graziers on this

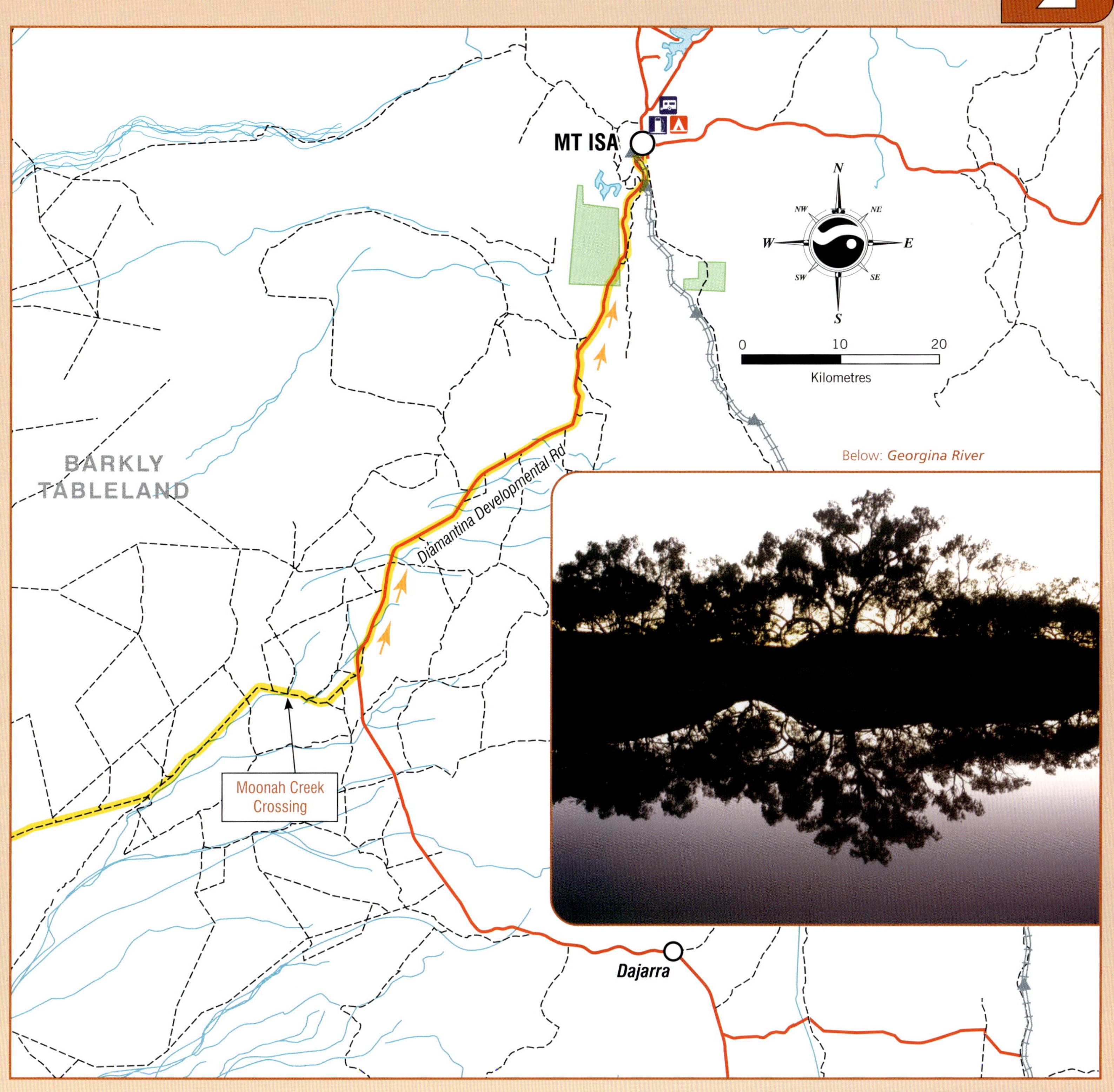

Below: *Georgina River*

stock route years ago. The toxic levels of fluoroacetic acid could kill stock which consumed the plant, and it was soon learned that grazing of this area was only viable when other pasture was abundant – a less than frequent event with only 250 mm of rain falling annually.

Head east out of town on the **Mount Isa road**, following a better run across the **Barkly Tableland**. You will pass turn offs to the outstations of **Warwick Downs** and Carandotta, before tracing and then crossing **Moonah Creek**.

You will travel some 95 kilometres from Urandangi through prime cattle country to a tee intersection on the **Diamantina Developmental Road**. Turn left onto bitumen and make a routine run through range country for about 90 kilometres, to arrive in **Mount Isa**.

This large mining town grew from a relatively recent mineral discovery, but expanded quickly following international investment. Visitors will find all services and supplies here with plenty of accommodation options. Those 4WDers heading north may like to consider our **Lawn Hill** trek as a possibility, while east bound travellers could choose to follow the **Diamantina River**.

TRACK 21

MIN MIN WAY

CHANNEL COUNTRY

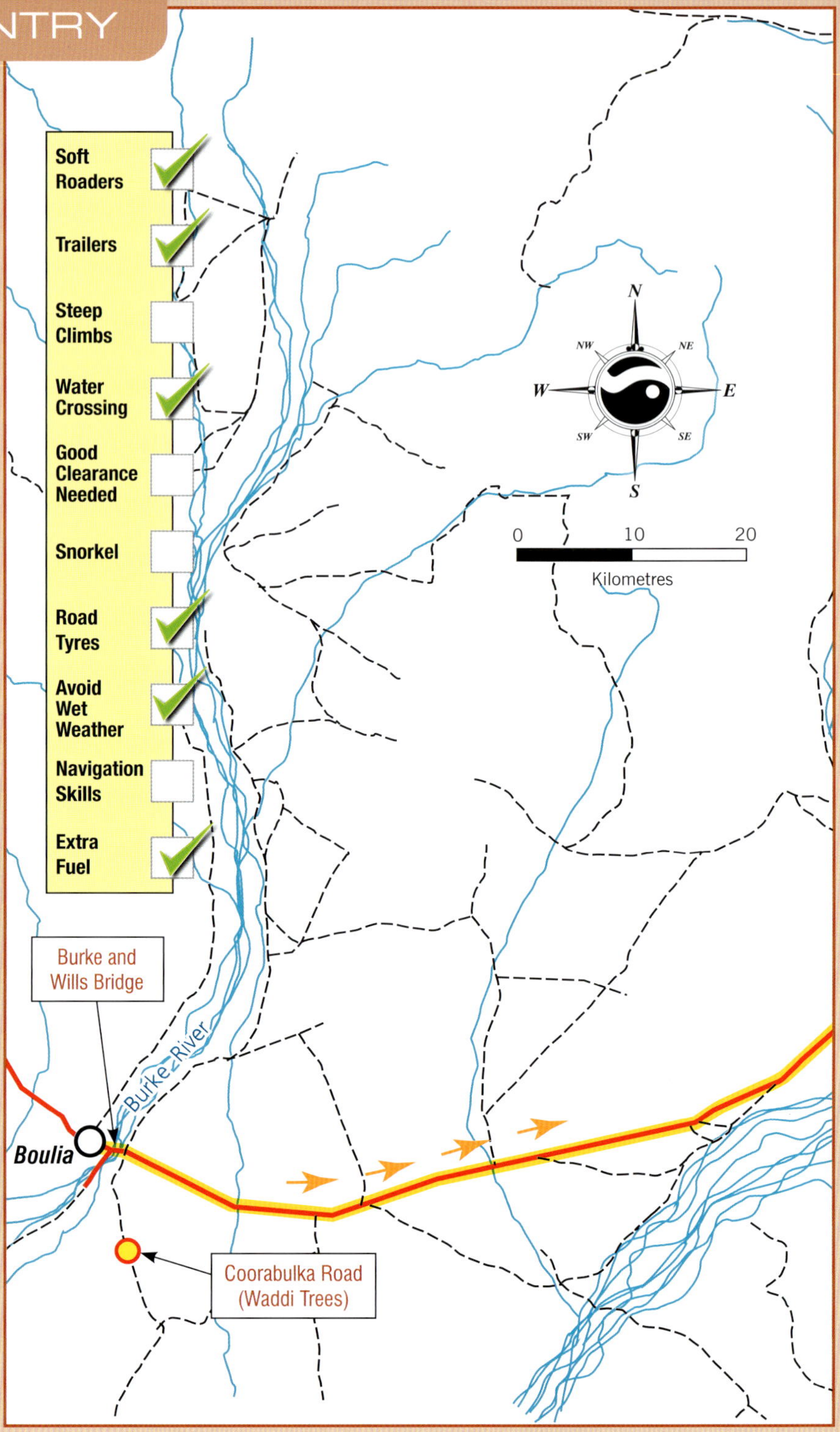

Track Snapshot

TOUR ROUTE:
Boulia to Winton via the Min Min Byway

DURATION AND DISTANCE:
The 360 kilometres can be easily done in a day, but some people choose to take two, stopping overnight at Middleton.

TRACK DETAILS:
A narrow but fully sealed journey that can be undertaken by any vehicle including trailers.

WHEN TO GO:
Suitable all year round, but the summer is quite hot out here, and remnant monsoonal rains can still close the road.

CAMPING:
Private parks at Boulia and Winton, with a less formal setting at Middleton (opposite the pub) and Mackunda Creek.

FUEL AND SUPPLIES:
Good range at Boulia and Winton – you can top up your fuel at Middleton.

MAPS:
Sunmap: Outback Queensland, Hema: Outback Queensland.

OTHER INFORMATION:
An easy run on bitumen, but still full of outback flavour and interest.

Soft Roaders	✓
Trailers	✓
Steep Climbs	
Water Crossing	✓
Good Clearance Needed	
Snorkel	
Road Tyres	✓
Avoid Wet Weather	✓
Navigation Skills	
Extra Fuel	✓

*The **Min Min** light has both baffled and captivated travellers for more than a century. Appearing as a fluorescent oval, the light seems to float across the evening skyline, then vanish just as quickly as it arrived. The Min Min has been reported by a broad range of people over the years, with only its geographic consistency providing any real material for scientific explanation.*

***Boulia** and district lay exclusive claim to this unpredictable phenomenon, with the **Kennedy Development Road** being the prime venue for this light show. Indeed this old Cobb and Co coach road linking Boulia with **Winton** is more popularly known as the Min Min Byway – though the appearance of floating balls of light is far from certain.*

*Fortunately the area offers other attractions with a much greater degree of certainty. Boulia itself is a modern outback town boasting a surprising range of services. Sporting and swimming facilities are excellent, and good meals are available at the local roadhouse or the **Australian Hotel. The Stonehouse Museum** is also worth a look, but the **Min Min Encounter** complex is a must.*

Visitors share in a theatrical experience spread over some 45 minutes. Animated sets usher patrons through a credible journey that attempts to give everybody a "Min Min" experience. A combination of facts, myths and creative special effects encourages visitors to formulate their own theories on this bizarre happening.

There is only one caravan park in **Boulia**, but the lack of competition hasn't brought with it a lowering of standards. The grassed river bank sites are particularly appealing, and the toilet / shower facilities are a welcome feature for outback tourers. The nearby **Burke and Wills Bridge** bears a plaque

Right: *Cawnpore Lookout*

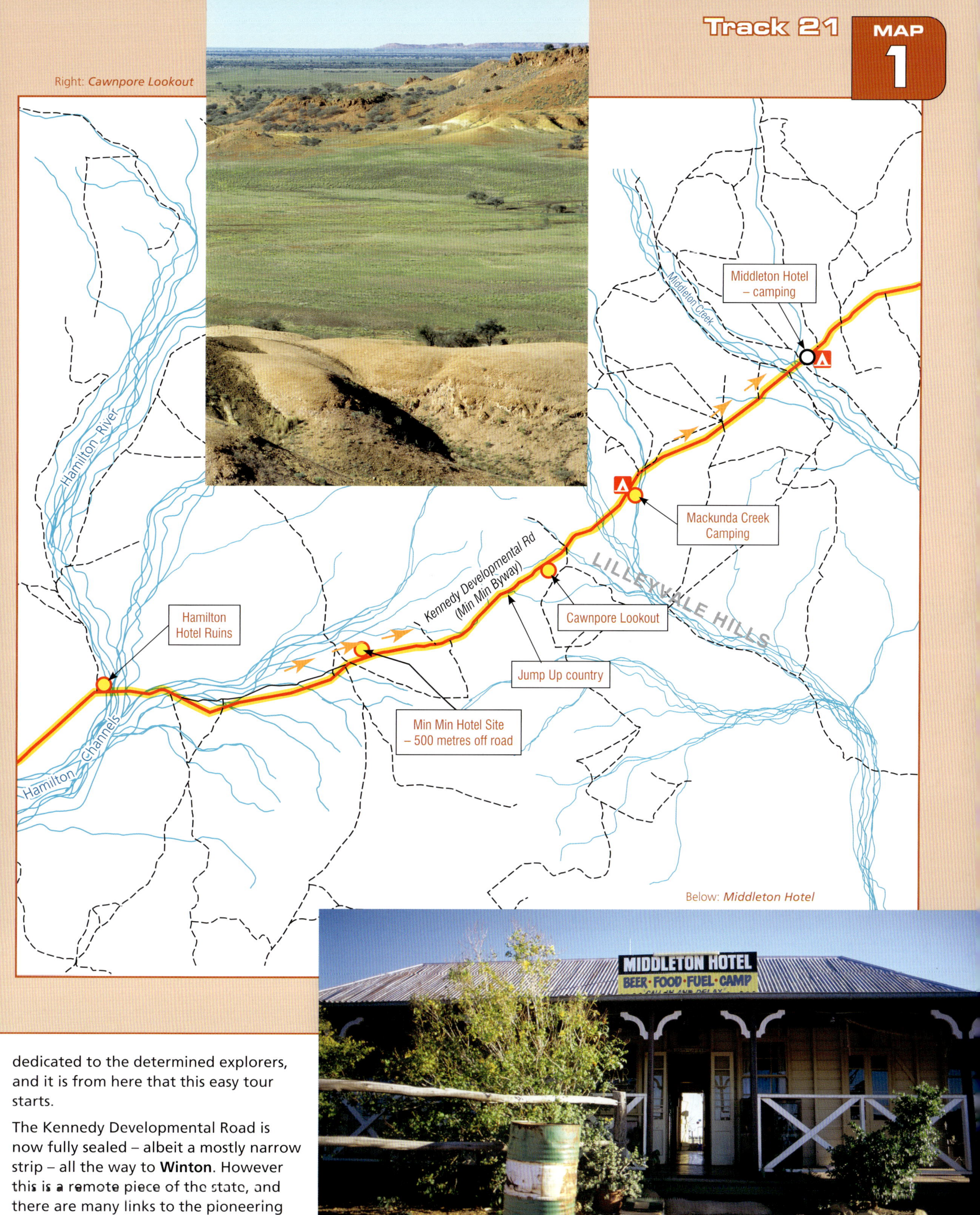

Below: *Middleton Hotel*

dedicated to the determined explorers, and it is from here that this easy tour starts.

The Kennedy Developmental Road is now fully sealed – albeit a mostly narrow strip – all the way to **Winton**. However this is a remote piece of the state, and there are many links to the pioneering days, together with some outstanding scenery.

MIN MIN WAY

Head east from Boulia on the Kennedy to pass the **Coorabulka Road** on your right just out of town (there is a stand of the distinctive waddi trees not far along this turn off if you are interested in viewing them; the wood is one of the hardest known to man, and mature trees may live for 1000 years). Concrete causeways span numerous dips along the Kennedy, with the occassional bridge, and vast acres of black soil grasslands where cattle graze.

Cattle have a long involvement with this area of Australia, with the Kennedy also known as the Winton Beef Road (the first road train journey in the country began at Boulia). Stock are often seen around watering points such as **Warenda Bore**, where a Cobb and Co marker indicates the site's linkage to our European history.

You will see an old stockyard nearby; its hand woven fence wire stands relatively low, making it more likely to have contained sheep rather than cattle. We found what was perhaps an old shearer's camp with rusting iron drums, and discarded bottles spread across the site. A makeshift chimney indicated where a rough hut once stood – on what would be at times, a quite desolate landscape.

Continue to follow the Min Min Byway to cross the **Hamilton Channels** some 78 kilometres from Boulia, at a series of floodways marked by depth indicators. The **Hamilton Hotel** operated here for many years as a way stop for Cobb and Co coaches travelling the route.

Today only the stone chimney and notched posts standing at a nearby stockyard, remain to preserve the memory of this once important site. A sheltered area complete with table and chairs allows modern day travellers to break their journey at this same historic site. Potable water can still be obtained here from the adjacent mill and tank system.

Further east from the Hamilton was the **Min Min Hotel** – an establishment also on the coach route, but infamous as a haunt for criminals, and as an outlet for "rot gut" liquor. The hotel was originally cobbled together with timber and corrugated iron, but burnt to the ground in 1917.

Little remains of the site today, except for a small cemetery and assorted rusting relics. Those with time to spare can roam the forlorn looking gibber plain, and piece together those clues still viable. Twisted bed remains and lots of broken glass offer a glimpse into the wild times that gave the hotel its notoriety.

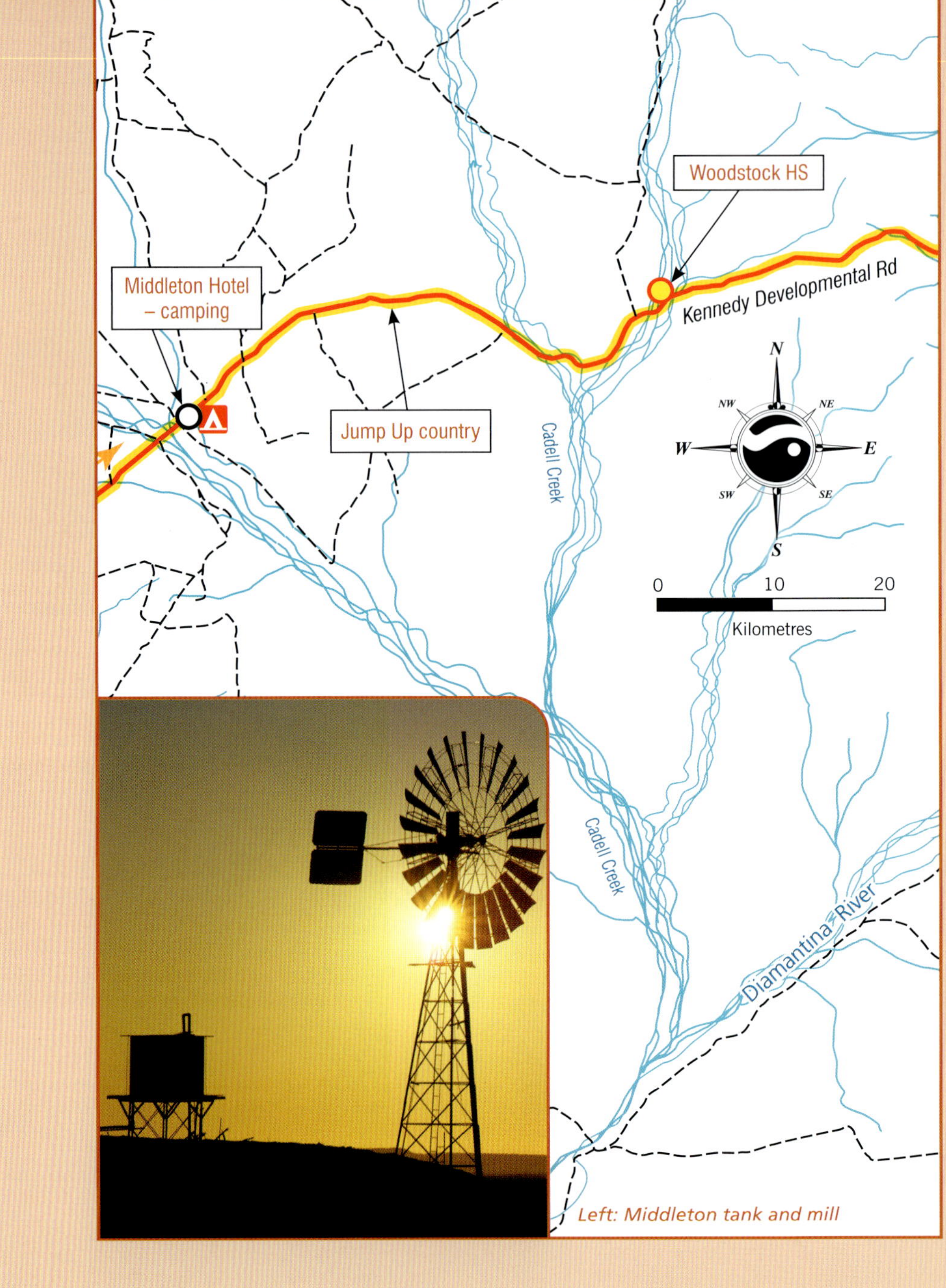

Left: Middleton tank and mill

Beyond **Min Min Creek**, a netting fence separates the shires of Boulia and Winton. Jagged mountain country rises around here, with flat topped mesas colouring the horizon in red and yellow tones. Vertical sides and eroded tops form a landscape that would appear at home on the set of an American Wild West movie.

Cawnpore Lookout offers a peek into this stunning range where the erosion began some 90–100 million years ago. Back then massive rivers (thought to rival the present day Amazon) pushed across a vast wetland. You will get excellent views from the picnic shelter, but broader expanses of the **Lilleyvale Hills** can be seen by carefully walking to a nearby viewpoint.

Mackunda Creek and its triple windmills, marks a return to flatter country and masses of yellow wildflowers in season. You will find a rest area here, some 146 kilometres from Boulia, where toilets and tables are provided, and short term camping (one night) is permitted.

The **Middleton Hotel** lies further east as a Cobb and Co establishment that is still

Left: *Cobb and Co marker*

open to this day. Its well worn verandah and tempting bar even now beckon travellers to stop for a break – if only to enjoy a cold drink or top up the fuel.

Travellers stopping the night will find free camping opposite the pub, with toilets and basic facilities provided. Hotel meals and hot showers are available at the Middleton, together with a friendly atmosphere and plenty of local knowledge.

The old public hall and nearby cemetery indicate a more populous community than is currently the case. You will find little tangible evidence of the busier times, but a rubbish dump littered with several abandoned vehicles can be reached following a short walk from the pub. The nearby Middleton football stadium declares an entrance fee of one stubbie – a prerequisite probably more welcomed by the players, as the solitary bench seat stand looks over a field of stony gibber.

You will leave Middleton to follow the gibber back to **Jump Up** country where the mesas and eroded mountain sides have left slabs of rock teetering on their balance. **Woodstock Station** on **Cadell Creek** flags yet another Cobb and Co marker, before the **Diamantina Channels** bring some colour to the landscape.

Concrete causeways span the Diamantina's braided arms, where muddy waters give moisture to rows of coolibah. Green undergrowth provides a lush element to the country, especially as you drive closer to the lagoons of **Wokingham Creek**, where the birdlife again multiplies.

A turn off to **Old Cork** is found on the east side of Wokingham, as you travel the final 50 kilometres into **Winton**. All services are available at this major town on the **Matilda Highway**, with ready access to both **Longreach** and **Cloncurry**.

TRACK 22

Dowling Track

CHANNEL COUNTRY

*As an alternative to our **Paroo River** trek out of **Hungerford**, you may wish to head further inland on this trek following the **Dowling Track.** Vincent James Dowling was a noted explorer and pastoralist on the Paroo, Bulloo, and Darling River areas, and this tour follows in his footsteps, albeit more than a century later.*

Head north from Hungerford to turn left onto the **Thargomindah Road**, just beyond the **Paroo Crossing**. Follow good gravel through **Currawinya NP** as you trace the NSW border to **Karto HS**, and begin to swing more northerly beyond the national park boundary. Scenic range country offers good travelling as you pass mulga woodlands and stands of bloodwood.

Follow the main road over **Cardenyabba Creek** to the northern signposted access track for **Kilcowera HS** (the southern access track follows Cardenyabba Creek, and requires some prior knowledge – check with the station manager before undertaking this option). Through travellers will continue straight, but those looking to experience a working station can turn right to drive the final 13 kilometres to the homestead.

Kilcowera Station offers powered and unpowered sites as well as lodge style accommodation in the shearers quarters. Visitors also have access to 50 kilometres of private station tracks, which are well signposted with mud maps provided. Driving these tracks will take the best part of a day, as you traverse some rugged range country with views over **Lake Wyara**. More details can be found at www.outbackbeds.com.au

Homestead visitors will return to the main **Thargomindah Road**, and continue north with the **Yaraka Hills** appearing not far beyond the homestead access road. A short stretch of bitumen paves the scenic range climb, before you reach the double causeway at **Gap Creek**. This crossing can be flood damaged, but is normally trafficable in the dry – and unlikely to be the challenge of last century when Cobb and Co operated a staging post at the crossing.

You will reach bitumen some 20 kilometres south of the **Bulloo Developmental Road**, before keeping right at the **Bulloo Downs** turn off. Turn left at tee six kilometres later to reach **Thargomindah's** town centre shortly after.

This town was a major centre for Cobb and Co operations in the late 1800s, and even today offers an unexpected range of services. Hotel and motel accommodation is available, together with a caravan park and permanent population of about 330. The township was founded late in 1861 after Thomas Brahe and his party camped on the Bulloo River here in their search for the missing Burke and Wills.

Stock up on fuel and food at Thargomindah, then head west on the **Bulloo Developmental Road** for eight kilometres to the alternative **Toompine Road**. Turn right onto gravel to pass a large clay pan and cross a **Bulloo** tributary. Follow mesa country to **Soonah Crossing** on the Bulloo River, about 44 kilometres from Thargomindah. Birdlife is prolific at this scenic stretch of river and it makes a great rest stop.

Cross the river via a concrete causeway to reach an unsignposted junction some 47 kilometres from Thargomindah. Keep left at the junction to pass **Kiandra HS** and trace the Bulloo River to a tee intersection on the main **Thargomindah – Quilpie Road**. Turn left onto bitumen for the short run into **Toompine**.

Toompine is now just a shadow of its former self when a cluster of houses and businesses surrounded the South Western Hotel. Cobb and Co used the hotel as a stop over, but today the houses have vanished, leaving the hotel as a sole reminder of the town's heyday. Free camping and motel style units make this a welcome stop with travellers however, while meals are available most days.

You will head north from Toompine for just a few hundred metres, before turning left onto a station track. Follow the route west to a crossing of the Bulloo, popular with bird watchers and anglers. Continue to a tee intersection, some four kilometres further on, swinging right (north) toward the signposted stations of **Piastre**, **Moble**, and **Whynot**.

Track Snapshot

TOUR ROUTE:
Hungerford to Quilpie via the Dowling Track

DURATION AND DISTANCE:
Three days is suitable for this 420 kilometre tour.

TRACK DETAILS:
Routine station tracks and a couple of river crossings (no problems when levels are low) make this tour suitable for all vehicles and trailers.

WHEN TO GO:
The Channel Country is best explored in the drier months from April to October.

CAMPING:
Facilities are provided at Hungerford, Kilcowera (station stay), Thargomindah, Toompine and Quilpie.

FUEL AND SUPPLIES:
Thargomindah and Quilpie offer fuel and all supplies. Hungerford has gravity fed drum fuel and basic supplies.

MAPS:
Hema: Outback Queensland, Westprint SW Queensland.

OTHER INFORMATION:
This tour follows just the Queensland section of the Dowling Track – a lengthy run extending from Bourke to Quilpie.

Yupunyah trees, coloured pink in summer, stand over the mitchell grass understorey, with unfenced cattle roaming the stations. Keep your speeds down (especially close to the homesteads) and enjoy the great views over the **Balbon Plains** as you continue northward.

You will leave Piastre Station and enter Moble Station where the Costello and Durack women waited nine months for the menfolk to return in the 1860s. These gallant pioneers were droving a mob of cattle overland to the Adelaide markets. You can read more about their exploits in that great classic "Kings in Grass Castles".

Cross Moble Creek (a major tributary of the Bulloo) to follow a scenic drive through to the **Cooper Developmental Road**, west of **Quilpie**. Turn right on the bitumen for the final 32 kilometres into Quilpie. This outback town has a good range of shops and services, with accommodation including hotels, motels, and a caravan park.

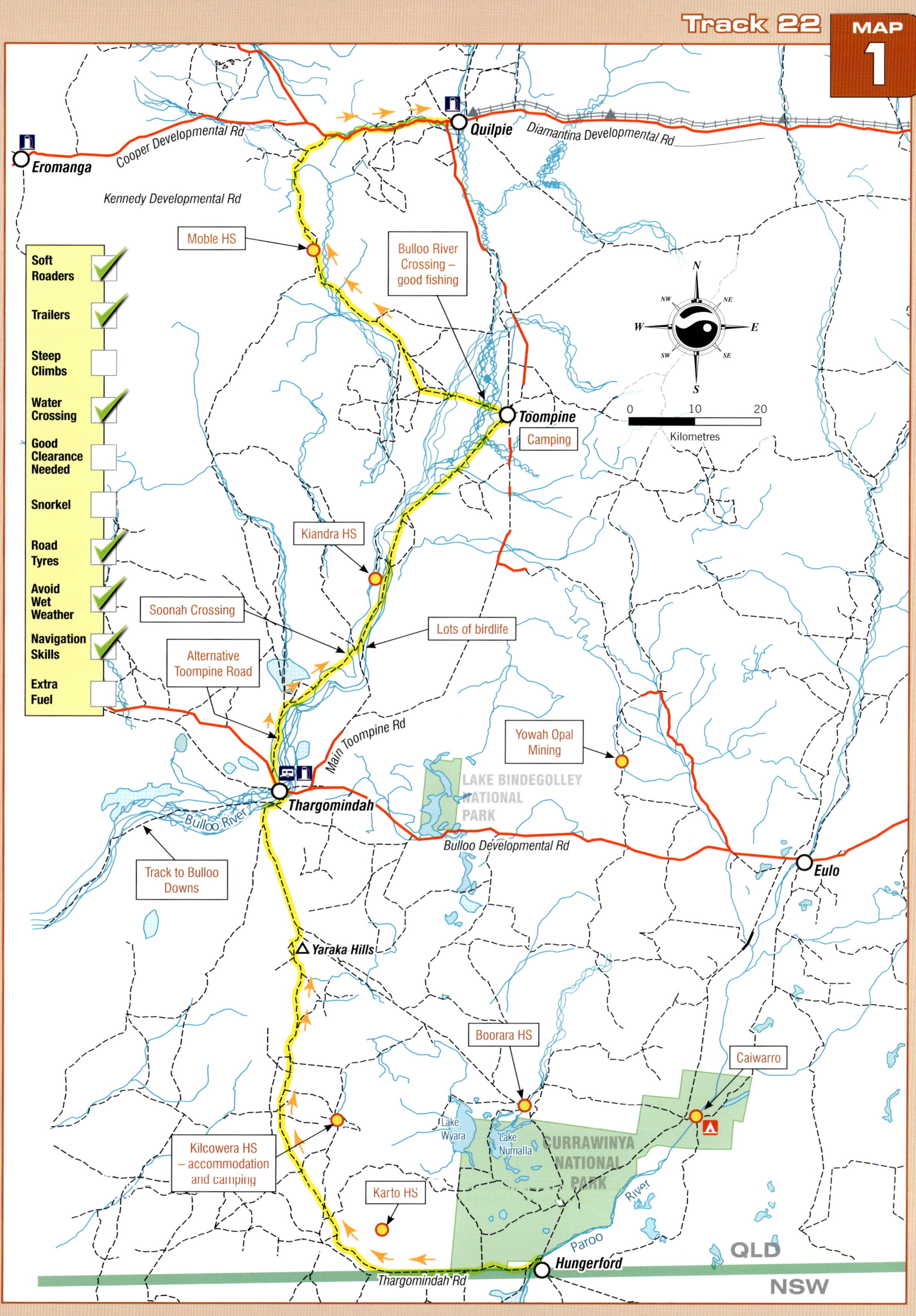

Eromanga
Cooper Developmental Rd
Kennedy Developmental Rd
Quilpie
Diamantina Developmental Rd
Moble HS
Bulloo River Crossing – good fishing
Toompine
Camping
N
NE
E
SE
S
SW
W
NW
0
10
20
Kilometres
Soft Roaders
Trailers
Steep Climbs
Water Crossing
Good Clearance Needed
Snorkel
Road Tyres
Avoid Wet Weather
Navigation Skills
Extra Fuel
Kiandra HS
Soonah Crossing
Lots of birdlife
Alternative Toompine Road
Main Toompine Rd
Yowah Opal Mining
Thargomindah
Bulloo River
LAKE BINDEGOLLEY NATIONAL PARK
Bulloo Developmental Rd
Eulo
Track to Bulloo Downs
Yaraka Hills
Boorara HS
Caiwarro
Lake Wyara
Lake Numalla
CURRAWINYA NATIONAL PARK
Kilcowera HS – accommodation and camping
Karto HS
Paroo River
QLD
NSW
Hungerford
Thargomindah Rd

TRACK 23 THE PAROO

CHANNEL COUNTRY

The Granites

Track Snapshot

TOUR ROUTE:
Hungerford to Quilpie via the Paroo River and Lake Dartmouth.

DURATION AND DISTANCE:
At least three days will allow you to get a feel for this 600 kilometre trek.

TRACK DETAILS:
Bulldust, river crossings and typical outback driving conditions limit this trek to full size 4WDs and capable Soft Roaders. Trailers are OK.

WHEN TO GO:
Dry weather is essential – Lake Dartmouth is regularly inundated (this trek crosses its northern tip) and flooding of the Paroo – Bulloo system will also close roads.

CAMPING:
Excellent bush camping on the Paroo in Currawinya NP (several camping areas) and informal sites at Langlo Crossing and Blackwater Creek. Other options include Hungerford, Quilpie and Eulo.

FUEL AND SUPPLIES:
Quilpie is the main centre on this tour, but fuel and basic supplies are available at Eulo and Cooladdi.

MAPS:
Sunmap: Outback Queensland, Hema: Queensland Outback.

OTHER INFORMATION:
Character rich outback pubs feature on this tour; Hungerford, Eulo, Cooladdi and Adavale are all well worth a stop.

*Those who have followed the **Paroo River** into **Hungerford** will not feel let down with this next leg, which follows the waterway to its origins. Remote station country and a couple of quirky towns are followed with a superb wetland at **Lake Dartmouth.***

Follow Hungerford's main street northward over a broad floodplain, etched with braided water channels. The Paroo River is crossed, as you pass the **Thargomindah Road** on your left about three kilometres from town. You are now within **Currawinya NP** – a Ramsar status wetland site, and home to over 200 species of birds.

A signposted turn to **"The Granites"** is reached about 17 kilometres from Hungerford, where you will turn left, then left again 400 metres later at a set of old yards. A 4WD only sign greets you for a one way return drive to Currawinya's major lakes.

A winding 40 kph zone takes you to **Lake Kaponyee** some 16 kilometres later, and a short diversion to the small salt lake. Parking is informal near an old fenceline, but in wet years the birdlife will be prolific; up to 200 000 birds visit Currawinya's lake system in times of flood.

The main track continues past a collapsed windmill and tank to a junction seven kilometres later. Take the right fork signposted **"Lakes Road"**, crossing a dry lake to a tee intersection. **Lake Numalla's** carpark is just 500 metres to the right, and visitors can walk another 500 metres to the lake shore. At 3000 hectares, Numalla is Currawinya's largest freshwater lake, but only walkers and canoeists can access the permitted areas.

Vehicles can turn left at the junction then drive five kilometres to the carpark overlooking **Lake Wyara**. This salt water lake is slightly larger than Numalla, and while there are no defined walks to the shoreline, birdlife is more abundant, with swans and pelicans frequenting the flooded margins.

Visitors need to retrace their steps to the main **Granites** intersection (about 34 kilometres) then turn left (NW) toward **Boorara HS**. You will drive for 11 kilometres to a signposted turn on your right. The Granites are reached following a two kilometre eroded gully ramble which finishes at a carpark. Vague pathways allow walkers to access the puzzling rock formations, spread over a large area.

Return to the main **Hungerford – Eulo Road** from here, turn north and proceed past the ranger station turnoff. **Warden Road** is reached 33 kilometres later when you turn right to reach the crumbling old **Caiwarro Ruins**. Stockyards and outbuildings are scattered near the rendered mud brick HS, with three large camping areas found nearby.

The **Paroo River** makes a great setting for those who camp, but there is only one toilet facility provided, and firewood must be brought in. However the broad stretch of river is sure to offer a quiet corner, and a lucky angler may pull in one of the resident yellowbelly.

Return to the main road and follow the corrugated gravel out of the national park and over a series of grids, to a tee intersection on the **Bulloo Developmental Road**. Turn right to cross the Paroo at a billabong before reaching Eulo.

Opal mining was the impetus for the first settlements in the **Eulo** area but today pastoral activity rather than

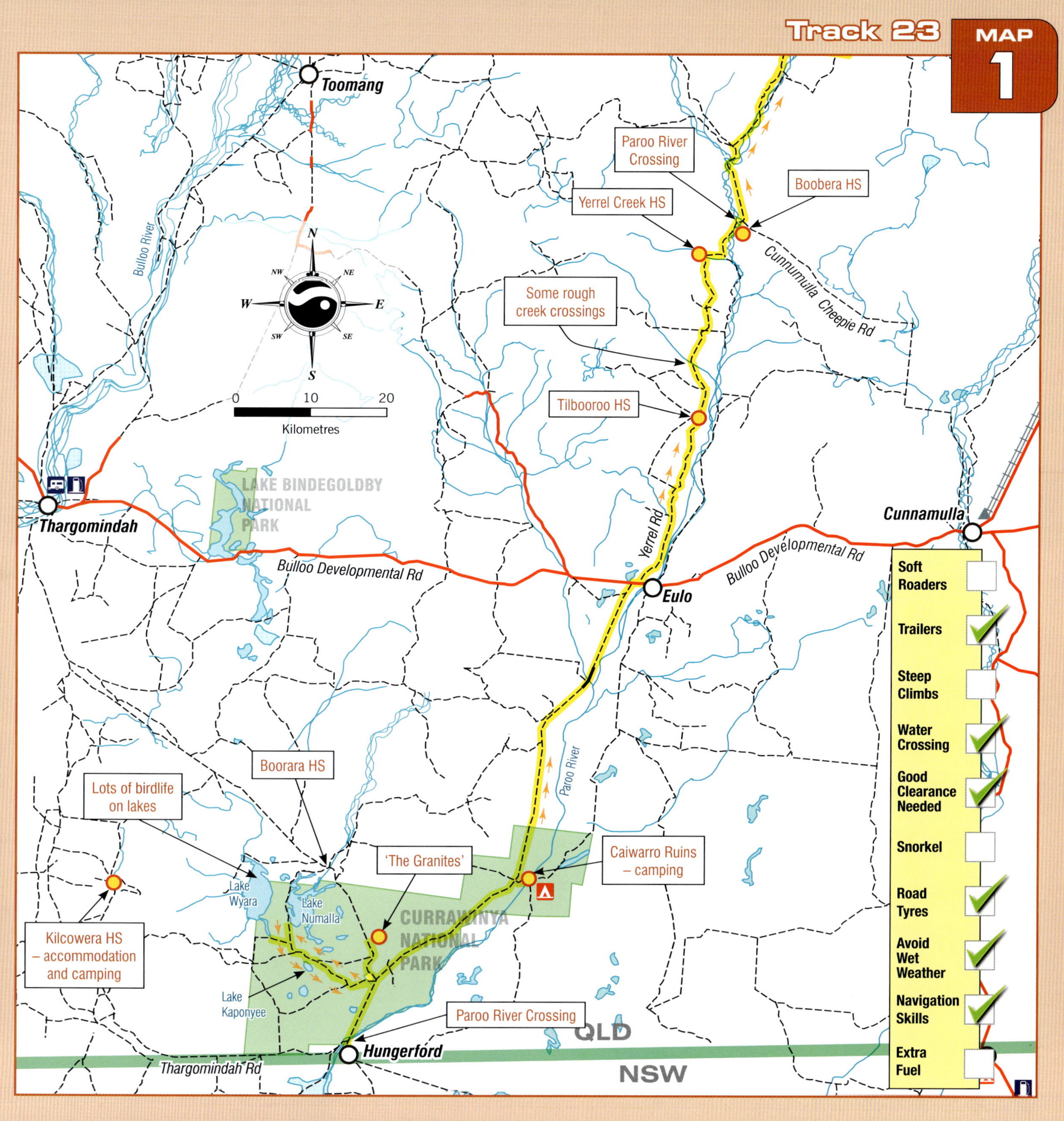

mining makes the town tick. Items of interest here include the ornate **Eulo Queen Hotel**, the mud springs (about eight kilometres west of town – and occasionally heard in the distance as the pent up artesian pressure is released), and the general store – worth seeing for its display of goods from yesteryear. Accommodation options in town are limited to the hotel and a camping area alongside it (the original caravan park has now closed).

Head west out of town recrossing the Paroo's concrete bridge, then turn right onto signposted **"Yerrel Road – Humeburn Crossing"**. Keep right 100 metres later, as you cross a gas pipeline and grid into **Penaroo Station**. Gibber, floodways and stockyards mark the journey northward past **Tilbooroo HS** (keep right) and some rough creek crossings. **Yerrel HS** is passed on your left, 82 kilometres from Eulo, then you cross the Paroo 12 kilometres later at **Boobera HS**.

Turn left onto the **Cunnamulla – Cheepie Road** for a better run back onto the Paroo 11 kilometres later. A scenic winding section of road passes old yards and pumphouse on a lengthy

Eulo Hotel

Caiwarro Ruins

river crossing, before you turn right at the **Wyandra** junction six kilometres further on. Bulldust and slow undulating country takes you through **Spring Creek Station**, then keep right at the **Mount Alfred** turnoff.

Modest range country is passed over the next 18 kilometres where you turn left just prior to a grid at signposted "**Quilpie via Doobibla**". Veer left as you reach the steel stockyards of **Doobibla**, crossing **Buckenby** and **Tumblebury Creeks** on a lovely drive within a gibber's throw of the Paroo.

Centre Creek and **Meeting Creek** are forded on a winding road through longer grass and complex drainage systems. Take the right fork just beyond the Paroo's crossing (likely to be dry), passing a stockyard on your left, then reaching **Yarronvale HS**.

Turn right at the tee intersection for another wide crossing of the Paroo, and an attractive waterhole on the river's eastern bank. Continue to a tee intersection, turning left at the airstrip, to follow **Quilberry Creek** through to the **Diamantina Developmental Road**. Swing right onto the blacktop for a nine kilometre run into the tiny town of **Cooladdi**.

Initially it is only the **Foxtrap Hotel** (rooms, basic supplies and fuel) that is evident, but an abandoned rail siding nearby indicates a larger town (once home to 250 residents) that would have been quite active in its heyday. Head north from the pub, first over **Inkerman Creek**, then **Yarram** and **Quilberry Creeks** to signposted "**Nimboy Road**", 24 kilometres from Cooladdi.

Keep straight at the junction, following the main road past **Norah Park** and **Cairns HS** to a broad crossing of **Peter Creek**. Taller trees and a couple of rather ornate gates herald your arrival onto **Warilda Station** – a character filled spread that is the centrepiece of **Langlo Crossing**.

You will drive close to the homestead buildings including original and more recent residences, shearers quarters, and even a tiled roof shearing shed. Leave via an amazing gate fabricated with hand riveted strips of steel, before reaching a tee intersection, where you will turn right to the **Langlo River bridge**.

A small cluster of buildings mark the location, where informal camping can be found on the west bank of the Langlo River.

Head west from the small community past **Billoola** and **Norah Park Roads** to an elevated section of road at **Oak Swamp**. A nice stand of sheoaks mark the two kilometre crossing before you reach the more significant wetland of **Lake Dartmouth**, 35 kilometres from Langlo Crossing. Following rain, the flooded landscape here comes alive with lillies, birds and vibrant forest.

The main **Charleville – Adavale Road** crosses the top neck of Dartmouth, and while it has been built up substantially here, wet weather will close the access.

Follow the road past **Varna HS** to **Mariala NP**. A winding pathway weaves through heavily treed landscape here, offering some views over the undulating terrain.

Beyond the national park, **Sherwood Park** operates as a commercial goat breeding operation (watch out for stock) as you head towards **Adavale** passing a number of sidetracks. A concrete causeway breaches **Blackwater Creek** just prior to the small town.

Adavale was once a bustling centre for the surrounding district, but it lost its way when the rail was pushed into **Quilpie** instead. These days the town boasts of a pub, police station and townhall, together with a group of elevated houses – built to cope with the

Lake Dartmouth

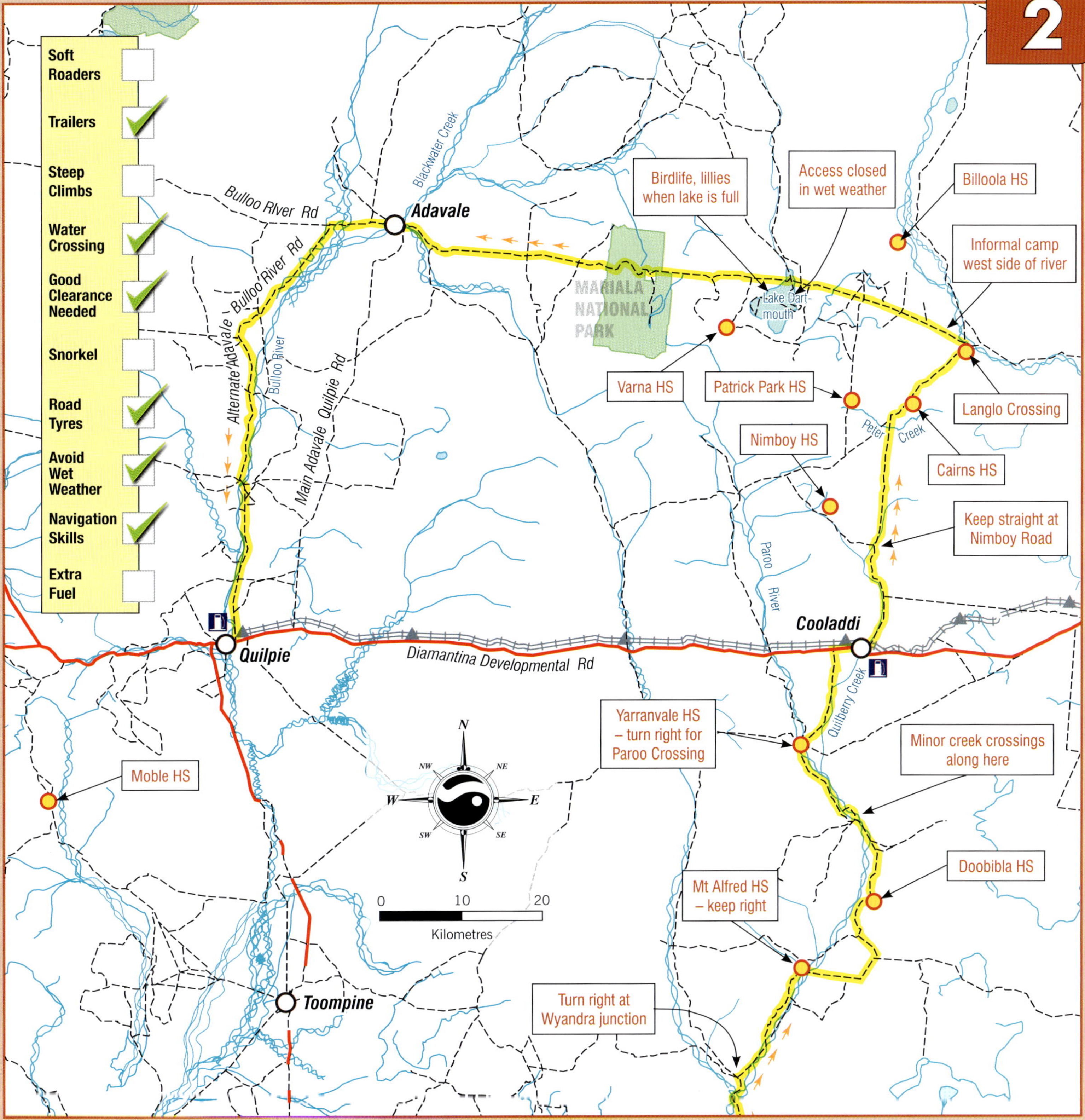

Soft Roaders	
Trailers	✓
Steep Climbs	
Water Crossing	✓
Good Clearance Needed	✓
Snorkel	
Road Tyres	✓
Avoid Wet Weather	✓
Navigation Skills	✓
Extra Fuel	

Adavale
Bulloo River Rd
Alternate Adavale - Bulloo River Rd
Bulloo River
Main Adavale Quilpie Rd
Blackwater Creek
MARIALA NATIONAL PARK
Birdlife, lillies when lake is full
Access closed in wet weather
Billoola HS
Informal camp west side of river
Lake Dartmouth
Varna HS
Patrick Park HS
Langlo Crossing
Peter Creek
Nimboy HS
Cairns HS
Keep straight at Nimboy Road
Paroo River
Quilpie
Cooladdi
Diamantina Developmental Rd
Quilberry Creek
Yarranvale HS – turn right for Paroo Crossing
Minor creek crossings along here
Moble HS
Doobibla HS
Mt Alfred HS – keep right
Turn right at Wyandra junction
Toompine
N NE E SE S SW W NW
0 10 20
Kilometres

regular channel country floods. Even the road maintenance Atco huts sit on stilts!

From Adavale follow the gravel to Quilpie some 100 kilometres to the south. Or if you are still yearning for dust and adventure, the **Bulloo River Road** is a similar distance option, offering good views of the **Grey Range**, and a lovely drive through braided channel waterways.

TRACK 24 THE THOMSON

CHANNEL COUNTRY

Track Snapshot

TOUR ROUTE:
Longreach to Windorah via Lochern and the Thomson River.

DURATION AND DISTANCE:
Allow at least two days for the 320 kilometre trek.

TRACK DETAILS:
A relatively easy run taking sealed sections and longer stretches of gravel and black soil. Wet weather will put a stop to travel as the flat country is transformed into a skating rink. Trailers and Soft Roaders OK, except for the optional short detour at Stonehenge.

WHEN TO GO:
April to November is the Outback travel season with the middle months of June, July and August being the most popular.

CAMPING:
Bush camping on the Thomson River at Lochern NP and on the Cooper just east of Windorah. More formal camping at Stonehenge and Jundah.

FUEL AND SUPPLIES:
Longreach, Windorah and Jundah have most supplies, with fuel and basic needs from Stonehenge.

MAPS:
Hema: NE, Hema: Outback Queensland, Sunmap: Outback Queensland.

OTHER INFORMATION:
Fantastic Channel Country touring with working stations and character rich outback towns.

*It is hard to believe that the **Thomson** and **Barcoo Rivers** coalesce to form a creek. But thanks to the conservative nature of explorer Charles Sturt, that is the title of the newly formed **Cooper,** as it picks up the waters of these two major rivers. The **Cooper Creek** continues to flow in times of flood with an impressive surge across kilometres of Australia's parched inland.*

Indeed Sturt himself was so taken by "this fine watercourse" that he named it in honour of South Australia's Judge Cooper in 1845. The explorer later confessed that he had considered christening the Cooper a river, but was "unable to locate any current along its length". The name stayed, and today the Cooper Creek holds a great deal of interest among Outback travellers.

The Thomson – Barcoo confluence is a particularly scenic and historic part of this country, and travellers can trace the channel linkage via a network of tracks and significant towns to arrive at the Cooper's birthplace.

You will begin the journey at **Longreach** – a larger regional centre that draws visitors by blacktop to the **Stockman's Hall of Fame** and other attractions. Leave town via the main **Windorah Road**, crossing **Elibank Creek**, but turning right onto the **Longreach – Tocal Road**.

The narrow bitumen finishes at a signpost declaring "Boggy when Wet" – a fact that appears quite evident given the dirt base, and prominent ruts dug by previous travellers. (It should be noted that travel on unsealed roads is not permitted in wet weather, even if there are no Road Closed signs erected – stay tuned to local radio stations for advice).

Brolgas and wild horses roam the station country out here, along side Santa Gertrudes cattle at **Strathmore Stud**. The remains of old telegraph posts – some still with insulators – can be seen standing, or more commonly lying, by the trackside as a reminder of the early pastoral days, when communications were not taken for granted as today.

The **Ernestine Hotel** stood here, halfway between Longreach and **Arrilalah**. The long running lease operated successfully for many years under the supervision of T. Pennington. Today just a pile of rubble marks the site that was so important as a rest stop for travellers.

Arrilalah also lies in ruin further down the river, 52 kilometres from Longreach. Once mooted as a possible rail terminus, Forest Grove as it was originally known, sprang from nowhere in the late 1870s. Three hotels defined the town's growing size, although only one survived until the second world war.

You can wander around the township site, looking at an enormous quantity of broken bottles and old cans. Tractor parts, tanks and even the remains of a steel hulled river boat are the limit of what can be seen at this site – a site that once forged the dreams of so many people.

Benares Station, then **Roseabel Station** mark travel further south, as treeless

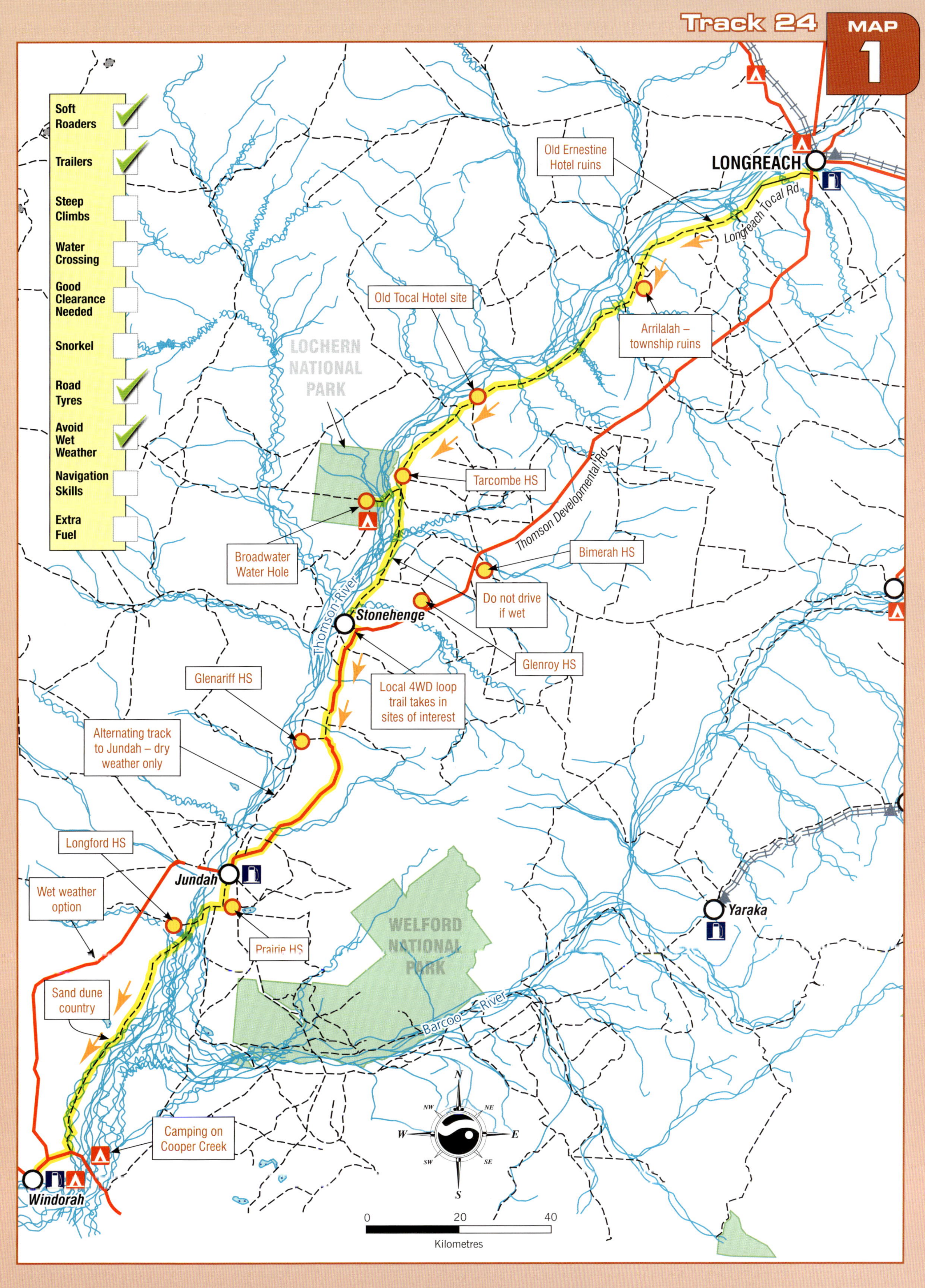
Soft Roaders
Trailers
Steep Climbs
Water Crossing
Good Clearance Needed
Snorkel
Road Tyres
Avoid Wet Weather
Navigation Skills
Extra Fuel
LONGREACH
Old Ernestine Hotel ruins
Longreach Tocal Rd
Old Tocal Hotel site
Arrilalah – township ruins
LOCHERN NATIONAL PARK
Tarcombe HS
Thomson Developmental Rd
Broadwater Water Hole
Bimerah HS
Do not drive if wet
Thomson River
Stonehenge
Glenroy HS
Glenariff HS
Local 4WD loop trail takes in sites of interest
Alternating track to Jundah – dry weather only
Longford HS
Jundah
Wet weather option
Prairie HS
WELFORD NATIONAL PARK
Yaraka
Sand dune country
Barcoo River
Camping on Cooper Creek
Windorah
0
20
40
Kilometres

Above: *Thomson River*

Right: *Prairie Station*

pasture and some native tobacco plants herald your arrival at **Tocal**, about 98 kilometres from Longreach. Another old hotel stood here from the late 1800s as a Cobb and Co mail exchange, although little remains as it burnt to the ground more than 50 years ago. Today, scattered tins and broken bottles are the only clues as to its existence.

You will turn right toward **Lochern NP**, about 23 kilometres from Tocal, at **Tarcombe HS**. A concrete bridge spans the **Thomson** at Lochern National Park, where a former grazing property was taken over by Queensland's then Department of Environment and Resource Management. The 24 600 hectares of mitchell grass and mulga fronts a 20 kilometre section of the Thomson.

Excellent camping is possible at **Broadwater Waterhole**, where secluded sites can be found on the riverbank. Yellowbelly, Barcoo Grunter and Spangled Perch can be caught from the waterhole on baited hooks (no nets are permitted on the river system). Dawn and dusk are usually the most productive times, when the coolibahs and bauhinias also glow gold in the low sunlight.

Camping is possible at the old shearer's quarters located near the park's office. Bunkhouse accommodation can be arranged, although it is necessary to book ahead for this. Birdlife is abundant at Lochern, while mulga snakes and the impressive yellow spotted monitor head the reptile list.

Return to the main **Tocal Road**, then continue south to **Stonehenge** following slower tracks through a series of floodways and braided channels. This 32 kilometre section should not be attempted if it is wet – instead head east to the **Thomson Developmental Road**, then turn south west through **Bimerah** and **Glenroy HS**.

Lochern National Park

Either way you will reach the curious township of Stonehenge. This small town gazetted in 1887 offers camping in the main street for a modest fee per vehicle, which includes solar showers, wood fired B.B.Q.s and power if necessary. The **Stonehenge Hotel** is sited just across the road, with rooms available for those so inclined.

A nine kilometre tourist drive (signposted "High Clearance Vehicles Only") takes visitors on a rocky amble to several viewpoints and sites of interest. White arrows have been painted on the track at useful points, keeping travellers to a defined path.

Sealed road continues south to **Jundah**, with the possible option of turning right to **Glenariff**, after a crossing of **Deep Creek**. The latter variation closely follows the Thomson past an elevated homestead and sandy floodways. This track follows an original stockroute into the larger town of Jundah; first settled by the Archer brothers in 1872 following a lengthy cattle drive from Warnambool in Victoria.

The main **Jundah – Windorah Road** crosses the Thomson River channels west of town following a sealed all weather route. If conditions are dry, a more scenic option follows the Thomson to an expanding channel network around **Prairie Station**. Leave town via an unmarked road to the south, crossing a grid then passing the airstrip.

You will cross a causeway on the Thomson, where fenceline posts strain against the river's flow – with twisted and tangled debris an obvious reminder of the potential surges. Turn south off the Thomson Development Road at Jundah, to follow the broadening channel system around Prairie.

Beyond **Longford**, a treeless plain extends with yellow wildflowers growing to the horizon. Then suddenly sand dunes appear out of nowhere, and fields of white ground cover grow so thick that they appear as snow. The **Cooper** is born somewhere on station country several kilometres to your left, but you won't see the coolibah lined waters until reaching the Diamantina Development Road near **Windorah**.

A single lane concrete bridge spans this silted waterway at its primary branch. Bush camping is popular here with toilets provided, and a choice of shady river bank sites or sandy beach locations. If water is flowing at the time of your visit, the resident pelicans will be lined up across a rocky bar, lying in wait for unsuspecting fish to jump the spillway.

This really is exceptional country here – the peaceful nature of the Cooper is illustrated by the prolific birdlife and the lazy flow of the life giving water through mulga and mitchell grass country. Travellers can restock supplies at Windorah, just a 12 kilometre drive away.

As one of the larger Channel Country town's, Windorah sits on the cross roads of the Diamantina and Thomson Developmental Roads – each now sealed to **Quilpie** and **Longreach**, but large tracts of dirt, gibber and sand still pave the way to **Bedourie** and **Birdsville** in the west.

Stonehenge Hotel

TRACK 25

The Barcoo

Channel Country

Track Snapshot

TOUR ROUTE:
Windorah to Blackall via the Barcoo River and Idalia NP.

DURATION AND DISTANCE:
This trek will require at least two or three days and 500 kilometres (more if you take the Isisford option).

TRACK DETAILS:
Most of this tour follows dirt station tracks and is suitable for all vehicles and trailers. There are some rougher tracks within Welford and Idalia that are optional and will require good clearances.

WHEN TO GO:
Head for this region between April and October, avoiding wet weather at any time of the year as the black soil becomes impassable. Winter nights can be cold.

CAMPING:
Welford, Idalia and the Cooper Creek at Windorah have bush camping with basic facilities, and there is a commercial caravan park in Blackall.

FUEL AND SUPPLIES:
Windorah, Blackall, Isisford are the major centres, with fuel available at Yaraka.

MAPS:
Hema: NW (most of trek), Outback Queensland, Sunmap: Outback Queensland.

OTHER INFORMATION:
Few visitors take the time to visit Idalia – if time permits make the drive; you will not be disappointed.

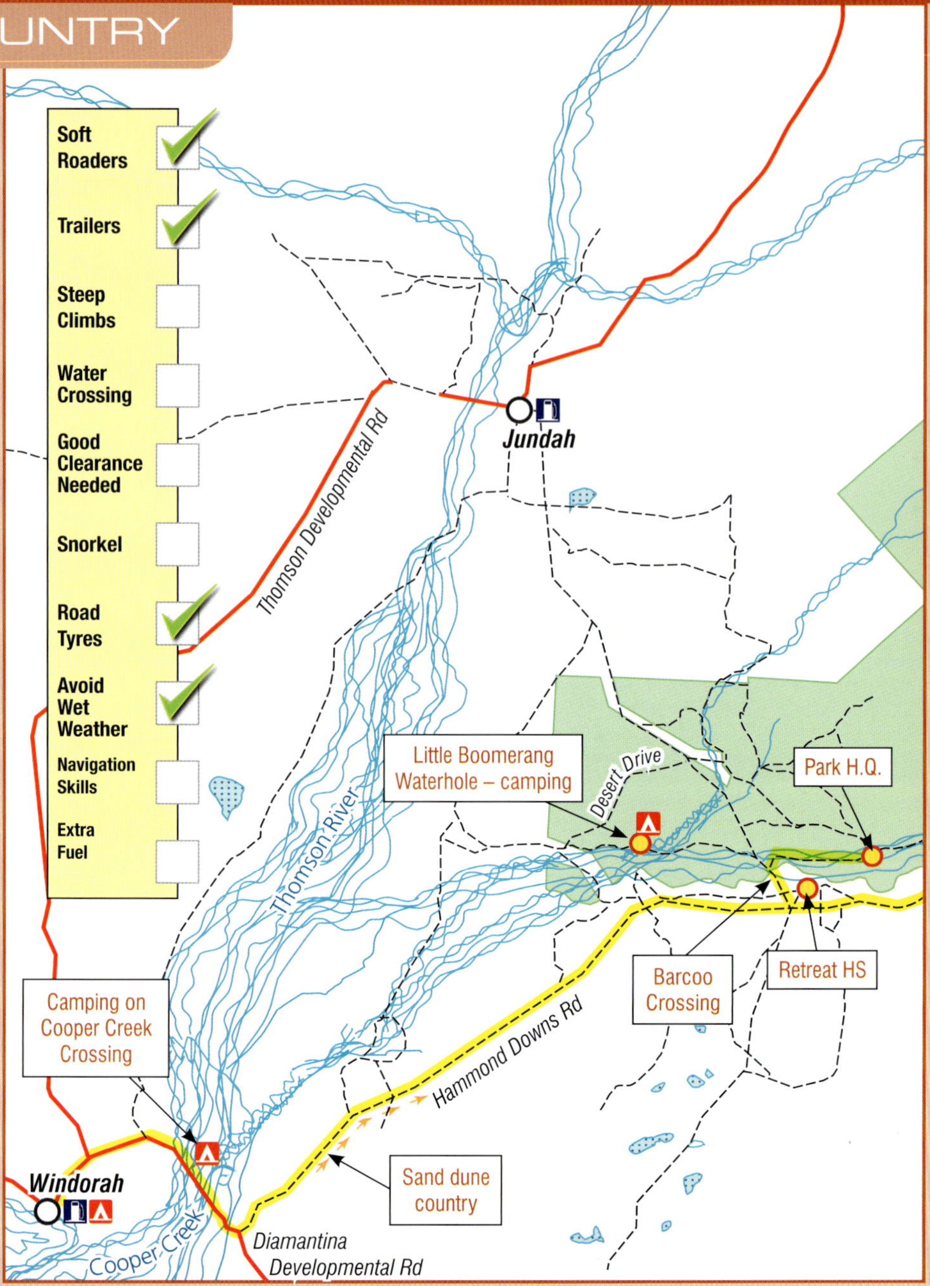

Rating	
Soft Roaders	✓
Trailers	✓
Steep Climbs	
Water Crossing	
Good Clearance Needed	
Snorkel	
Road Tyres	✓
Avoid Wet Weather	✓
Navigation Skills	
Extra Fuel	

*The drive from **Windorah** to **Blackall** via **Welford** and **Idalia** is without doubt one of the highlights in **Queensland's channel country.** You will stop at superb waterholes on the **Barcoo River,** visit a couple of small outback communities, and find some amazing landscapes in the **Gowan Range.***

Leave Windorah via the **Diamantina Development Road** in the direction of **Quilpie**, crossing the **Cooper** on a concrete bridge, adjacent to the popular bush camping site. If the weather has been dry, turn left 22 kilometres out of **Windorah** on the signposted "**Hammond Downs**" road. You will follow a rutted dirt station track to the Barcoo River and a series of floodplains. The journey takes in arid grazing country and noticeably red sand dunes before coolibahs and a shimmering mirage indicate the **Barcoo**.

You will cross the river at **Retreat Station**, some 80 kilometres from Windorah, before entering **Welford National Park** and a choice of camping areas. No camping is permitted on Retreat Station at the Barcoo crossing, even though its sandy beaches and rocky outcrops look quite appealing. **Little Boomerang Waterhole** is located at the western edge of the national park and offers riverside camping on a sweeping bend. Fees are payable within the park, but the peace and quiet is priceless.

Welford was established as a grazing property in 1882, and is now managed by Queensland's Department of Environment and Science. The original rammed earth homestead, together with a shearing shed and stockyards are visible, but not accessible, to the travelling public. Other evidence of the pastoral history including tanks, wells and fencelines are scattered across the national park.

Two designated 4WD trails allow access through different environments within Welford. The **Desert Drive** meanders through wind blown sand dunes, with spinifex and acacia woodlands breaking the journey. **Mulga Drive** passes by **Old Gum Bore**, then finishes at a waterhole on **Sawyers Creek**.

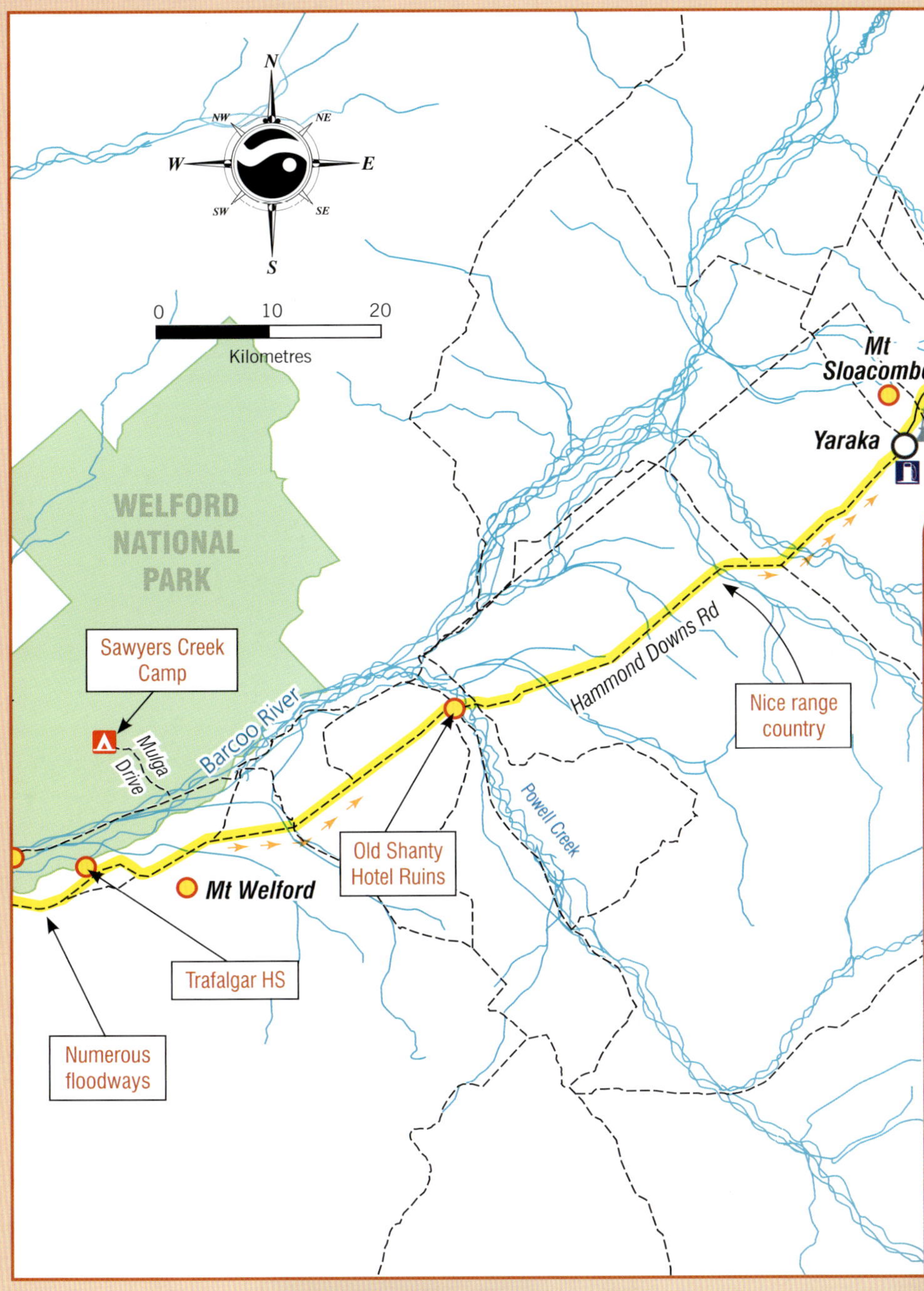

N
NE
E
SE
S
SW
W
NW
0 10 20
Kilometres
to Isisford
Emmet
Numerous floodways
Mt Sloacombe
Yaraka
WELFORD NATIONAL PARK
Sawyers Creek Camp
Mulga Drive
Barcoo River
Hammond Downs Rd
Nice range country
Powell Creek
Old Shanty Hotel Ruins
Mt Welford
Trafalgar HS
Numerous floodways

Above: *Cooper Creek, Windorah*

Left: *Yaraka Hotel*

Redgums line the waterway here, with reeds defining the particularly clear water. Crumbling red rock throws vivid reflections into the pool, which is usually deserted, and certainly one of the highlights of the Barcoo System.

Return to the main **Blackall Road,** crossing the Barcoo and turning east onto the reasonably robust gravel road (although it is worth noting that the black soil surface beyond **Emmet** gets very slippery following just a little rain).

A number of causeways mark travel past **Trafalgar HS** and prominent **Mount Welford** on the right. **Jebburgh** and **Sedan HS** are passed before you reach

Rainbow Gorge

Idalia National Park

an old shanty pub lying in ruins on **Powell Creek**. A single lane bridge spans the waterway, some 130 kilometres from Windorah.

Stockyards and dam at **Wandsworth Station** precede some nice range country views over the next 40 kilometres. The **Yang Yang Range** features prominently as you reach **Yaraka** at a tee intersection. A clutch of 20 or so houses, together with fuel, store and pub make up the township, whose main claim to fame seems to be that it marks the end of the **Rockhampton** rail line.

Leave town passing the station track option to **Isisford** on your left, and the **Mount Sloacombe Lookout** track, also on the left. Numerous floodways punctuate the 52 kilometre run from Yaraka to a tee intersection at Emmett.

The left turn takes you into **Isisford**, about 50 kilometres to the north, and located right on the **Barcoo River**. A large camping area just out of town at the Barcoo Crossing offers bush camping for a very modest fee, and consequently attracts large numbers of visitors. Toilet facilities are provided not far from the informal camping sites.

Isisford dates back to the 1870s when the town's first hotel, the **Teddington Arms**, provided refreshments to local graziers. Today, **Clancy's Overflow Hotel** offers similar hospitality in a setting where little has changed over the years.

If you have time to make a side trip to Isisford it is well worthwhile, otherwise turn right to the old rail siding of Emmett. There are a couple of prominent buildings here together with a collection of old steam driven apparatus and farm equipment.

Take the signposted "**Blackall Road**" out of Emmett through **Springleigh Station** to **Thornleigh Creek**, some 44 kilometres from Emmett. Turn right after the creek, just before a set of yards, along the signposted "**Idalia Road**".

This is a one way in and out station track that services a number of properties. Follow the main track past a few turnoffs for 33 kilometres to the border of national park. A 40 kph zone applies to vehicles within the NP as you reach the ranger's residence and airstrip (both on the left – so keep straight at the junctions).

The ruins of **Old Idalia** are found on the right, 18 kilometres into the NP (this park was established following the surrender of pioneering grazing country). A short drive takes you to a set of stockyards and old slab hut ruins. From here follow a 600 metre walk through stunning box and silver leaved ironbark woodland to **Wave Rock**.

Idalia's campground is found 10 kilometres further into the park from Old Idalia. A number of sites are clustered around a dam with basic facilities, but no views from within the forested area.

Idalia's wildlife includes echidnas and possums, together with rare bat species and the endangered yellow footed rock wallaby.

Continuing north from the camp you reach **Rainbow Gorge** – a beautiful creek that descends through gnarly trees and colourful boulders. It is a short unmarked walk from the vehicle track to a water pool 200 metres downstream.

Beyond the gorge you will pass a couple of tracks on the right, with **Bullock Gorge** being a rewarding option. You will need to negotiate some rocky steps in the vehicle, before reaching a tee intersection 13 kilometres from camp. Turn left to a carpark, and follow a relatively flat 2.7 kilometre walk trail through a treed area coloured with yellow foliage. There are a couple of lookout points on the loop walk, with views extending over the **Gowan Range** and beyond.

There are many other possibilities for walks and nature study within Idalia, and those with time to spare will certainly be satisfied. On leaving it is necessary to retrace your way in, returning to the **Windorah – Blackall Road**.

Turn right toward **Blackall**, following sealed road for a further 26 kilometres, before blacktop continues to a tee intersection on the **Blackall – Isisford Road**. Turn right here over a series of floodways (and the more significant

Isisford
Barcoo River
Popular camping on Barcoo River
Thornleigh Creek
Ravensbourne Creek
Blackall
Side trip to Isisford
Benalla HS
Blackall – Emmet Rd
Idalia Rd
Emmet
Bullock Gorge Walks
Emmet Pocket Walks
Rocky steps in track
Rainbow Gorge
Old Idalia HS and Wave Rock
Monk Tank Camp
Ranger Residence
N NE E SE S SW W NW
0 10 20
Kilometres

Soft Roaders	✓
Trailers	✓
Steep Climbs	
Water Crossing	
Good Clearance Needed	
Snorkel	
Road Tyres	✓
Avoid Wet Weather	✓
Navigation Skills	
Extra Fuel	

Right: *Barcoo River*

Ravensbourne Creek) for a routine drive into Blackall.

It is worth stopping at this town for a day or two to absorb its history and other attractions. Local gun shearer Jack Howe clipped 321 sheep with blade shears in a day here back in 1892 – a feat left unchallenged for nearly 60 years, and only bettered then by belt powered shears! Blackall was also the first Australian town to sink an artesian bore in 1885, and the **Aquatic Centre** maintains this link today with a heated spa bath available all year round.

Chapter 5
NORTH QUEENSLAND

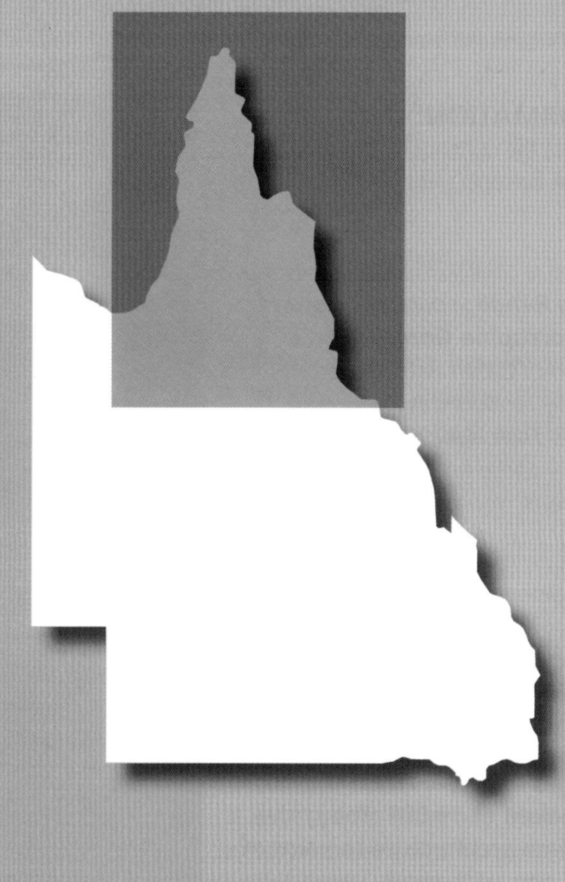

◀ *Fishing at Seisha*

LAWN HILL

The gravel road from Adels Grove to Lawn Hill Gorge weaves past prominent bluffs, some jutting out at a 45 degree angle, and capped with a treeline tracing the landscape profile. You enter a gap in the Constance Range, then continue to a carpark at Lawn Hill Creek.

From here walkers can take a stroll along the creek or head skyward on some scrambly tracks that culminate at expansive viewpoints. **The Island Stack Walk** for example offers good views over Lawn Hill Creek and its associated waterholes. Less energetic walkers could try the **Cascades Walk** – an interesting amble past calcium rich rock formations to natural spa pools.

Nearly all visitors will hire a canoe to explore the waterway system of Lawn Hill, taking in some superb waterfalls and stunning refections. Those who paddle their way to the upper gorge will be rewarded with a scenic network of pools and rivulets.

Vehicles exit the National Park via Adels Grove, passing a turn off to the currently working **Century Mine**. Some 15 kilometres from Adels, you will reach a tee intersection with most traffic turning right toward **Gregory Downs**. This is the quickest and easiest exit, but those looking to use the capabilities of their 4WD will enjoy the possibilities available via **Lawn Hill Station**.

Bowthorn Station

Tufa waterfall

Turn left at the tee intersection onto the "**Savannah Byway**", where a signpost recommends the use of high clearance vehicles. Navigation can be tricky along this route, but a series of **KFC** signs (no, not the roast chicken, but **King Fisher Camp**) help point the way.

Shoulder high monsoonal grassland ushers the journey to Lawn Hill Station, where a grid, cattleyards and ramp mark the outskirts. Turn right at the machinery shed to pass a stockyard and generator, then veer left through a gate and over a grid. Keep left through grassland, with the station's airstrip on your right.

Narrower tracks continue through another gate and over Lawn Hill Creek (can be deep). The track now opens up across Savannah country with lush grass, ghost gums and hibiscus flowers. **Musselbrook Creek** and its floodprone basin presents a major obstacle on the journey northwards, before you meet a tee intersection, some 64 kilometres from Lawn Hill Station.

Turn left at this junction and fight the Dry Season bulldust for 27 kilometres to **Bowthorn Station**. Lookout for birdlife on the journey as remnant waterholes remain viable in The Dry with lush green tussock grasses fringing lily topped lagoons. Black headed pythons are quite common throughout this country and you may spot one of these non-venomous (but quite intimidating) reptiles on the roadway.

The track heads northwards past Bowthorn HS along a rocky and uneven path. Some bypass tracks avoid areas of substantial erosion, so plan your route carefully. Orange grevilleas and yellow flowering shrubs lift the tone of the trek though, as you enter "**Gidgee Paddock**" before crossing the **Nicholson River**.

A series of channels zig-zag along the river, as you arrive at **King Fisher Camp** some 30 kilometres from Bowthorn HS. In fact the camp forms part of the 900 square mile spread of **Bowthorn Station**, where Brahman breeders number up to 5 000 beasts in a good year.

Mustering normally takes place twice per year, but travellers are kept away from most station activities. Fishing is a popular past time at King Fisher Camp with good possibilities from the banks of the Nicholson River. Even non-anglers will enjoy pleasant walks and plentiful wildlife. Camping offers basic facilities, and a remote escape from the busier Savannah Way venues.

It is a seven kilometre drive northward from King Fisher Camp to a tee intersection, and the better road to **Doomadgee**. You will pound the gravel for 33 kilometres, before reaching a tee intersection on the wider **Savannah Way**. From here it is 51 kilometres west to **Hells Gate**, or alternatively 126 kilometres east to **Burketown**.

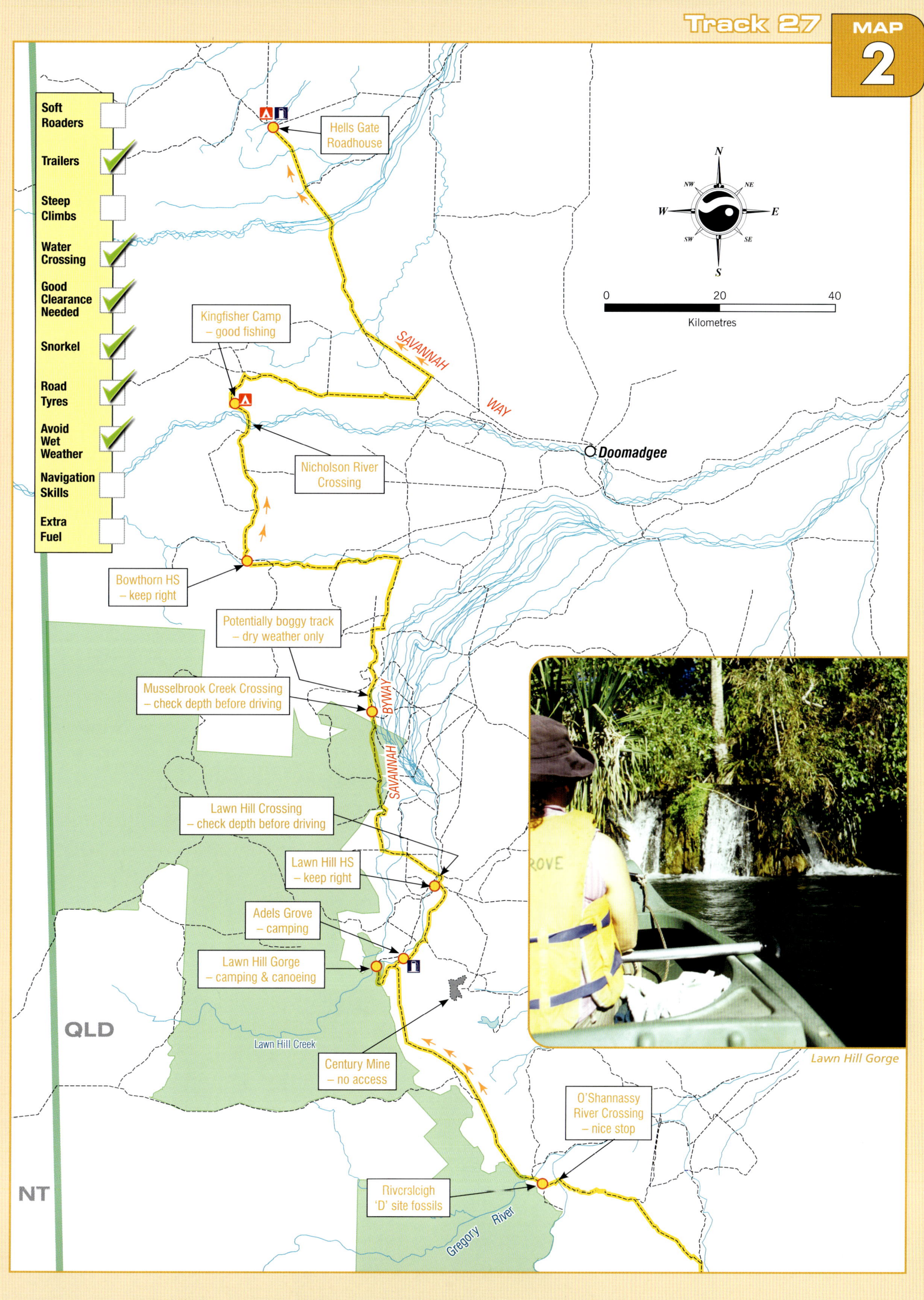

Lawn Hill Gorge

TRACK 28

LAKEFIELD

NORTH QUEENSLAND

Track Snapshot

TOUR ROUTE:

Cooktown to Coen via Rinyirru (Lakefield) NP

DURATION AND DISTANCE:

Allow at least five days for the 400 kilometre run.

TRACK DETAILS:

These sandy and dirt tracks are regularly flooded and can be difficult when first opened. Trailers can be taken with care, but not Soft Roaders, as good clearances and low range will be required for some water crossings.

WHEN TO GO:

May to October is the usual dry season, but rivers can be a problem early in the season and humidity later in the year.

CAMPING:

Bush camps are located throughout Lakefield NP in designated areas, with private parks available at Cooktown, Endeavour River and Musgrave Roadhouse. National Park camping must be booked online www.qld.gov.au/camping or by phone on 13 7468. 'Touch Screen' booking stations are located at Cooktown, Coen and Rinyirru (Lakefield) NP ranger sation.

FUEL AND SUPPLIES:

Cooktown and Coen are the major centres with fuel and basic needs obtainable at Musgrave Roadhouse.

MAPS:

Hema: Cape York.

OTHER INFORMATION:

Mosquitoes and sand flies can be a problem, but more than compensated for by the amazing scenery and fishing opportunities. Don't turn back at Coen – the trip ahead is a beauty!

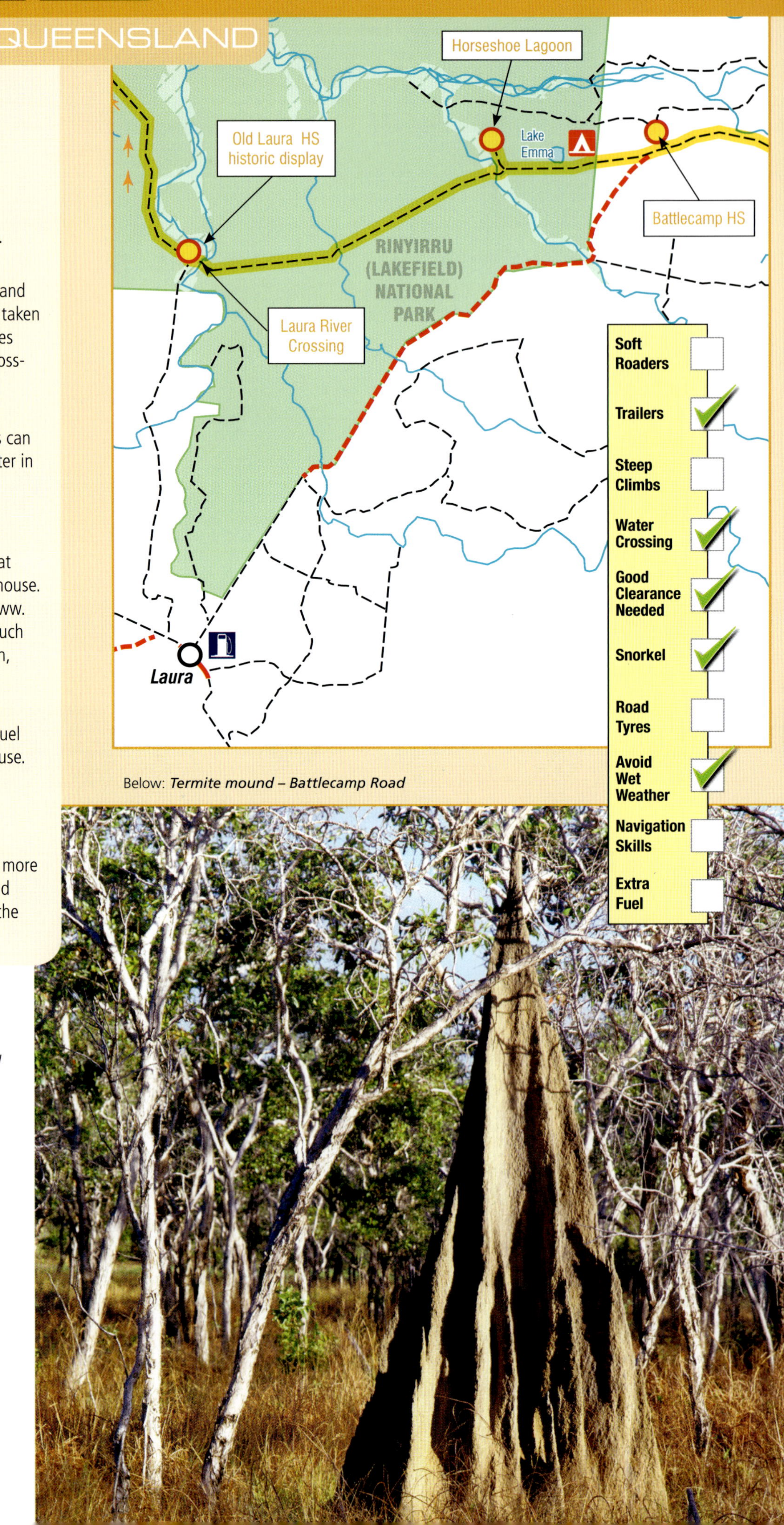

Below: *Termite mound – Battlecamp Road*

Iconic ***Cape York*** *would have to rate as one of the most dreamed about 4WD destinations in this country. The most northern reaches of the Australian mainland conjure up images of tropical rainforest, productive fishing, and relaxed carefree days far removed from the city's hustle and bustle.*

In addition, the 4WD challenges dished out on The Cape appear thick and fast, as travellers cross pristine creeks, slither under a canopy of verdant jungle where sunlight comes in as runner up, and vehicles reach some of the best campsites in Queensland.

Visitors to ***Cape York Peninsula*** *require robust and well equipped vehicles, together with appropriate experience, but the rewards are well worth the effort. The Cape can be tackled by lesser vehicles (even*

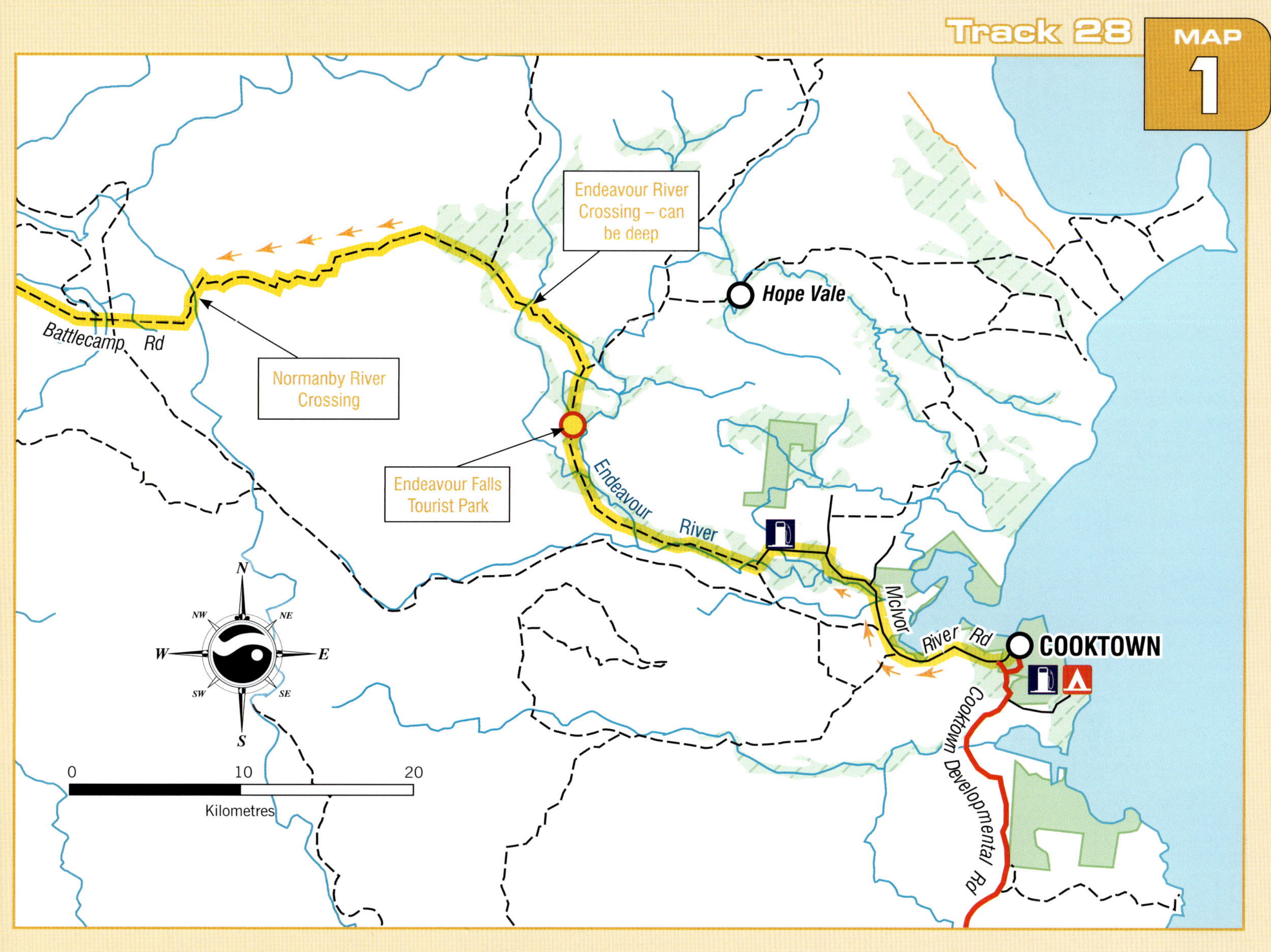

bicycles are routinely seen) though groups of well prepared 4WDs will be better able to reach destinations that typify the remote frontier country of far north Queensland.

This first stage of our tour into Cape York will suit most capable 4WD vehicles and reasonably confident drivers, and may whet your appetite for our more challenging tour ***(The Telegraph Track)*** *that follows on. Alternatively, travellers who complete this trek but don't wish to tackle anything harder, can still visit The Tip via the* ***Telegraph*** *and* ***Bamaga*** *Roads.*

We begin this tour in **Cooktown**, as there are two distinctly different options for arriving at this point from **Cairns**. You may choose the longer distance, but shorter driving time route via **Mareeba** and the **Mulligan Highway**, or follow the coast through **Mossman** and the **Daintree National Park**.

The former choice follows bitumen all of the way making it a reliable route in wet weather as you climb onto the **Atherton Tablelands**, then head north through historic mining towns. A series of roadhouses mark the route, which weaves through savannah country and cattle stations.

Those following the coastline will also enjoy bitumen to **Cape Tribulation** – albeit narrow and winding, and with a barge to ferry you across the **Daintree River**. The scenery is superb however, with lookouts offering great views over the **Coral Sea** as you invade coast hugging rainforest.

The unsealed **Bloomfield Track** heads north from Cape Tribulation crossing numerous creeks and following steeply undulating country (take care if the surface is still moist). You cross the **Bloomfield River** via a concrete causeway, then head inland to meet up with the **Cooktown Development Road**, arriving in **Cooktown** shortly after.

Cooktown itself is a pleasant stop with numerous colonial buildings marking its early European heritage; a settlement that dates from 1873 when gold was discovered inland from here. However this town's claim to fame occurred more than a century earlier, when Captain James Cook sailed into its sheltered river mouth here for urgent ship repairs.

These days you will find all of the trappings of tourism available, and the town is a good place to top up on supplies before heading further up The Cape. **McIvor River Road** leads the way out of town, on the south side, as you follow the **Endeavour River** past mangrove flats and feeder creeks.

Blacktop paves the way past the airport, and over a bridge spanning the Endeavour River, to unsealed road and the usual corrugations. **Scrubby** and **McLeod Creeks** are breached as you reach the **Endeavour Falls Tourist Park** on your right, about 33 kilometres from Cooktown.

Keep left four kilometres later (right turn leads to Hopevale Aboriginal Community), and follow signposted "**Battlecamp**" to a crossing of the Endeavour River's east branch about six kilometres after the intersection. This ford can be deep early in The Dry so

LAKEFIELD

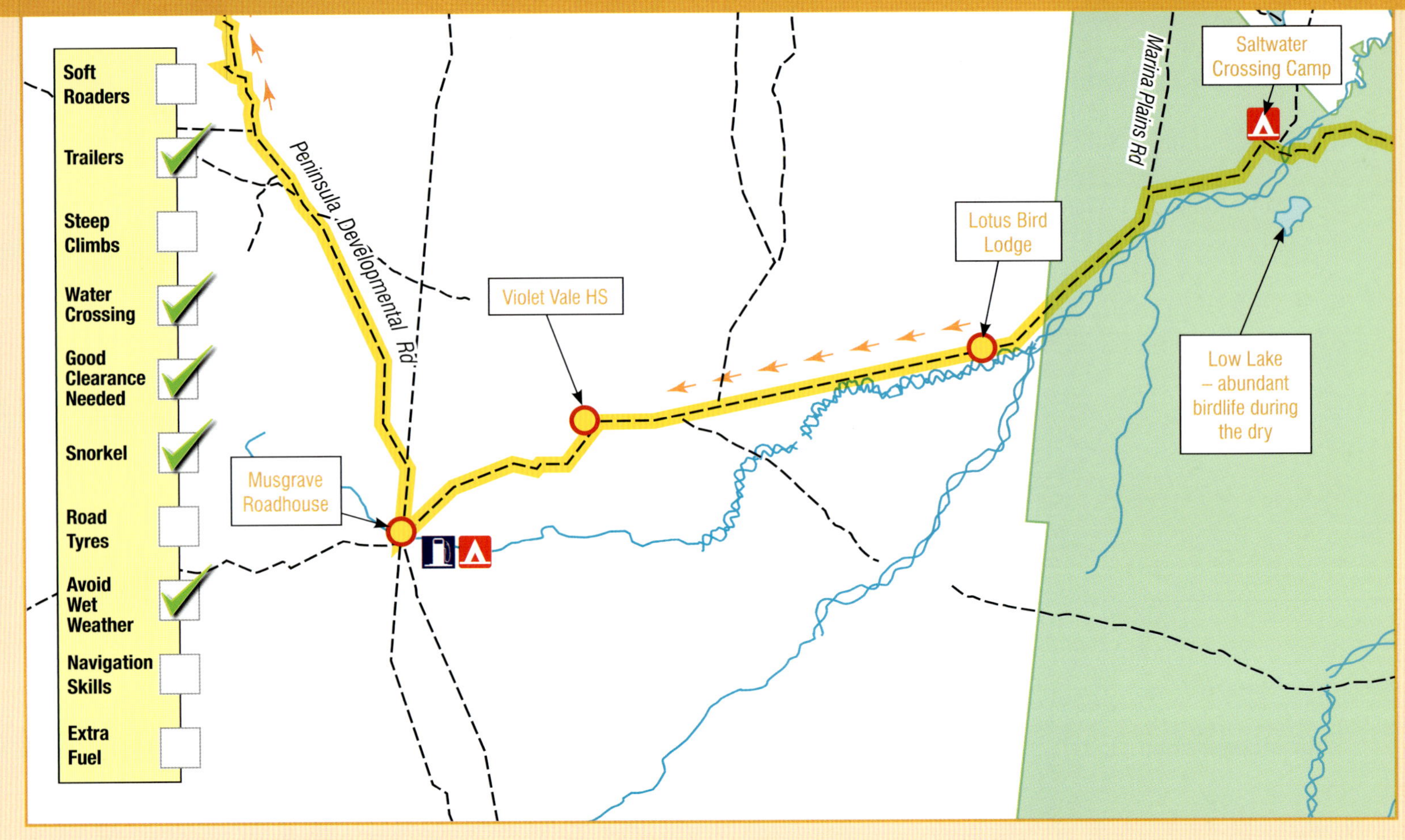

check its depth if unsure. A scenic falls tumbles over rocks downstream of the crossing, and would make a good rest stop if time permits.

Follow the main dirt road west through grazing country as a pocket of rainforest flags an opening in the approaching range on **Battlecamp Road**. This section of road was opened up during the 1870s to provide access from Cooktown to the **Palmer River Goldfields**. An unfortunate incident in 1873 gave rise to the "Battlecamp" name, when a large group of Aboriginals clashed with some travelling miners, leading to the loss of many lives.

The **Melsonby Station HS** turn off is passed on your right some 20 kilometres beyond the falls, with the **Normanby River** reached two kilometres later. This crossing is usually dry, so stay on the main road, avoiding any side tracks as you pass Battlecamp HS. Leave any gates as found while you enjoy a view of the rising Battlecamp Range to the south.

You will enter **Rinyirru National Park (Lakefield)** about three kilometres beyond Battlecamp HS and find an information shelter together with camping self registration details. It is necessary to register here if you plan to camp prior to the ranger's station located at **New Laura**, some 50 kilometres away.

Lakefield National Park encompasses some 537 000 hectares of grassland, rivers and estuarine habitat, where native wildlife abounds. The region is basically inaccessible in The Wet, but dries quickly leaving remnant waterholes and some excellent fishing opportunities.

The **Lake Emma** turn off is reached three kilometres into the national park and may be accessible by vehicle depending on seasonal flooding. Receding waters are variable in their timing so obtain local advice if heading into Lakefield early in The Dry. This is especially important in this south eastern section where drainage is poor.

If the entry track is open, Lake Emma offers bush camping typical of the national park, with no facilities (there are toilets at only two camping areas across Lakefield), and nice water hole access. Nearby **Horseshoe Lagoon** presents a lily topped billabong with plenty of birdlife and the likelihood of saltwater crocodiles; play it safe, don't swim or stand near the water's edge – appropriate behaviour right across the northern tropics unless you receive other advice from rangers or knowledgeable locals.

Follow **Battlecamp Road** for about 19 kilometres to a wide gravelly crossing of the Laura River. A lot of permanent water sits here and the fording can be deep, so take care. The **Old Laura HS** is reached just after the crossing, and makes a good stop to inspect this area's pioneering history.

Originally selected by two Irish immigrants in 1879, the homestead and grounds were improved over the years until the last occupants vacated the buildings in 1966. Hostile country made grazing a tedious occupation, although a succession of owners persevered – information boards detail the trials and tribulations faced by these hardy individuals as they worked to develop the land.

You will reach a tee intersection just beyond Old Laura, where you will

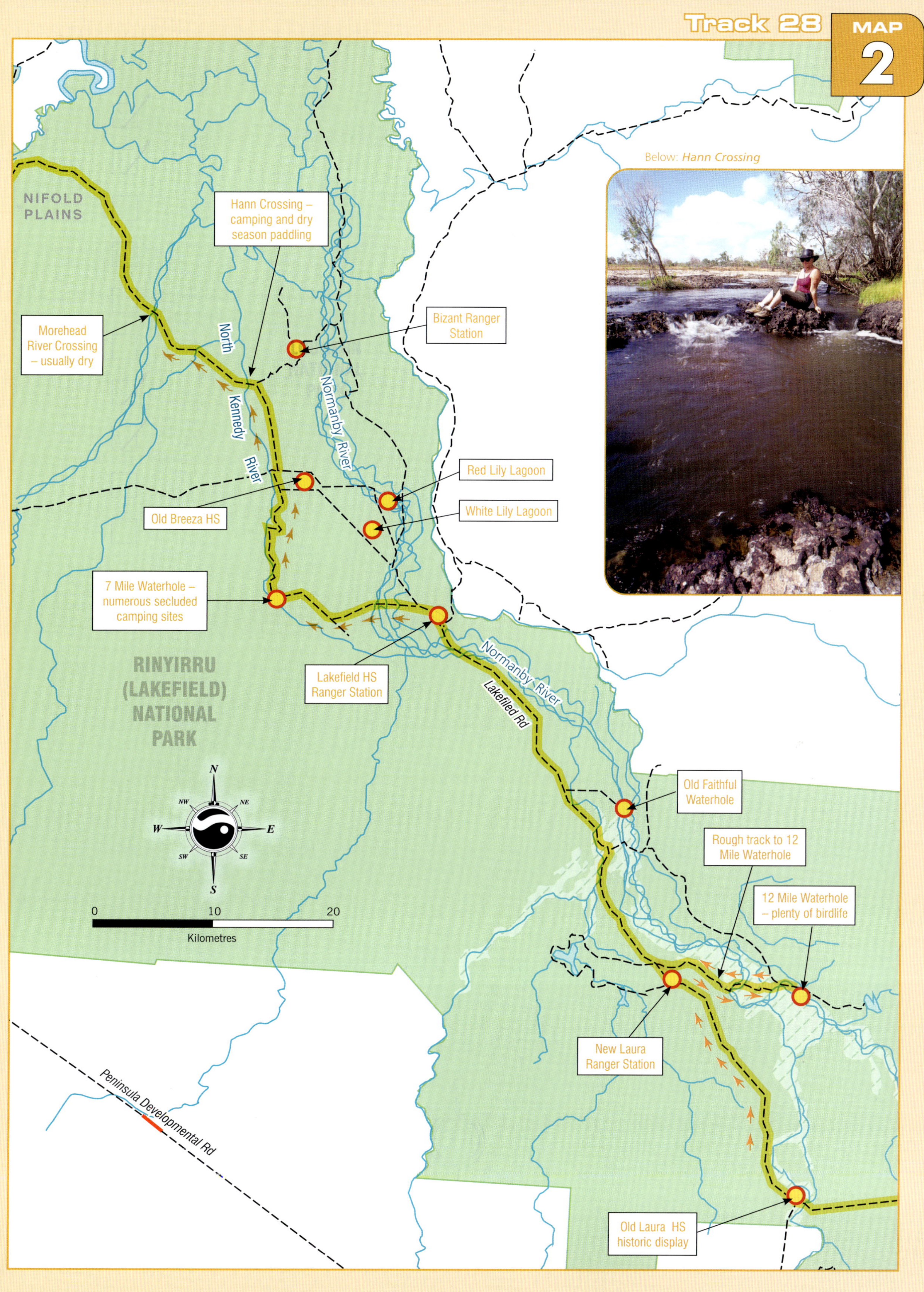

Below: *Hann Crossing*

turn right, away from the better road heading south to the **Laura** settlement.

Head north for eight kilometres along the **Lakefield Road**, passing the **Six Mile Waterhole** turn off (camping), then reach the **New Laura HS** (ranger's station) about 15 kilometres later on the left. A track leading to **12 Mile Waterhole** begins directly opposite the New Laura turn off, taking visitors on a rutted and adventurous journey to the confluence of the **Laura** and **Normanby Rivers**.

Birdlife is prolific here; you may spot brolgas, magpie geese, and ducks together with bustards and other grassland species. Cormorants and darters gravitate to the wetlands looking for food, but are most often seen drying their unoiled feathers in the sun after each session in the water.

Return from 12 Mile and head north again for 20 kilometres, passing the turn off to **Old Faithful Waterhole** (suitable for small boats). Five kilometres further on you will pass the turn off to **Mick Fienn Waterhole**, before pounding the baked clay and bulldust to **Lakefield HS** about 12 kilometres further on.

A ranger's station is located at the old homestead grounds, which also marks an intersection on the main road. You can continue straight ahead along the main road via **Red** and **White Lily Lagoons**, but a good alternative is found by heading west at the homestead junction, taking a loop along the **North Kennedy River**.

This 26 kilometre detour visits **Seven Mile Waterhole** and its numerous secluded camping sites. Most river bank sites are shaded, and barramundi is regularly taken from the lengthy waterhole. Small boats can be launched from some camps, although others are sited well above the waterline.

Follow the detour road to a tee intersection, and turn left onto the Lakefield Road at **Breeza** – an old homestead site marked by mature mango trees on the edge of a floodplain.

Cross open country for nine kilometres to an intersection on the **North Kennedy River**. Swing left here to pass some camping opportunities, then drop into low range for a pot holed causeway breaching the river. This is **Hann Crossing** and a superb place to cool off in the rapids, where shallow water and rock bars keep the salties away!

Musgrave Roadhouse

Camping is by self registration, although some numbered sites must be prebooked at Lakefield Ranger Station, such is the popularity of this location. Toilets are also provided here, and a defined walking track follows two feeder branches of the river on a seven kilometre circuit amble. A shorter walk takes you to **Boggy Creek** and its confluence with the North Kennedy, where tidal waters reach a small falls.

Continue heading in a north westerly direction before you negotiate the usually dry **Morehead River** at a rocky crossing. Smoother floodways etch the enormous **Nifold Plains**, with the **Princess Charlotte Bay** now only 15 kilometres away as the crow flies. Countless termite mounds stand across the landscape here, looking rather like tombstones within a borderless graveyard.

The turn off to **Low Lake** is reached 17 kilometres after the Morehead, and is a good spot to visit at the end of The Dry. With some other waterholes now dried up, this last freshwater reserve will attract birdlife in huge numbers. There is no camping at Low Lake, but nearby **Saltwater Crossing** offers some possibilities.

Marina Plains Road branches right about 10 kilometres from the Low Lake turn off. Keep left here and continue straight past **Sweetwater Lake** to the national park boundary, seven kilometres away.

Improving road paves the way past **Lotus Bird Lodge** on your left as you pass Violet Vale HS and reach the **Peninsula Development Road**, 36 kilometres beyond national park boundary. You will drive directly into **Musgrave Roadhouse** at the junction, to find fuel, basic food, accommodation and welcome hot showers.

Musgrave owes its origins to the **Overland Telegraph Line** which linked The Tip with Brisbane, allowing morse code transmissions from 1887. This homestead still stands much as as it did more than a century ago, when defence of the asset proved to be as important as its functionality.

Heading north from Musgrave will see you cross numerous floodways and creeks. The road is part sealed, but generally good with the usual corrugations, and occasional potholes when unsealed. You will pass a couple of tracks to either side; ignore these and keep heading straight, eventually reaching **Coen**, some 108 kilometres from Musgrave Roadhouse.

The township of Coen sits on a river of the same name and marks this tour's end. As one of the larger centres on The Cape it is a good place to stock up on supplies or see to any mechanical issues. Travellers can arrange accommodation in town or drop into the **Exchange Hotel** (commonly known as the Sexchange Hotel).

There is excellent bush camping on the Coen River three kilometres north of town at **The Bend**, with a pit toilet provided. You may stop here to consider your travel options – either head south back along the Peninsula Development Road, or push on north via the main road, or,as an entertaining option, follow our tour notes through the **Iron Range** and across the **Telegraph Track**.

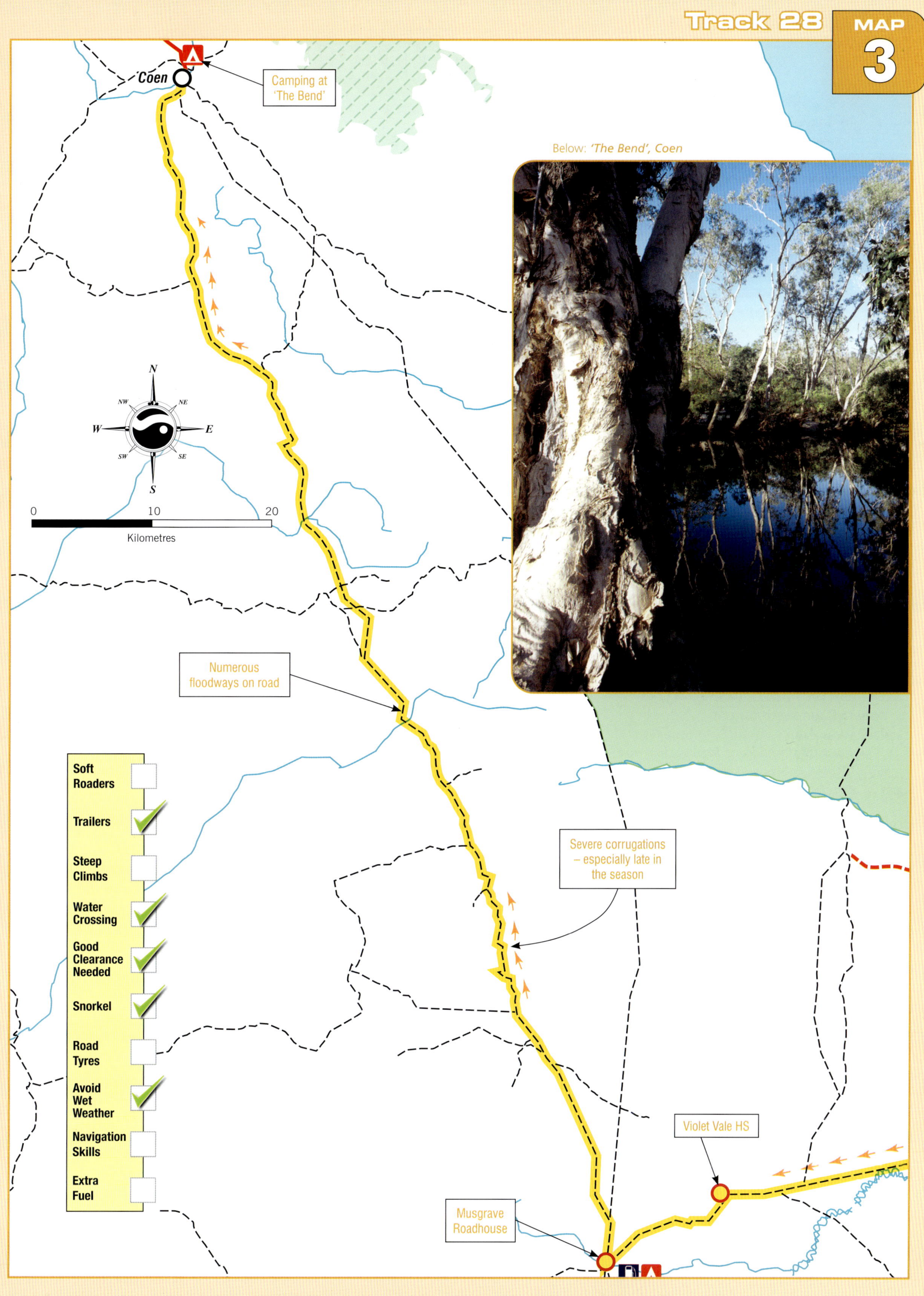

Below: *'The Bend', Coen*

TRACK 29

Telegraph Track

NORTH QUEENSLAND

Iron Range Creek

Track Snapshot

TOUR ROUTE:
Coen to The Tip via Iron Range and the Telegraph Track

DURATION AND DISTANCE:
Allow at least a week to enjoy all that this 460 kilometre trek will present.

TRACK DETAILS:
The Telegraph Track is a rough and rugged experience demanding experienced drivers and capable vehicles. Water crossings can be deep (up to a metre), with tricky entry and exits. The Iron Range track is usually wet and slippery. Soft Roaders are well out of their depth, and only very experienced travellers should contemplate towing a trailer.

WHEN TO GO:
May to October offers the best travel, with water crossings at their deepest early in the season.

CAMPING:
Superb bush camping at most river crossings along the Telegraph Track (as always take your rubbish out, and preferably any left by others) and at Chili Beach. Online booking www.qld.gov.au/camping or by phone on 13 7468. A number of 'touch screen' booking facilities are located across the peninsula. Commercial camps at Seisha and adjacent to the peninsula's roadhouses.

FUEL AND SUPPLIES:
Coen, Archer River, Bramwell Junction and Bamaga offer fuel and supplies. The Lockhart River Community is another option for those heading to Chili Beach.

MAPS:
Hema: Cape York.

OTHER INFORMATION:
A fee is payable for the Jardine River ferry, as it is impossible to cross this river by fording. All vehicles must have a raised air intake (snorkel) for this tour, and a winch may prove useful.

***Cape York's** northern half offers some real adventure for 4WDers with its action packed **Old Telegraph Track** and a wild detour to **Chili Beach**. This is low range travel at it best, but the excitement is not limited to vehicle gymnastics alone – you will reach some superb rainforest and find waterfalls that rank among this country's finest.*

This tour demands a serious vehicle with good clearances and a separate transfer case. Soft roaders are not suitable for the difficult terrain, and even full size vehicles will need an experienced hand at the wheel to keep them out of trouble.

*It is possible for less capable vehicles to reach the tip of Cape York via the **Telegraph** and **Bamaga Roads**, so given the choice of not going or following these roads, we would recommend undertaking the easier journey anyway. However those travellers looking for action packed touring will find it on this trek.*

We begin this tour at **Coen** (follow tour notes "**Lakefield**"), or simply follow the **Peninsula Development Road** from north of **Cairns**. As the major town on this section of The Cape, Coen is the best place to top up on supplies before heading northward.

Bitumen paves the way out of town as you cross a bridge over the **Coen River**, then reach a camping area at **The Bend**, two kilometres later. The Coen Airstrip marks the end of blacktop, and a quarantine check point that will prevent you from taking produce south on your return trip.

Once back on gravel, your route enters **Kulla NP**, then continues through **Oyala Thumotang NP**. You will then reach a track heading left toward the **Rokeby Ranger Station** (60 kilometres away with bush camping on the **Archer** and **Coen Rivers**). Ignore the turn off and follow some winding road through floodways on the Archer headwaters as rocky bushland flags your exit from national park.

You will reach the **Archer River Roadhouse** some 65 kilometres from Coen, and find a great spot to stop for the night with hot showers, bar facilities and the legendary Archer Burgers. An alternative bush site can be found at the **Archer Crossing** just beyond the roadhouse, although only pit toilets are provided here.

Camping is popular at both the roadhouse and crossing with some excellent possibilities on the Archer's tree lined sandy flats. Take care if you wish to drive along the river's edge as the sand is soft, and it will probably require a tyre pressure reduction for successful progress. Although salt water crocodiles do inhabit this river, the fast flowing rapids and shallow rock pools of the crossing are unlikely to attract these potentially dangerous reptiles in the dry.

Crossing the Archer by vehicle is easy in The Dry with a concrete causeway spanning the broad piece of water. You will reach a turn off to the right some 20

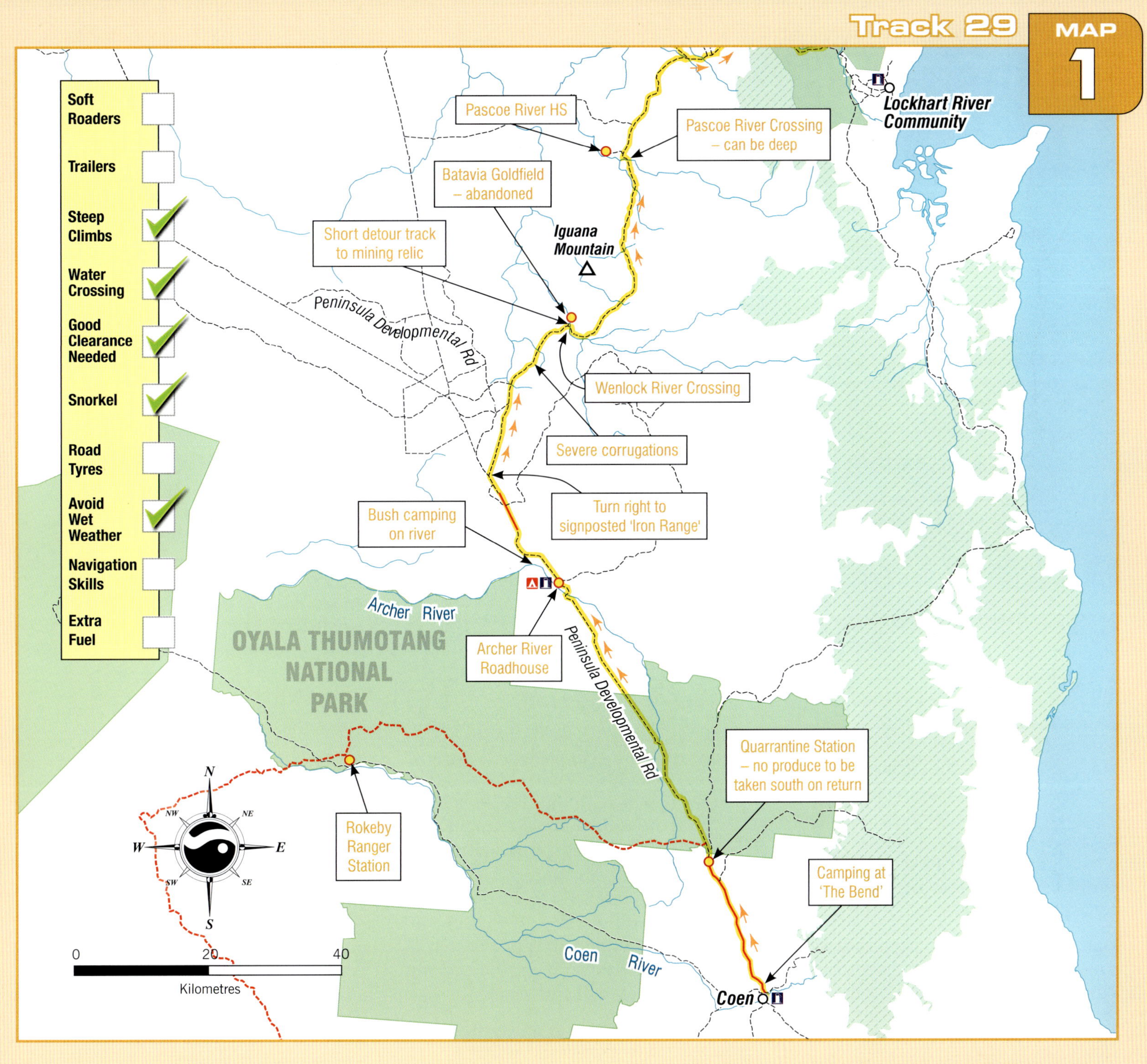

kilometres north of the Archer, where a signpost points to the **Iron Range** and **Lockhart River**. Those not wishing to undertake a detour via the Iron Range, can continue straight here, following the **Peninsula Development Road** onto the **Telegraph Road** and picking up these notes again at the **Frenchmans Track** junction, some 79 kilometres to the north.

The Iron Range leg is well worth undertaking however, so veer right at the junction and follow the main track, avoiding a couple of tracks on your left that lead back to the Peninsula Development Road. You will cross a couple of creeks on this narrow track that features sharp gutters and some extreme corrugations.

You will reach the **Wenlock River** some 26 kilometres into the track, where it may be necessary to slip into low range as you tackle the cut up entry and exits. Once across, a side track to the left will take you to the old **Batavia Goldfields**, where mining activity began in the 1890s.

The access track follows the river past an old headstone, before it deteriorates into a low range lurch. Relics and machinery are spread over an extensive site here, with steam engines and rusting trucks marking a reasonably productive mine, which continued intermittently for almost a century.

Beyond the Wenlock you will climb into the **Great Divide**, with **Iguana Mountain** and **Bare Rock** guiding your travel over some more creek crossings. The **Pascoe River** is reached 34 kilometres from the Wenlock, and it too throws a challenging crossing your way, although low range, slightly bagged tyres and radiator blind (if the water looks deep) are the ingredients for success.

TELEGRAPH TRACK

Left: *Frenchmans Track*

About five kilometres from the Pascoe you will reach a minor track on your left that leads to Pascoe HS. Ignore this turn and continue for another 14 kilometres to the next left turn, and note this location as it is easy to pass on the return journey. This is the turn off to **Frenchmans Track**, and it may be your chosen route out from the Iron Range – if its alternative crossing of the Pascoe is trafficable! You must check and get permission from Batavia Downs (ph 07 4060 3272) before using the track.

Veer right at this junction to ford a couple more creeks, with a deteriorating World War 2 bridge visible on the second crossing. This timber bridge dates from the 1940s when the defence forces were moving north across the country. Slippery exits are very possible on many creeks in this region as rainfall is a regular feature of the coastal forest, even during the Dry Season.

You will reach the boundary of **Kutini – Payamu National Park (Iron Range)**, with **Mount Tozer Lookout** taking in the adjacent Janet and Nelson Ranges. **Tozers Gap** marks a saddle in the hills as you ford a couple more paperbark lined creeks, then reach the **West Claudie River** some seven kilometres from Mount Tozer Lookout.

It is usually rutted and muddy on the descent to the **West Claudie**, and you will deal with a challenging exit (especially on the return journey), but stick to the ruts and try to keep some momentum on the climb out. A few camping opportunities can be found around the river area, although no facilities are provided here.

Continue along the main road to a bridge over the **Claudie River**, where you will reach a tee intersection on the eastern side. A right turn here will take you past the Rangers Station (arrange camping permits here), and onto the **Lockhart River Community**. Visitors can purchase food and fuel from the Community Store, but note that alcohol may not be carried into the township, there is no visitor camping, and cameras cannot be used in the precinct.

If you turn left at the bridge intersection you will make your way through a pocket of rainforest where eclectus parrots, palm cockatoos and cassowarys make their home. Several rainforest camping areas mark the next five kilometres with **Cooks Hut** being a possible site. The fenced off hut ruin was once home to a local prospector who built the rough dwelling here under a canopy of mango trees following the end of World War 2.

Gordon Creek Camp marks the last of the rainforest options as you weave through national park and occasional coastal views, before crossing **Chili Creek** (lots of brush turkeys around here). Two kilometres later you will reach a three way intersection, with the left fork heading to **Portland Roads**, and the right hand option going to **Chili Beach**.

Both options are dead end journeys, and both are worthwhile destinations. Those veering left to Portland Roads will drive for five kilometres to a sheltered mangrove flat, where prawn boats and smaller fishing craft are anchored. Portland Roads was once the site of a substantial military presence, built in preparation for a feared Japanese invasion. That outcome disappeared, and with it nearly all of the township. Today a few lucky locals call the tropical haven home, but note that camping is not permitted here.

You can camp at Chili Beach however, with informal sites located at the end of the rough nine kilometre access track. Toilets are provided, although drinking water should be brought in, and the prevailing winds are certainly more troublesome here than at Portland Roads.

Fortunately there is a great outlook from Chili Beach with an offshore island, together with smaller granite formations, and sweeping views across **Albatross Bay**. Coconut palms provide a relaxing backdrop, while clear freshwater creeks run across the sand into the **Pacific Ocean**.

The journey back from the Iron Range follows the same route as you took in, but with a challenging exit via **Frenchmans Track** if you feel confident, and you have permission from **Batavia Downs**. The turn off to Frenchmans is found 27 kilometres west of the Claudie bridge in open woodland.

Turn north at the junction to follow granite outcrops as the forest opens up to broader views of the surrounding ranges. Distinctive brown rock, giving rise to the Iron Ranges name, is seen across an enormous eroded area, as sandy soil with orange grevilleas herald a return to heathland.

You will negotiate some difficult rutted sections on this leg of the track, where erosion has opened up deep gullies. Traverse these obstacles with care, perhaps with the reassurance of a spotter in front of the vehicle, giving directions as you crawl along.

Narrow track descends to the **Pascoe River**, 10 kilometres beyond the main Iron Range intersection. This river is

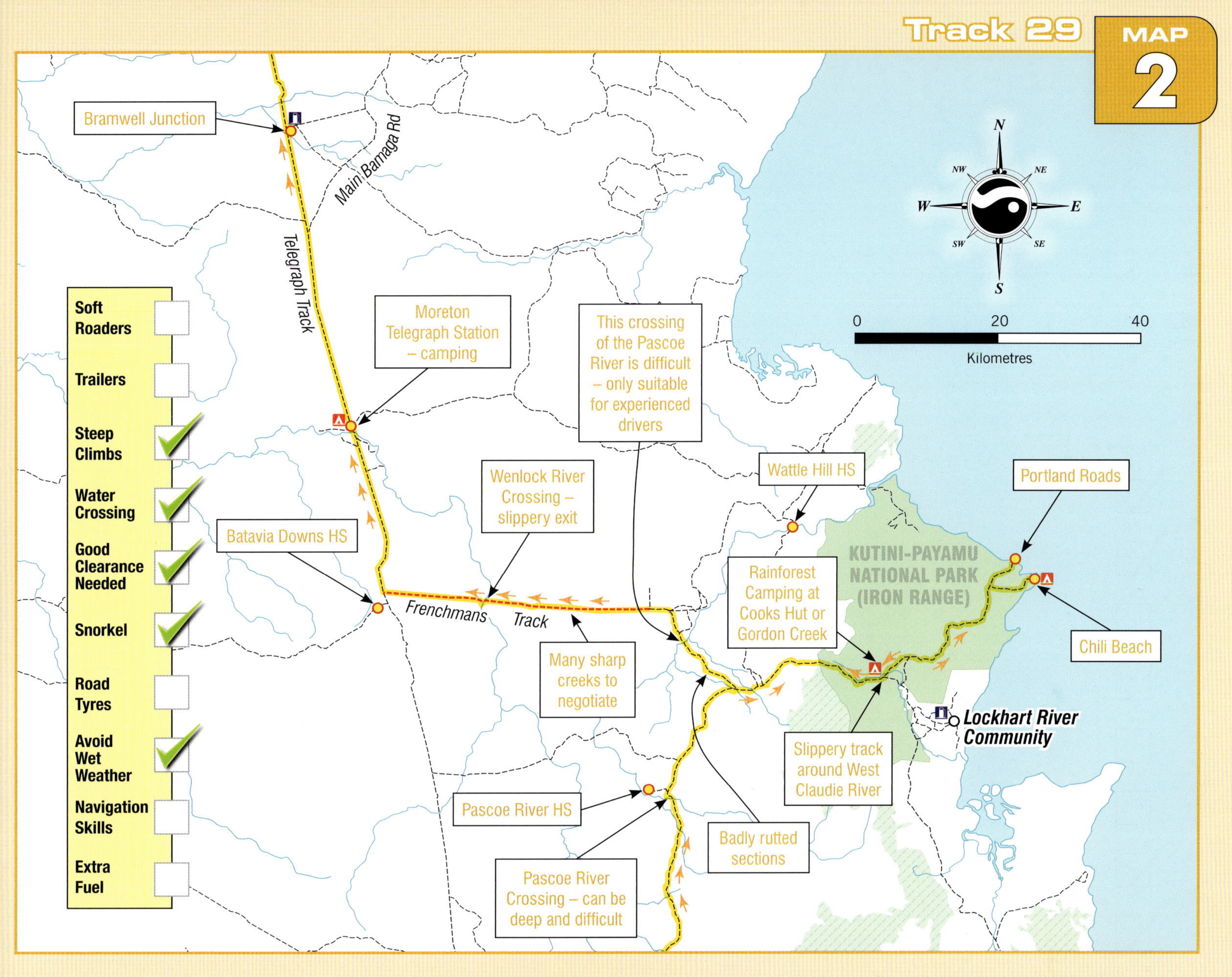

often deep (up to one metre, or possibly more) so obtain local advice before attempting the crossing, and fit a radiator blind or tarp across the front of the vehicle. Deep holes and potentially damaging rocks (especially on the exit) are also a feature of this notorious ford, so hold yourself back in the lowest gears (1st or 2nd low range) and follow a line that should be first checked on foot.

Once across, follow the main track for five kilometres to a tee intersection, where you will turn left away from **Wattle Hill HS**. Continue west through the **Wenlock** headwaters (some sharp creeks to negotiate) as you cut through grass tree forest. Numerous diversion tracks are a feature of the drive, as you avoid eroded and cut up obstacles.

You will reach the Wenlock crossing about 29 kilometres beyond the Pascoe, but find the sandy base of this much wider waterway to be relatively easy. Some vehicles may struggle up the slippery exit, before reaching a multi-track junction about one kilometre later. Keep right at this intersection and follow the main track to a tee junction on the **Telegraph Road**, some 12 kilometres later.

Turn right onto this more frequently used road and pound the gravel north to a bridge spanning the Wenlock. This civilised crossing links **Moreton Telegraph Station** on the northern bank, where camping and basic mechanical repairs are available, but fuel is not.

Head north from Moreton, passing the signposted turn off to **Bramwell Station HS**, and reach **Bramwell Junction** about 40 kilometres later. Top up your fuel at this rest area, and stop for the night if you need to, but note that some excellent bush camping possibilities are just around the corner.

The main **Bamaga Road** heads east at this junction (the quickest way to The Tip) but the **Old Telegraph Track** also heads north from here to **Bamaga**. This latter option crosses some pristine waterways and is easily the most scenic option – albeit at a slower pace. If you wish to travel the Telegraph Track as one leg of your trek to The Tip, we recommend that it be done in this northerly direction, as **Gunshot Creek** is then tackled as a descent, rather than as an intimidating winch assisted climb.

Veer left at Bramwell onto narrow track as you follow the **Overland Telegraph Line** (OTL) along its original route. This construction project took place in the 1880s, remaining a viable morse code line until 1964, and even served as a telephone link up until the 1980s. These days the line is dismantled, and although some poles and cross arms mark the route, most are bent over and have no insulators.

You will pass a few of these once vital relics enroute to the **Heathlands Reserve**. **Palm Creek** is found three kilometres into the track and is really the litmus test for travel further up the Telegraph Track. Its entry is steep and intimidating, while the exit could require a winch. Consider taking the Southern Bypass Road if this obstacle proves too difficult.

The **Dulcie River** follows up a few kilometres later with similar characteristics to Palm Creek although the water level is often bonnet high – use a tarp or radiator blind if you are not sure. **South** and **North Alice Creeks** are breached with few difficulties, before you arrive at the **Dulhunty River** about 29 kilometres from Bramwell Junction.

This is a superb river with sandy sections and some rock pools that dot the rapids area like natural spa baths. Shady trees provide some good camping possibilities on the southern banks of the river, although this crossing is very popular and no facilities are provided.

If you find this river too busy, **Bertie Creek** offers a good alternative just a kilometre further on. Drivers should take particular care at this fording, where rock shelves are a potential trap and usually hidden by the flowing water. It would probably pay to walk this crossing and identify the most suitable route across, perhaps by using a volunteer to stand in any of the deeper holes. You will continue beyond Bertie Creek for two kilometres, before reaching the **Gunshot Bypass**.

Telegraph Track

Most visitors avoid **Gunshot** and take this right turn, undertaking a loop drive through heathland reserve, and possibly via a ranger's station. Those wishing to at least size up Gunshot will continue over another creek, keeping right at a minor junction four kilometres later, and arrive at the notorious southern bank, usually meeting up with other travellers, who are looking in disbelief.

Generally the view straight ahead is disturbing to say the least, with an almost sheer drop off to a waterhole below. Standard vehicles will certainly be in for a workout (read: "possible crunch") if you choose this entry point, but at least the exit is no worse than anything you have conquered so far.

Fortunately Gunshot presents several approaches to the crossing, and their current condition will depend upon recent vehicle activity and flooding from the previous Wet Season. An alternative crossing to the east may be a possibility (although it too can be cut up and steep), but the downstream option is often trafficable. It will pay to watch other vehicles tackle the obstacle first, so that you can visualize what your strategy should be.

Don't be forced into a crossing of Gunshot if you are not confident – the bypass alternative is only a few kilometres back, and you are in country far too remote to risk vehicle damage, or worse! Once across Gunshot (or you have reached the northern side of the **Bypass**) you will skirt grevillea and banksia bushland to **Cockatoo Creek**, about 10 kilometres later.

Camping is a possibility on the southern bank, with an Aboriginal outstation located on the other side. Vehicles crossing the creek face a sandy descent and climb out, but with a set of underwater rock steps, best tackled in a clockwise arc, beginning at the downstream end.

Track conditions improve beyond the Cockatoo as you pass **Sheldon Lagoon**

MAP 3

Pajinka 'The Tip'
TORRES STRAIT
Somerset Ruins
N
NE
E
SE
S
SW
W
NW
0
20
40
Kilometres
Seisha
Bamaga
Jardine River Ferry and Permit Station
Sanamere Lagoon
Old Jardine River Ford – no longer used
Northern Bypass Rd
Nolans Brook – deep
Scenic stretch with several difficult water crossings
Eliot/Twin Falls – excellent stop
Fruitbat Falls – day use only
Cockatoo Creek Crossing – rocky river base
Gunshot Bypass
Heathlands Ranger Station
Gunshot Creek Crossing – eroded and difficult – use bypass if necessary
Telegraph Track
Southern Bypass Road
Palm Creek crossing – very difficult, possibly requires a winch. Check out on foot and get advice from recent travellers.
Bramwell Junction
Moreton Telegraph Station – camping
Soft Roaders
Trailers
Steep Climbs
Water Crossing
Good Clearance Needed
Snorkel
Road Tyres
Avoid Wet Weather
Navigation Skills
Extra Fuel

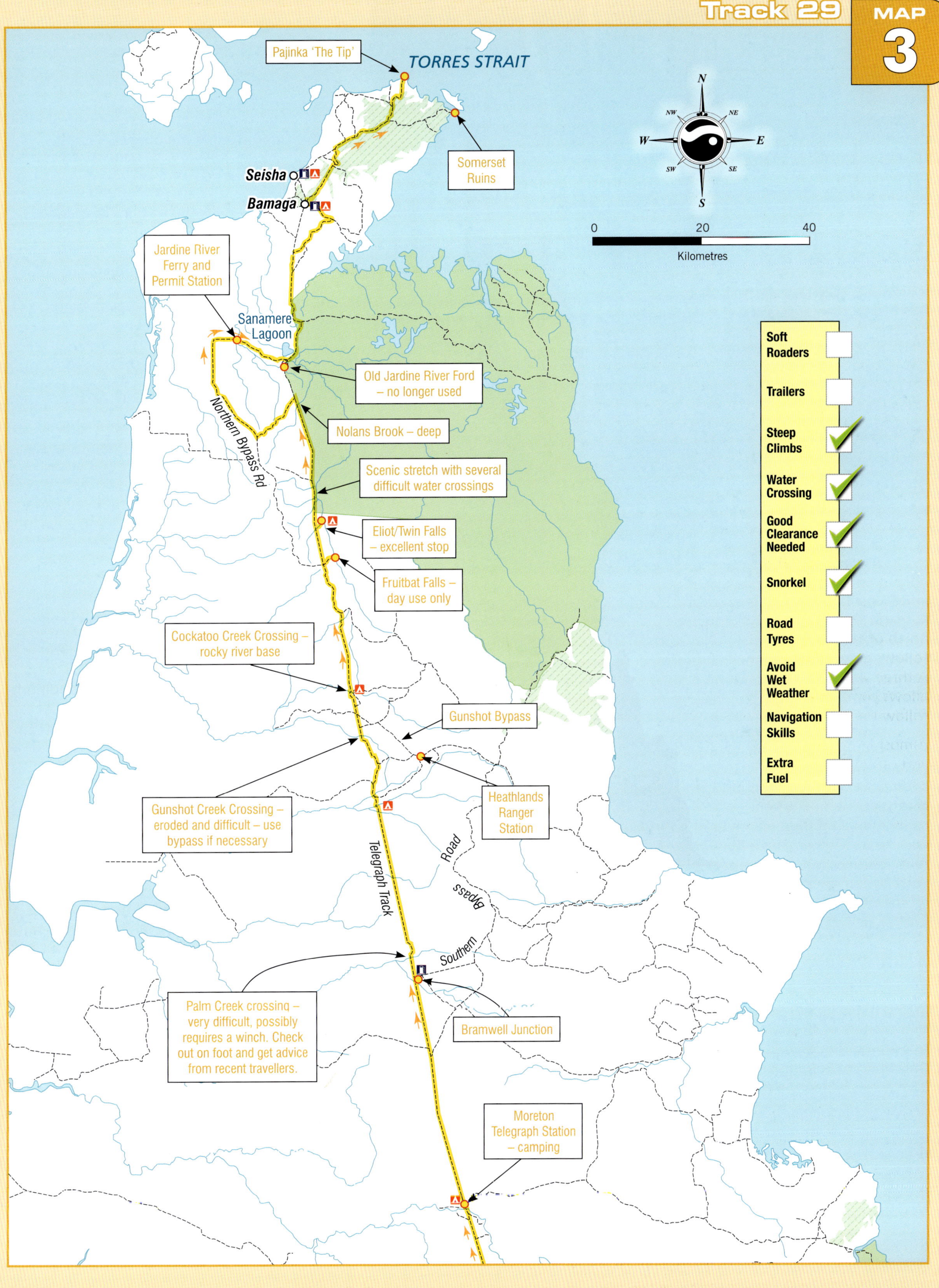

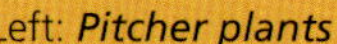

Left: *Pitcher plants*

and **Sailor Creek**. You will reach the main Bamaga Road a couple of kilometres north of Sailor Creek, where a left turn follows good road for nine kilometres. A three way intersection at this point allows you to veer right, to once again follow the Old Telegraph Track.

Almost immediately after the junction, you can swing right for a couple of kilometres, to reach **Fruit Bat Falls**. A carpark marks the vehicle track conclusion, and the beginning of a short walk to a swimming hole beneath the falls. Fruit Bat is a day visit area only, with no camping allowed, but is still well worth seeing.

Camping is permitted at **Eliot / Twin Falls** just seven kilometres up the road. It is a popular location with toilets and showers, and the picturesque setting makes it a compulsory stop. The crystal clear waters of **Eliot Creek** race over smooth golden brown rocks, with sandy bottomed swimming holes clustered above and below the falls.

A gash cut in the landscape across the creek, allows a broad wall of water to drop several metres from the verdant forest above. Twin Falls tops off this paradise with a natural spa bath formation.

When you finally leave this tropical oasis, slip the transfer into low range for a wheel lifting passage over **Canal Creek**. This uneven crossing is punctuated with large potholes and some chassis twisting terrain. Good camping is also possible here if Eliot Falls seems too busy, with superb fern and paperbark forest shading an understorey of delicate vegetation, including pitcher plants.

The drive from Canal Creek to the **Old Jardine Crossing** is especially rough and demanding, so only undertake this section if you feel confident. Less capable vehicles can return to the Bamaga Road near Fruit Bat Falls and swing right to the **Jardine River**.

Otherwise you continue north through slow country with **Turkey**, **Mistake** and **Cannibal Creeks** testing your clearances, fording depth and strategies alike. **Cypress Creek** is reached some 10 kilometres from Eliot Falls, and differs from other waterways on the Telegraph Track, with its log bridge, rather than unmade fording.

The term "bridge" may appear too generous on your arrival though, as the crossing requires you to balance your vehicle on loose logs laid longitudinally across the deepish ravine. It is doubtful that any road engineer has assessed this structure for some time, so tread cautiously (one vehicle at a time) and follow the instructions of a spotter who can give hand directions from the opposite side as you crawl across.

Beyond Cypress, follow some poorly drained country over **Logan Creek**, to a potentially deep crossing of **Nolans Brook**, about 13 kilometres later. Walk this crossing first to identify the shallowest route, and locate any obstacles that may not be visible from the driver's seat.

Two kilometres later you will reach a track junction, where you need to swing left to reach the main **Bamaga Road**. The straight ahead option reaches a camping area on the Jardine where vehicle fordings are no longer permitted (or indeed, viable).

Follow the link for 11 kilometres back to the main road, then turn right onto good gravel for another 24 kilometres to the **Jardine River**. A ferry crosses this wide river here, and while the cost may seem fairly hefty, the permit issued does allow you to camp on **Injinoo Lands** north of the Dulhunty River. Be aware of current alcohol restrictions north of the Jardine too; there are substantial penalties for any breaches. Ring the Injinoo Community Council (07 4069 3252) ahead for up to date information regarding permits and other restrictions.

Beyond the Jardine, follow the main road past **Sanamere Lagoon** to a major road junction some 28 kilometres later. Keep left at this intersection (although the right option also leads to Bamaga), and follow it to the outskirts of the **Injinoo Community**. Swing right onto bitumen here, before reaching the township of **Bamaga** about seven kilometres later.

Most supplies and services are available here, but good camping is located on the **Coral Sea** at **Seisia**, **Loyalty Beach** or **Punsand Bay**. The final trek north to **The Tip** follows corrugated road through the **Lockerbie Scrub** and **Carnegie Range** to a carpark at **Pajinka**.

From here walkers head through rainforest and a beach leg (at low tide) to a rocky tip facing the **Torres Strait**. The 90 minute return hike is not particularly strenuous, but an essential conclusion to this marathon tour.

Notes...

Notes...